Radicalized Loyalties

Radicalized Loyalties

Becoming Muslim in the West

Fabien Truong

Translated by Seth Ackerman and supervised by Fabien Truong

polity

First published in French as *Loyautés radicales. L'islam et les "mauvais garçons" de la Nation* © Éditions La Découverte, Paris, 2017

Polity Press
65 Bridge Street
Cambridge CB2 1UR, UK

Polity Press
101 Station Landing
Suite 300
Medford, MA 02155, USA

ISBN-13: 978-1-5095-1934-7
ISBN-13: 978-1-5095-1935-4 (pb)

A catalogue record for this book is available from the British Library.

Library of Congress Cataloging-in-Publication Data

Names: Truong, Fabien, author.
Title: Radicalized loyalties : becoming Muslim in the West / Fabien Truong.
Other titles: Loyautes radicales. English
Description: Cambridg, UK ; Medford, MA, USA : Polity, 2018. | Translation of: Loyautes radicales. | Includes bibliographical references and index. Identifiers: LCCN 2017052169 (print) | LCCN 2018005535 (ebook) | ISBN 9781509519385 (Epub) | ISBN 9781509519347 (hardback) | ISBN 9781509519354 (pb)
Subjects: LCSH: Muslim youth--France--Attitudes. | Children of immigrants--France--Attitudes. | Male juvenile delinquents--France--Attitudes. | Muslims--Cultural assimilation--France. | Islamic fundamentalism--France. | Suburbs--France--Social conditions.
Classification: LCC DC34.5.M87 (ebook) | LCC DC34.5.M87 T7813 2018 (print) | DDC 305.235/10882970944--dc23
LC record available at https://lccn.loc.gov/2017052169

Typeset in 10.5 on 12pt Sabon by Servis Filmsetting Ltd, Stockport, Cheshire
Printed and bound in Great Britain by Clays Ltd, St. Ives PLC

For further information on Polity, visit our website: politybooks.com

CONTENTS

NOTE TO THE READER

I hope you will make your way through this book comfortably. It is at once a tale, a study, and an essay. In it you will find life stories, known facts, theory. All invite you to move beyond your initial reactions, whether the experiences of the boys recounted here are familiar to you or foreign.

If you are keen on details, references, and sources, the notes will be useful to you. They are essential if you want to go further, and they acknowledge the texts to which I am indebted. If you don't like being interrupted, please ignore them. They will still be there for you at the end of the book.

The quotations are from transcripts of hundreds of hours of interviews and conversations. The words are those of the subjects of the study. To have dispensed with them would have been to pretend. Almost all of these conversations were recorded. As for the rest, it will be understood that in certain situations it would have been neither desirable nor respectful. This book, then, is also to some extent Adama's, Marley's, Tarik's, Radouane's, and Hassan's. Other than Amédy Coulibaly, all of the names have been changed to protect their anonymity. Certain identifying details have been altered. If you think you recognize someone you know, you are certainly mistaken. But it will not be by accident. All of these boys carry with them the weight of a social world that overshadows them. They represent.

Expressions in italics denote concepts and ideas that will be built up as we go. These are the linchpins of my argument. I hope you will be able to make critical use of them.

Finally, forgive me for addressing you, the reader, so informally. Carrying out research, practicing social science, and writing all have certain common purposes: to move about, to keep a record, to seek understanding. I like to think that these help us articulate our differences and better see how we are ultimately so much alike. When it comes to such a task, I am more comfortable in the mode of "you" and "I." Especially in an era afflicted with so much "them" and "us."

Fabien Truong

ACKNOWLEDGMENTS

This book is dedicated to Tarik, Radouane, Adama, Marley, and Hassan, as well as all those who appear in cameos or who disappeared from the text in order to be present in the study. You know who you are, I know what I owe you. I hope I have been worthy of your trust and generosity.

Thanks to Souleymane, Hélène, and Raymonde for guiding my initial steps in Grigny, along with Gérôme; and to all the local boys and other residents who in one way or another crossed paths with them. The work continues. My profound gratitude goes to Amar for his hospitality and his sense of "interlocution": this study simply would not have been possible without him.

This book benefited indirectly from daily discussions with all of my academic colleagues, "subjects," friends, and comrades with whom I engage on other fronts. You, too, know who you are and you have my warmest regards: if sociology is a martial art, it is also a collective sport.

The book benefited more directly from Gérôme Truc's close reading, our nightly debriefings, as well as astute comments from Nicolas Duvoux and Stéphane Beaud. They are in no way responsible for the content of this book, however. I cannot neglect the invaluable logistics that underpinned the research and writing: Jean-Pierre and Christophe at Saint-Ouen; support from the Université Paris-8, the Cultures et Sociétés Urbaines staff at the Centre de Recherches Sociologiques et Politiques de Paris, and from the CNRS with the Institut des Sciences Sociales du Politique and the REAT project; the invaluable behind-the-scenes work of "team Vladimir" (Margot, Pauline, Laurianne, Ilan, Maxime, and Vlad). For the English version, many thanks to Seth Ackerman and his clear insight during our linguistic ping-pong games, Marc Saint-Upéry for putting us in touch so quickly, as well as Emily Luytens and Les Back for their initial comments.

Thanks go to my publishers: Hugues Jallon, Rémi Toulouse, Marie-Soline Royer – who read the manuscript with her customary attention to detail – and Pascale Iltis for enthusiastically welcoming this project to La Découverte; John Thompson at Polity Press for his early confidence and suggestions – and all the editing and publicist team. Special thanks go to Loïc Wacquant for generously initiating that encounter.

A final word for my family and friends, who have been so understanding. And then, a "more-than-thanks" to Rachael for everything that I cannot write here but that mattered so much.

To Oscar and Félix for having been so curiously unperturbed. I hope someday you will better understand the meaning of those days and nights spent far from home.

To the memory of Pierre-Yves, and of Anne who is with him.

INTRODUCTION: THE CALL OF THE GROUND

The only things that ever trickles down to poor people
is rain, and that ain't much more than God's piss.
Percival Everett, *I Am Not Sidney Poitier*

Friday the 13th

It was an overcast late afternoon on November 13, 2015, when I first visited Grigny, in the southern suburbs of Paris. Accompanied by my friend and colleague Gérôme, I met up with a neighborhood group that had formed the day after the January 2015 attacks targeting the staff of *Charlie Hebdo* and the Hyper Cacher supermarket near the Porte de Vincennes in Paris. Grigny, like many working-class towns in the Paris suburbs, has long held a sinister reputation among outsiders. But ever since "Charlie," it has borne an extra weight: Amédy Coulibaly, the Hyper Cacher killer, was one of its children. Its tower blocks were swiftly branded as breeding grounds of hate. In reaction to what they experienced as yet another punishment, the locals collected hundreds of anonymous responses from residents through the streets of the town. Now, ten months after the attacks, an idea took shape: to display the messages in a ceremony of peace and commemoration. The group was overwhelmed by the outpouring of words they'd gathered, and they put out a call for help. Gérôme and I responded, as sociologists. It was a chance to work together and contribute to what we saw as a thoughtful initiative. Our first meeting, on November 13, stretched on into the evening. The encounter was full of promise. For several hours we spoke about the January attacks and daily life in the neighborhood. As night began to fall, we made plans for next steps. Gérôme went back to Paris. I stayed in the southern suburbs to meet up with two childhood friends, musicians in Alfortville: for nearly 10 years we had made the rounds of all the concert halls with our punk-metal band – a time that now seemed as if from another life. Gradually I shed my sociologist's skin and prepared to spend a relaxed evening with old companions. As I arrived at my destination, I did not yet know that a few kilometers away, a black VW Polo was about to start up. Inside were three "boys,"* not yet in their thirties, armed with assault rifles. They were headed for Paris. Destination: the Bataclan.

When the first rounds of gunfire broke out, Tarik grasped immediately that lives were being lost in rapid succession. He was a few hundred meters away, about to see a show by Dieudonné, the comedian convicted of "defamation, insult, and incitement to racial hatred" and accused of fanning the flames of social separatism in the French suburbs. Tarik lives in one of these infamous suburban towns: La Courneuve. He happened to have chosen that evening to go see for himself whether the controversial comic was any good. Now, none of that mattered. He knew the sound of explosions too well to be left in any doubt as to their consequences. The crackle of gunfire hurtled him back to a childhood marked by the bloody raids of the Groupe islamique armé in Algeria.† And it brought back the turmoil of an adolescence spent rising through the ranks of the drug trade, where claiming a piece of the pie means carrying a piece, too. When word came that these murders had been carried out in the name of the religion he espouses, his anger exploded. By contrast, Radouane was untouched by anger when he read the news on his phone. Unlike Tarik, he didn't linger on the endlessly looping images. Sitting on the couch in his family's living room, he felt nothing. Not disgust, not empathy; no rage, not even joy. He stopped watching television and barely read the press, sickened by what he saw as an industry of permanent lies. He felt empty. He knew that yet another line had been breached in the all-round loathing of "us Muslims." The idea that

* *Translator's note*: In familiar French, *garçons* (boys) is sometimes used to refer to males of any age – not unlike the colloquial English expression "good old boys," or "the boys on the bus." Throughout the text, I have preserved this usage by translating *garçons* as "boys," even when the word refers to individuals who are well into their adult years.

† The Groupe islamique armé (GIA) appeared in Algeria following the cancellation of legislative elections won by the Front islamique du salut (FIS) in 1991, and sought to install an Islamic state. In the 1990s, it carried out a long series of targeted attacks and civilian massacres – a period of conflict described as a "dark decade," claiming some tens of thousands of victims.

this really was a war between two camps seemed that much closer to crystallizing.

I had first met Tarik and Radouane eight years earlier, along a different frontline. Then, we were divided by the surface of a gray desk and the frame of a whiteboard. I was starting out as an economics and social science teacher in Seine-Saint-Denis, another unpopular area encircling Paris, on the north side; Tarik and Radouane belonged to the multi-hued ranks of "my" students. That was now in the past: Tarik had left school a long time before, Radouane had gone on to pursue lengthy studies. I now teach in Saint-Denis at the University of Paris 8, having become a scholar studying the personal trajectories of my former students.[1] My sociologist's skin has thickened since then, and the setting of our initial acquaintance has become a web of lasting connections. But that Friday evening, this shared history was an insignificant detail, lost in the growing maelstrom.

In Alfortville, anguish turned to shock when my friends learned that two close acquaintances of theirs had been in the crowd at the Bataclan – a venue we knew well, and which we feared had attracted friends from our circle that night. Phones lit up, and the statistics were grim: one of their acquaintances would emerge from the carnage alive, the other would not. At this point we were still unaware that Pierre-Yves, one of "our" sound engineers, had been executed at point-blank range along with his wife. It was three days later that we discovered his death. I hadn't seen him in several years. The echoes of his big, generous laugh now stay with me: a dim memory, tracing the contours of another life, cut down by the absurd.

Behind absurdity, the social world

Such events force us to confront the meaninglessness of existence, to acknowledge those moments when, in Albert Camus's words, "the stage sets collapse" and we are condemned to "keeping the absurd alive."[2] And yet there's something unsatisfying about turning senseless events into solitary observation posts, sustaining the narcissistic fiction of our isolated egos when in reality the ordeal is assuredly collective. That Friday night, the shock was compounded by the chasm between the premeditation of those on one side and the insouciance of those on the other, ignorant of the violence that was about to befall them. It was as if the stench of killing had laid bare the unsteady points of our social compasses.

As the enormity of the carnage became clear, the whole of society raised its voice. The fabric of interpersonal relations and the drama of what was collectively happening to "us" were all put on display in an uncontrolled unspooling of individual emotions. That is what Gérôme meant when he observed, in a study of the attacks in New York in 2001, Madrid in 2004, and London in 2005, that with "a multiplicity of meanings of 'we,' our reactions to attacks demonstrate a heightened sense of 'I,' which leads us to sympathize with the fate of the victims on the basis less of a shared belonging than of a shared singularity."[3] For Tarik, memories flooded back of the paternal shotgun enthroned in the living room of his Algerian home. Radouane noted the strange disjuncture between his feeling of numb disillusion and the emotion stirred in him by the misery of Syrian or Palestinian children, in a confused juxtaposition of guilty parties. For me, nights spent with Pierre-Yves, and our band's farewell show, where he'd brilliantly handled the sound, came back like flashes of light. Such is the web of impressions spontaneously linking together our jolted individual selves – alongside a rather indistinct "We."

Each wave of Islamist attacks on European soil heightens the fragility of a "We" that seems parachuted in from above, stripped of its trappings of "givenness" the more it is chanted like a slogan. The periods of official tribute and reflection that follow such attacks no longer yield unanimous assent: they're also becoming times of suspicion and tension. Such moments are about being together, but also about being counted, being seen, feeling out the apparent fissures – as if, amid such emotion, differences can't coexist without being reduced to sealed-off blocs. It's as if "to be Charlie" or "not to be Charlie" were the only question that mattered, inviting us to sport distinctive outward markers: *je suis* or *je ne suis pas*.[4] The connection between "We" and "I" seemed to vanish in the face of "Us" versus "Them." Scapegoats, demons, moral panics, outsiders – the logic of blame is well known.[5] Today, the threat has a generic name: Muslims.

Such Manichean binaries give meaning to the absurdity of violence by replacing careful explanations, connections between cause and effect, and collective responsibility with "culture talk."[6] They feed the reassuring prophecy of a "clash of civilizations" while expressing that "attitude of longest standing, which no doubt has a firm psychological foundation, as it tends to reappear in each one of us when we are caught unawares, [which] is to reject out of hand the cultural institutions ... which are furthest removed from those with which we identify ourselves."[7] On the Western side, the old colonial image of Islam, layered with "cultural antipathy," morphs into a "cultural war" against a supposed Muslim International.[8] As the political scientist Arun Kundnani writes, "in the West, people make culture; in Islam, culture makes people."[9] Islamist discourse deploys a similar, if more direct, rhetoric, proposing to "manage barbarism" and "liquidate the gray zone" between Muslims and infidels.[10] It stresses the depravity of Western society, an amoral world of "unbelievers" driven by passions and impulses, where culture is mere window-dressing to camouflage the basest proclivities. Ostracized "Muslims" and "unbelievers" share the same failing: they are prisoners of nature, their nature. They are "Jews" in Jean-Paul Sartre's sense: a problem to be solved, men subject to others' gaze, rather than fully fledged individuals.[11]

In such a setting, the Muslim religion becomes "racial,"[12] as the essayist Moustafa Bayoumi puts it: its visible features are turned into problems and symbols. Beards, kaftans, hijabs, or burkinis eerily resemble the skin and hair of the "Negro" described by W. E. B. Du Bois in his day.[13] France, in this war of imaginaries, possibly represents an even more powerful symbol than the United States. If 9/11 could appear as a strike against the West's financial power and military dominance, attacking Paris – its cafés, streets, magazines, football stadiums, concert venues – is a declaration of war on entertainment, hedonism, or aestheticism. The fight to eradicate terrorism is no longer just a struggle for freedom of thought or the free market. Now it's about defending a liberal and open way of life against the dictatorship of a closed and fundamentalist world.[14] In this sense, the images of France under siege may well add a dash of soul to the axis of evil sketched by George W. Bush in 2002.

But what does such an imaginary tell us about Tarik, seated with his friends at the café terrace next door to that of "La Belle Equipe," a few minutes before 19 people lost their lives in that multicultural bistro? What does it tell us about Radouane's impassiveness in the face of these murders, at the end of a long day spent in his Paris office as an accounts manager, a day that began at five in the morning in his neighborhood mosque? Almost nothing – except perhaps that the world runs on categorizations that reduce reality to acceptable representations. Amid so much confusion, only one certainty remains: humans are, most often, social animals without knowing it.

The magic of "radicalization"

One word has come to the fore to give meaning to these dilemmas: "radicalization." Though now used by journalists, intellectuals, and ordinary citizens, the term was first popularized by decision-makers and policy experts after September 11, 2001. According to Peter Neumann, director of the International Centre for the Study of Radicalisation and Political Violence in London, the rapid spread of the term is explained by its vagueness: "the idea of radicalisation" makes it possible to talk about everything that happens "before the bomb goes off" without having to grapple with the "'root causes' of terrorism" – a notion always suspected of fostering an irresponsible culture of excuses.[15] For profiling purposes, "radicalization" narrows the focus to the various milestones along the path taken by the "terrorist next door." It allows us to name the indescribable, to shield ourselves from terror by placing a label on its origins.[16] But as Guy Debord observed about the use of the word "terrorism": "what is important in this commodity is the packing, or the labeling: the price codes."[17]

"Radicalization" aims to describe a specific phenomenon: the emergence of what psychiatrist and former CIA officer Marc Sageman calls the new generation of "homegrown terrorists," groups of friends who turn against the countries where, for the most part, they were born.[18] As long as the enemy still came from outside, there was no cause to speak of "radicalization." The word "terrorism" was quite sufficient: the attacks were committed by foreigners, radically "other." When the enemy comes from inside, the question of betrayal arises: the tipping point where "us" becomes "them." The stakes here are considerable: to protect ourselves from these locally grown enemies, we must first know who they are. In France, the 1990s witnessed the rise of what the sociologist Farhad Khosrokhavar terms "Islamism without Islam": marginalized individuals whose life-courses begin in social and emotional poverty, leading to delinquency and prison, and then to an ostentatious religiosity aimed at regaining a lost dignity.[19] Twenty years later, "radicalization" now helps to fill in this picture of failed "integration." How could such hardline fundamentalism meet with a wish for murder and death – here, in France?

"Radicalization" is both a practical and an analytical category. As a practical category it's deployed in a variety of arenas that aim to improve public safety, as a way of giving meaning to ordinary life experiences: teachers ask themselves whether this or that pupil has been "radicalized"; appeals for vigilance proliferate; the public is called upon to report "signs of radicalization"; politicians finance "de-radicalization programs." As an analytical category, radicalization is mobilized by social scientists to denote everything that happens "before the bomb goes off," but with different and sometimes contradictory meanings, none of which commands unanimous scientific assent.[20] Despite this semantic cacophony, all these usages share something implicit: radicalization is about wayward individuals, the culmination of a succession of steps in a biographical trajectory. A slippery-slope motif emerges in all the posthumous commentaries on "homegrown terrorists" – those anti-stars whose anonymous pasts are suddenly dissected to identify the moments of personal failings and failures that led to the irreparable. The psychologist Fathali Moghaddam's so-called "staircase" model, often used in deradicalization programs, gives a typical picture: involvement in terrorism depends on an individual's capacity to cope with feelings of injustice and frustration, and this capacity is challenged over a succession of steps.[21] That means better individual profiling is needed, a task that became all the more urgent as the portraits of would-be martyrs grew more complex over the 2000s. After Daesh supplanted Al Qaeda and Syria went up in flames, the territorial conflict moved closer to the gates of Europe. Now school graduates, members of economically prosperous families, "converts," "whites," girls, even children, are climbing an increasingly accessible staircase, further blurring the relationship between the "us," the "them," and the "I." If sociological variables no longer seem decisive, and if free will and voluntary servitude aren't politically acceptable explanations, then a narrative comes to the fore in which fragile individuals gradually tumble into a violent ideology. This, in turn, calls for a struggle against the persuasive force of that ideology's accredited conduits ("the Koran," "imams," "Salafists," "the Internet," "Daesh," "prison," etc.). The label is bolstered with each new case, but it's as if the word is always trying to catch up with the reality. The increasingly innovative updated versions of it – "pre-radicalization," "high-speed radicalization," "solitary radicalization," "self-radicalization," "online radicalization" – merely underscore its inability to make sense of the world. It has become a rallying cry for preventive and remedial action: as the sociologist Stuart Hall would say, it is a veritable "conductor" of the crisis.[22] It seems wiser to abandon the term and, instead, to observe what it seeks to explain: the seductive power of the ideology of "martyrdom," the call for political violence, and Islam's attraction for a whole swath of young people.

Ideological explanations are, at best, tautological: it's obvious that any young person ready to die for the glory of the Prophet adheres profoundly to a firm system of belief. But political allegiance and moral justification are at least as much consequences as causes. Scott Atran, one of the finest ethnographers of Middle East jihadism, made this clear when questioned by the US Senate about the threat posed by radical imams. He suggested that such clerics stand at the end of a long-distance race. Rather than genuine recruiting agents, they act more as "attractors," thriving on convictions already deeply held.[23] Radicalization by ideology functions as a myth. It offers a narrative about the origins and spread of evil, but ultimately says little about the phenomenon it supposedly describes. Its primary function is to "empty reality," thus revealing our intimate relationship to it.[24] Its focus on ideology signals a magical conception of religious belief, common to both jihadist propaganda and Western fears of radicalization. Faith in radical Islam is seen as leading to either paradise or barbarism, as if ideas float – and strike – in the air. But no religious belief or conception of the world can have sufficient weight to guide what people do unless it resonates in some way with their needs, practices, power relations, institutions. In short, it must deal with pre-existing social expectations and constitute an effective and acceptable response to concrete problems. As Max Weber says, ideas are mere "switchmen" on the "tracks of action," not impetuses to it. This was one of sociology's very first findings.[25] There is no religious essence contained within pure texts, impressing itself into blank minds – however adrift those minds may be. Islam is no exception to this universal dependence on historical context and sociological setting.[26] If there is something like a staircase of terror, its woodwork is made from composite raw materials, a mix of social, economic, and political forces without which no one will ever ascend to their death in the serene certainty of their own election.

This *magic of radicalization* is a result of "culture talk" that pictures Islam as a body of frozen beliefs guided by an irrational logic (faith versus reflexivity), by withdrawal (a lack of integration versus civic participation), and by subordination (submission versus contestation). Such a uniform picture has no empirical basis. Every specialist in Islam contests it – starting with Gilles Kepel and Olivier Roy, though they frontally oppose each other in the debate on the origins of Islamist terrorism.[27] Kepel sees contemporary jihadism as the expression of a "radicalization of Islam," while Roy instead stresses an "Islamization of radicalism." Kepel points to changes in the tone and targets of Islamist propaganda, and in interpretations of religious texts. In his view, these interpretations advance an increasingly uncompromising reading of the sacred texts and address themselves to the social margins of Western countries, assuming a seductive posture of victimhood. For Kepel, therefore, the spread of radicalization and the emergence of "third-generation jihadists" have been brought about by changes in ideology and Arabic texts. Olivier Roy instead sees continuity in the attacks France has experienced since the 1990s, pointing to their shared connection with working-class, outer-city neighborhoods, and the disappearance of any transformational political horizon in the era of globalization: Islamist fundamentalism now serves as the black flag of a "nihilist generation." These alternatives – "third-generation" versus "nihilist generation" – besides being wholly theoretical, show where we end up when we start with a label that reduces everything that happens "before the bomb goes off" to the consequences of an ideological degeneration within the Muslim culture or faith. The issue then becomes a matter for Islamologists. Such experts are solicited for their opinions about "homegrown terrorists," whom they only know from posthumous portraits in the press, and working-class neighborhoods which they don't visit, or no longer do. Gilles Kepel's explanation, centered on the ideology of Arabic texts, is puzzling in light of the fact that the young people who seem to be "radicalized" come to religion initially knowing little Arabic, and with only a sketchy understanding of the hadiths or the Koran. Unless we assume that beginners are always manipulable (though in that case, the number of terrorists should be significantly higher), this means we have to situate religious instruction within the context of tumultuous social, familial, educational, emotional, and spiritual trajectories. As for Olivier Roy's thesis of the "Islamization of radicalism," it frees itself of the "radicalization" label by providing an explanation centered on nihilism. But this is rather empty: "Islamization" rests on convictions, decisions, aspirations, projections, links of reciprocity or antagonism – not on "nothing."

A bad religion for "bad seeds"?

We thus need to return to the patient observation of human beings. We must trace the connections between headlines and social reality, between minority life and majority life, between ordinary paths and extraordinary paths. Although French law prohibits tallying the population by religious adherence, in 2015 the Muslim population was estimated at around 4 million individuals – 6.8 percent of metropolitan France.[28] For a majority of Muslims, religion is an important dimension of social identity, accentuated by higher levels of attendance at houses of worship and, above all, the ritual practices that punctuate daily life (consumption of halal meat, Ramadan, wearing a veil or a beard, etc.), especially among the youngest and descendants of immigrants.[29] This phenomenon is made all the more visible by the fact that Muslim houses of worship are few in number and Muslims highly concentrated in neighborhoods relegated to the periphery of French cities.* The so-called "radical" version of Islam, usually associated with the Salafist current, remains a small minority. According to the Interior Ministry, it involved between 12,000 and 15,000 individuals in 2012, with the highest estimates ranging up to 30,000 individuals.[30] As for the use of physical violence in the name of Islam, the government in November 2015 had official files on 10,500 individuals for "membership in or links with the Islamic movement." For those who actually go on to take action, the primary outlet is overseas: departures for Syria and Iraq reportedly involved between 1,200 and 1,800 individuals, including around 250 who returned to France, with a recent increase in departures recorded since 2015.[31] Finally, 21 "homegrown terrorists" have carried out deadly strikes on French soil since 2012. They are known for their repeated attacks, claiming 335 victims so far.†

Underlying this funnel-shaped set of figures is a *relationship between continuities and ruptures*. The staircase metaphor sketches a kind of continuity between religious faith, submission to dogma, increasingly rigoristic religious practice, and advancing to the point of violent action, punctuated by moments of psychological rupture that, through a weeding-out process, lead individuals to climb the ladder of radicalism. When we sound out the woodwork of the staircase and situate the turn to Islam within the time-scale of individual life-courses and collective histories – rather than the lightning speed of biographical radicalization – intermediate-level questions crop up, involving distinctions between the three principal objects of collective

* According to the Interior Ministry, in 2014 there were 2,368 prayer halls in France, including 90 mosques.

† Since 2012 (and through November 2017), responsibility has been claimed for 10 fatal attacks on French soil: Toulouse and Montauban in 2012; Paris and Montrouge in January 2015; Villejuif in April 2015; Saint-Quentin-Fallavier in June 2015; Paris and Saint-Denis in November 2015; Magnanville in June 2016; Nice in July 2016; Saint-Etienne-du-Rouvray in August 2016; Paris in April 2017; and Marseille in October 2017.

concern: (1) "homegrown terrorists" who want to strike their own country; (2) "candidates for departure" to Syria or Iraq; and (3) adherence to so-called "rigoristic" religious practices that are prescriptive in terms of lifestyle.

For "homegrown terrorists" who see themselves as being at war *here*, there is, indeed, a typical profile: boys, with immigrant backgrounds and "culturally Muslim" parents; working class, living in stigmatized urban outcast neighborhoods, with pasts in petty or large-scale crime; arriving late to religion. There are two overlapping questions here. First, how do these elements combine to form a system? And how do they constitute fertile soil for terrorism? Such consistent patterns are never trivial. If psychological fragility were the trigger in the majority of cases, the profiles of "homegrown terrorists" would be more heterogeneous.[32] And, second, how do we explain the fact that these elements, even when combined, ultimately result in a small number of individuals actually taking action? Why don't hundreds of thousands of young people with similar biographical details climb the staircase of terror more quickly? Are they stuck on lower levels, like time bombs? Or simply somewhere else? What is it that continues to act as a safety valve for them, despite all the difficulties? And what is the role of Islam in all of this? Can religion also be a pathway to certain forms of integration, pacification, or remediation for the nation's "bad seeds"?

As for the "candidates for departure," what attracts them to a religion of combat? What image do they hold of the war *over there* before their departures actually take place? Can an act resembling an escape to some "better" place really be put in the same category as obsessive planning and execution for a local attack – a classification that heedlessly adopts Daesh's rhetoric about an International of "soldiers of the Caliphate"? Are these exactly the same logics? Compared to "homegrown terrorists," the jihadists-in-training who cross borders to join the ranks of Daesh are more diverse in terms of background and gender. This should give us pause. Does it suggest a random distribution of individual fragility? Or is it, conversely, a sign that there are common logics running through the entire social body, crossing lines of gender or age? And now, another population which cannot be solely contemplated as "candidates" has emerged: the returnees.

Finally, what of the attraction to Islam and the value placed on an apparently "rigoristic" way of life, where religious rites and obligations mark the rhythm of daily life – this in a country that was built on the expulsion of God from the organized life of the polity? What accounts for the greater visibility of these practices, which serve as sources of tension in public spaces? How have they evolved over time? Why do a growing number of young people seem to adopt the Muslim religion as a second homeland, or as what Karl Marx called a "chimerical nationality"?[33] What leads them to such powerful symbolic categories when, ultimately, religious practice governs a relatively small portion of the day? What demand for meaning and transcendence are such practices responding to? Are sacred values always about "identity"? What is the significance of this generational experience of faith and fidelity, which seems to reach beyond the circle of so-called "culturally Muslim" families? In this sense, is the usual distinction between "converts" and "non-converts" really relevant?

Finding Allah at street level

I am neither a Muslim, nor an Islamologist, much less a prophet. And if it must be confessed, I don't think I believe in God. I'm a sociologist who has been crisscrossing the working-class neighborhoods of the Paris suburbs for more than 10 years. To put it simply, I observe and participate in the social life of people who inhabit the world differently from the way I do. I try, as Germaine Tillion has written, to watch and to live at the same time.[34] That is how the presence of "Allah" revealed itself to me, how it appeared without my looking for it.

It started in 2005 in Seine-Saint-Denis, in the northern suburbs of Paris, when I received a teaching appointment at several high schools (*lycées*) located in neighborhoods where the statistical indicators fool no one: large majorities of immigrant families, parents with unskilled jobs when they're not unemployed, school achievement below the national average and inversely proportional to the surrounding economic poverty. After I left high-school teaching for a university post in 2010, I continued to track the fortunes of some of my former students. Over the course of their personal journeys marked by spells of crime and early school-leaving, I regularly found Islam along the way. In the social lives of many young people, religion unquestionably has become a moral resource with few equivalents, even as it has also become a mark of stigma vis-à-vis "the outside." Above all, it generates a malleable set of practices, the result of a constant bricolage that changes depending on the moment, the place, the individual.

It was on the back of that work that I first set foot in Grigny, a town with serious difficulties: almost one in two Grigny residents lives below the poverty line, compared to one in three in Seine-Saint-Denis. The fateful turn taken by the night of Friday, November 13, 2015, became the point of departure for a new study, which I carried out both alone and with Gérôme.[35] In Seine-Saint-Denis, I had learned to move with my former students, both in time and in space. In Grigny, I lived on the ground several days per week. Time was swallowed up by multi-sided encounters that intensified each time I returned. My repeated stays yielded their share of local references and habits. Back in Seine-Saint-Denis, the trust others were willing to place in me had been the chance result of an imposed situation: the classroom. That trust solidified over time, as the masks and the scenery changed, with the former teacher becoming a university professor, a confidant, an advisor, and then just "someone who writes books." In Grigny, there was nothing I could cite in my personal life to justify my presence. And yet at the same time there was every reason in the world for me to be there, in a town accustomed to dodging journalists inquiring about its young people and its famous homegrown terrorist. To get started, I had to explain my way of working in detail. The moral contract was transparent: I knew "*la banlieue*" and its youth well, but didn't know the first thing about Grigny; I would give the floor to whoever wanted to speak – so I could learn and possibly make public what I heard, but also so that I could take it on board and make my own meaning from it. I enjoyed spending time with the people I met and didn't know exactly what I would do with what I saw. Most importantly, I came back. Things started moving more quickly than I'd imagined. I soon met people whose stories and engaging personalities made them first-rate allies: because of the rich conversations I had with them, of course, but most importantly for their role as protecting guides. Thanks to them, I met individuals who would have avoided me had I introduced myself directly. When suspicion is a rule of survival – and my presence was, inevitably, a suspicious curiosity – being seen in public with figures who mattered, pillars of neighborhood life whose motives were above all reproach, was almost a necessity. It was absolutely indispensable if I wanted to glimpse what lay behind the surface of distrust, the narrow circles of solidarity: generosity and hospitality, which loosen tongues, open doors, and allow respect to be earned, step by step. Trust is built through persistence: calling, insisting, coming for no reason, calling back, coming at the last minute, showing your face, hanging around, turning up, helping, surprising, coming again. That is how, little by little, I came to be identified alternately as either "the sociologist" or "so-and-so's friend."

These behind-the-scenes details about my work are essential. Making clear where one is speaking from, restricting oneself to talking only about what one has seen and seen again, is a question of morality and mutual consideration. That is what I owe to Tarik, Radouane, Pierre-Yves, and others. It's also an intellectual safeguard. To work over an extended period of time – time spent with people, time that passes in their lives – is to think in terms of repeated visits, testing the soundness of each little discovery through constant re-checking. That is the challenge of what the sociologist Michael Burawoy calls the "ethnographic revisit": trying to "disentangle movements of the external world from the researcher's own shifting involvement with that same world, all the while recognizing that the two are not independent." That way, ethnography can "emancipate itself from the eternal present" rather than remaining "trapped in the contemporary."[36] Revisiting sites, individuals, situations, sentiments, means cultivating what, for me, is the heart of my vocation, what sociologist Les Back calls "the art of listening."[37] It's almost an anachronistic art in a society where everyone can claim their 15 minutes of digital glory, where everyone has the freedom to speak without having to listen to those who, actually, have an urgent need to articulate the contradictions of their lives. It was by devoting myself to this with perseverance and humility that I learned to know Tarik, Radouane, Hassan, Marley, Adama – and a ghost: Amédy.

These six boys from the *cité* (housing project) will be the main characters in this story. But not the only characters. Since "the real is relational," they exist only in their relationships with others – parents, brothers, sisters, friends, girlfriends, etc. – whom we will encounter by extension.[38] And then there are all the absent figures, boys and girls, for whom this group stands in.[39] This sextet did not emerge from random encounters or the vagaries of the writing process. Rather, it represents "the evolution over time of a system of relationships between characteristics borne by individuals."[40] These boys form an ensemble: because they are bearers of characteristics repeatedly observed in many studies; but also because the differing arrangements of their individual characteristics help to bring out the meaning of the differences, the divergences. The characteristics function in relation to one another. They're significant, as well as rich in their density and uniqueness. Finally, each of these characters embodies something that is regularly defined as a problem: involvement in the Muslim religion by marginalized Western youth. My answers will be imperfect: some points will appear head-on, others will emerge through mirroring effects. But they will be grounded in facts – "won, constructed, and confirmed."[41]

Tarik and Radouane are two former students whom I've known since 2008. They are now 25 and still live in Seine-Saint-Denis.

Marley, Adama, and Hassan are residents of Grigny, from different generations. Marley is the same age as Tarik and Radouane, Adama is entering his thirties, Hassan his forties. Hassan and Adama knew Amédy Coulibaly: the former rather distantly, as a street educator; the latter intimately, as a close friend. They are two physical points of contact with Amédy Coulibaly; others will almost always remain in the background. For a sociologist, researching a deceased person or a celebrity is an almost counterintuitive pursuit. It requires clear choices. In my case, I've preferred to examine "Amédy" and leave "Amédy Coulibaly" aside. Of the latter we know a great deal, thanks to detailed portraits in the press and a meticulous police investigation. One can follow his trajectory as a terrorist, as well as the logistics of the attacks, rather precisely. It's as if – and this was probably his intention – the jihadist had effaced the person "from before," the one his friends and acquaintances described to me. This is the Amédy I was told about, though few wished to discuss him openly, out of a combination of delicacy, incomprehension, uncompleted mourning, and shame. In addition, a number of archival materials make it possible to follow his itinerary, and even to hear him speak. This Amédy will be the book's sixth character. I did not personally know him, my information is obviously partial, but I have chosen to write "as if." As if Amédy had his place with the living, and as if the episodes and emotions that will bring him into being were the result of direct observation. There are two main reasons for this: the promises I made to those who spoke to me to protect their anonymity by making them disappear from this text; and a determination to find a measure of humanity and ordinariness in his trajectory, despite the atrocious nature of the acts he committed. Not to accept this measure would, I believe, be a failure to fully acknowledge the issues at stake. Accepting it also makes it possible to move beyond moral condemnation, impulses toward hate or resentment, deterministic miserablism, or bleeding-heart indecency. It is about trying to better understand the loyalties and reversals that make what people become, between well-worn paths and back-road crossings. The turns are sometimes sharp, as Amédy and Adama knew all too well. These were two children cut from the same timber, two friends who passed through the same predicaments and were ultimately separated by their fates, or, to use the sacred terminology, their *takdir*.

What if the real ruptures and continuities lie not where we assume they do, but in hidden, long-lasting loyalties – and the conflicts between them?

What if the loyalties that lie at the heart of the desire for Islam among marginalized Western youth have their roots – as the word "radical" implies – in a collective history still not fully aware of itself; in a troubled model of society, in anguish about an uncertain future?

What if the forces at play arise from an ensemble of *radical loyalties* – in the here and now – rather than from some titanic clash maintained by a permanent state of emergency?

And what if learning to know "them" could help "us" better understand ourselves?

— 1 —

COMMON HISTORIES

In the appreciation of the passage of time, the first step is the hardest.
Marcel Proust, *Time Regained* (trans. D.J. Enright)

Making a home in public housing: a French history

To grow up in a housing project in Grigny, or in Seine-Saint-Denis, is to inherit a part of France's history. At the end of the Second World War the country was morally divided, enfeebled by profound human and material losses, practically a ward of the United States. Didn't France owe its salvation to the Marines? Wasn't it the Marshall Plan keeping the economy afloat? The postwar reconstruction years were focused on reconquering and rebuilding a defeated country that had always seen itself as a beacon of global influence.

From utopia to U-turn

France now had to restage its entry into the twentieth century: to fully embrace modernity, find a new path to prosperity, and fulfill the founding myth of a generous Republic in solidarity with its most disadvantaged. For a long while, this new departure seemed to be birthing an "affluent society": a "second French Revolution," as slow and protracted as the revolution of 1789 had seemed sudden.[1] From the 1950s to the 1970s, the nation's blossoming housing projects embodied this promise. The proliferation of collective housing, grouped into towers and compact blocks, was intended to meet the challenges of the times. The rational architecture of these projects eased congestion in aging and bourgeois central cities, bringing modern comfort to young white-collar families as well as to an incoming stream of manual workers – those from the French countryside and, later, those imported from the far-off lands that served the metropole: the colonies. Nearly every city, in its updated form, displayed the same pattern: a historic central city filled with stone-built dwellings of a glorious past; in the thriving suburbs, the concrete of a radiant future. It represented a new deal between center and periphery. The urban landscape was expanded and divided. And triumphant colonization had its last gasp: instead of colonists moving abroad to exploit an overseas labor force, now that labor force would have to migrate. Meanwhile, working-class solidarity within the neighborhood was strained by perpetual economic growth.

An initial turning point came in the 1960s: white-collar workers left the *cités*, auguring an end to social mixing. Meanwhile, immigrant family reunion policies and the 1970s changed the color of the scenery. Dark-skinned workers were officially recognized as heads of families: what was once seen as a temporary immigration of unattached individuals became a new population putting down lasting roots.[2] At the urban periphery, poor neighborhoods became immigrant neighborhoods, and then neighborhoods of immigrant children. In the wake of the 1981 Socialist Party victory and the success of the 1983 "*Marche pour l'égalité et contre le racisme*,"* these children became politicized, asserting their rights to full recognition. Grassroots organizations proliferated, but the most dedicated activists struggled to obtain positions of responsibility. The rupture with the traditional elitist political system grew more pronounced; the bitterness was all the greater given the high hopes for representation that were now dashed.[3] The 1990s confirmed the implosion of the working class. Factory work became scarcer and more precarious, the service industries were proletarianized, commutes became longer and more costly, and the democratization of education gave the children of manual workers hope that they could rise in the social hierarchy. The period marked the end of Fordism and the erosion of a form of collective pride forged by workers' struggles. Such struggles, though they often excluded immigrants, had kept workers together. Now they gradually became invisible.[4] The social question became an urban question, urban policy eclipsed the fight against unemployment,

* Organized by a small group in the Lyon *banlieue*, the "March for Equality and Against Racism" started in Marseille on October 15, 1983, receiving relatively little attention, and ended in Paris on December 3 with a demonstration attended by more than 100,000 individuals.

and little by little politics was replaced by the art of keeping up appearances.[5] Immigrant neighborhoods became "problem neighborhoods": sieves to distribute a marginalized population for whom success meant getting out.

A utopia of ultra-modern neighborhoods looking outward to the world gave way to an other-worldly landscape. Quick to hang familiar labels on an obvious case of social and ethnic separatism, commentators drew facile analogies to the American ghetto or apartheid: France's problems, it was said, were ultimately the same as those of the United States or South Africa. But as Loïc Wacquant has shown, such an analogy cannot withstand comparison, at least it could not in the early 1990s.[6] The traditional function of a ghetto is to prevent contact between a stigmatized group and the "legitimate" population, while providing the former with secure living conditions so that society can benefit from its labor without being sullied by proximity to it. That was the case with the Jewish ghetto in sixteenth-century Venice or the black ghetto in the United States of the 1950s and 1960s. But the apparent post-Fordist symmetry between today's American "hyper-ghetto" and the European "anti-ghetto" is deceptive. Their inhabitants share the same grievous lack of opportunities and the same social opprobrium. They've both become superfluous in an economy that no longer needs the manpower it once did. They live in disreputable neighborhoods, outcast zones, embodiments of an idleness and social dysfunction that are said to threaten the whole social body. Yet marginality is still a product of specific histories and geographies. The American "hyper-ghetto" is racially homogeneous; it spreads beyond the horizon over vast autarkic zones, a desolate space where police, prisons, and the underground economy regulate social life. In the hyper-ghetto, low levels of life expectancy seem as inalienable as the right to bear arms. The European "anti-ghetto," though the majority is non-white, is ethnically more diverse. Rather than being an offshoot of racial segregation, it is the distorted mirror of the old European colonies, more narrowly concentrated in pockets that still look outward to the city center, despite great poverty. The constant flow of departures and arrivals is as decisive as the effective impossibility of escape for many. While police, prisons, and the underground economy are central, their sway is contested by the possibility of working elsewhere and by a welfare state that's embedded in daily life. Nevertheless, rising numbers of young people born in the 1990s and afterward were forced to grow up with the feeling of being locked out. In France, the *cités* are not so much "another world" as a "world of others": taxi, bus, or truck drivers, housewives, warehouse workers, the unemployed – but also, more rarely, football players, actors, or high-achieving students.

Fears

In France, the great fear is the prospect of voluntary secession by a group of people who seem like the neighbors one never speaks to. That would mean the end of republican integration, confirming that a nation that managed to make room for its children from deep in the nineteenth-century countryside has failed, in the early twenty-first century, with the children of the children of its overseas colonies. This anxiety can be boiled down to a distinctively French phobia, one so deeply rooted in national history that foreigners struggle to understand it: "*communautarisme*."

In a nation that achieved unity on the basis of universal and abstract ideals ("liberty, equality, fraternity"), particularistic or "communalist" claims seem to threaten social cohesion, as if open displays of belonging were inevitably mutually exclusive.[7] According to this logic, *because* residents of the *cités* live by rules, values, and beliefs that are their own, they go against the nation. An era of mounting inequality has become an era of "others": "Arabs," "blacks," and, now, "Muslims."

The Muslim religion is assumed to serve as a unifying force within the ethnically heterogeneous neighborhoods of this anti-France, resembling a kind of revolt, a return to the past. A Republic that thought it had replaced God once and for all in the race to mold people's minds now finds itself confronting Him once again. For many, indeed, sacred commitment has become a way to engage in politics at a time when the professionalization of French political life has exacerbated an already glaring democratic deficit, and when the fencing-off of decision-making arenas is seen as an embodiment of a latent racism.[8] Organizing around Islam can thus provide a sense of honor, history, and collective life. This implicit rebuke by "problem neighborhoods" has led outsiders to imagine them as Muslim enclaves, dens of potential Islamists. Since the Bataclan attacks, the Molenbeek neighborhood of Brussels, where some of the terrorists lived, has seen its name become a generic identifier. Within these "Molenbeeks," marginality has been conflated with a religious identity, placing secular France at the forefront of a new struggle. In a country that esteems its literary luminaries, Michel Houellebecq's latest bestseller epitomizes the spirit of the times in the concision of its title: *Submission*. Submit or succumb, in other words.

This, in broad outlines, is the tone of the "culture talk" in which boys like Tarik, Radouane, Marley, Adama, Amédy, and Hassan are immersed.

"Boys will be boys"

In the *cités*, age makes a difference. A boy's age gives him a place in local society, positioning him vis-à-vis others and embedding him in a neighborhood's history. The passage of time and the succession of generations take place in a three-part cycle: "kids," "grown-ups," "old-timers."

Three "kids" ...

Tarik, Radouane, and Marley are 24, 25, and 26 years old, respectively. They belong to the same "generation" – a roughly three-year period during which one cohort of boys in a *cité* will succeed another at the local school, in the community centers, on the football fields, or in the streets. They entered adolescence in the early 2000s: the post-September 11 world, and the France of the 2005 suburban riots.

Tarik has never walked and is confined to a wheelchair. A series of lethal abnormalities were diagnosed while his mother, Aïcha, was pregnant with twins. Though she and her husband Mohamed had planned to move to France permanently, they returned to Algeria instead, convinced they would have to bury a stillborn son in the land of their ancestors. Tarik survived, unlike his brother. He spent the first 11 years of his life in Kabylie, in limbo: between school, Koranic instruction, and daily care, his childhood was marked by lengthy stays at the Hôpital Necker in Paris. There it was confirmed he would survive, provided he received continual medical attention – an impossibility in an Algeria rocked by terrorism. Mohamed decided to move with his son to the northern suburbs of Paris, leaving Aïcha and Samia, Tarik's little sister, 11 years his junior, in the family home. Mohamed left behind a business that had offered him a livelihood and recognition in Algeria, becoming a warehouse worker in several factories around the Paris region – a job he still holds today. With his meager pay and help from the welfare system, he took care of his son, who alternated between six months in a rehabilitation center and six months in school. School is where I first met him, when he was 16.

Tarik heaps praise on "France's public services," to which he owes his life, though there are many wounds they can't heal. Father and son never speak of this family saga of exile and paternal care. Such sacrifices aren't meant to be dramatized or explained. Among men, certain things are done rather than talked about: Mohamed did what he had to do, without complaint or emotional display. Tarik attributes this to the inexorable divergence of the sexes: "My father let my mother and sister have an easy life over there, and since he's a man and I'm a man, we came here and had a shitty life!" Mohamed didn't hesitate to wield his belt when Tarik strayed from the narrow path – not because he couldn't understand what was driving him in his early flirtation with crime, but because that is what has to be done between father and son. Tarik was hardly a scrawny or timorous teenager. In fact, his handicap spurred him to take calculated risks; he had to plan on the assumption that his studies would be interrupted too often to be finished. For a few years, he prospered in the drug trade. His savings made it possible for his mother and sister to be "brought over" to France, and gave him his independence. He paid cash for a high-end wheelchair and left his father's apartment. Gradually he quit "*le business*" (crime), and today he's "white as snow."

Radouane grew up a few hundred meters from Tarik's neighborhood. He had a less eventful trajectory. Petty crime really only took up two years of his life: to fill out his wardrobe, he would steal GPS systems in Paris. This "weakness" could not be long hidden from the accusing eyes of his father, Chérif, who saw jeans in his room worth several hundred euros each and questioned their dubious origins. As an only son, Radouane was the center of his parents' attention, and never felt his childhood lacked for anything. His parents had come from Morocco to pursue a French Dream that, for them, never became a nightmare. Chérif arrived alone and penniless in the 1970s and rose up slowly over a decade or so: once homeless, now renting an apartment in the northern suburbs of Paris. A temporary warehouse worker his whole life, he ended his career at the Galeries Lafayette, working in the stock rooms of the capital's most fashionable department store. Ultimately, night work, erratic schedules, and heavy lifting took a toll on his health. Since his retirement, he has had frequent hospital stays, and Radouane helps out in his spare time. His mother, Latifa, is 12 years younger than her husband. She received what Radouane considers a "modest education" and now works as an assistant in a dentist's office near home. Radouane is very close to his parents and can't bring himself to leave the family apartment, especially now that his father requires daily care. In a sense, he has already repaid them in kind. After a year during which I and some other teachers made special efforts to help him, he passed the baccalaureate exam. The day he got the results, he heard his father "sob" for the first time, over the phone. That was also the moment I first realized, through Radouane's misty eyes, how the impact of such an exam can reverberate over several generations in families like his. He went far in his studies: a degree in accounting, another in management, acceptance at a business school in Paris, plus a Master's and a job at a multinational to boot. In retrospect, there was nothing predictable about Radouane's trajectory: a fun-loving student, he hid his serious side with outbursts intended to amuse his classmates and conceal anxieties that, at the time, I could hardly guess at.

Marley never left his childhood apartment, located in one of Grigny's main *cités*. His parents are from Guadeloupe. They came to France, like many others, seeking a better life. Marley's father soon deserted the family home, moving to another outer-city town. For Marley, he remains nameless and faceless: "For me, my father is nobody, I owe him absolutely nothing," as he put it the first time we discussed the latter's existence – which is mainly an absence. His mother, Monique, worked in Paris as a teacher's aide in an elementary school. She left early in the morning and got home late, taking the commuter train every rush hour to support her two sons and her daughter. It was Marley who caused her by far the most worry. He got into an endless series of "scrapes," some of them becoming real crises – such as when Monique lost 20 years of savings, around 20,000 euros, owing to a fraudulent bank transaction in an arrangement where Marley had acted as the middleman for a bankrupt company, an injustice resolved only after years of exhausting legal proceedings. Monique prayed to Jesus for her son, but she didn't rely on God alone. She knew how to "wear the pants" in the family. To straighten Marley out, she sent him back to the "old country" to work in a restaurant for a year and a half. But after his return, she continued to accept the shopping bags Marley kept depositing in their apartment's small kitchen, with the help of his brother, Caleb, a trucker two years his junior. His older sister, Janice, left the city when she got a job as a secretary. Once Monique moved back to Guadeloupe to enjoy her retirement, the household the four of them once shared shrank to just the two brothers. Now Monique visits Grigny only occasionally, to see her sons and catch up on neighborhood news. Marley never really liked school and quickly turned to petty crime. Or maybe school didn't like him. That's how he describes it when he tells of how he was assigned to a special school for "hyperactive children." He dropped out of a bakery training program, ending his schooling with no diploma of any kind. Soon the streets were his whole world: he was involved in a series of burglaries and muggings of commuter train passengers; he sold drugs and offered his services to any of the older boys who might need them. He alternated such "hits" with prison stays – five so far – and countless spells on probation, which limit his movements with electronic bracelets.

... two "grown-ups" ...

Adama and Amédy, almost 10 years older, were, as they say in the *cités*, "big brothers" to Marley. They entered adolescence earlier, in the mid-1990s – a less tense ideological and geopolitical context, perhaps, but one that already contained sparks of future conflagrations. The issue of racism was central, and its normalization came with the demise of the full-employment era. Jacques Chirac personally embodied this political shift. It was Chirac, as a young prime minister with a bright future, who said on television in the mid-1970s: "A country with 900,000 unemployed but with 2 million immigrant workers is not a country where the problem of jobs can't be solved."[9] A decade and a half later, as mayor of Paris and undisputed leader of the French right, Chirac added cultural incompatibility to the list of grievances:

> Foreigners aren't the problem, it's that there's an overdose of them. It might be true that there aren't any more foreigners than there were before the war, but they're not the same ones, and that makes a difference. There's no doubt that having Spanish, Polish, and Portuguese working here causes fewer problems than having Muslims and Blacks. [...] If you add in the noise and the smell, it drives the ordinary French worker crazy.[10]

The first National Front election victories followed in 1995, bringing an openly xenophobic party to power in several towns in southern France. For the French political class, this was an earthquake. For Adama or Amédy, it seemed more like a slow continuum; at ages 11 and 13, they saw in such "culture talk" nothing but a blatant rejection of them and their families. Their parents had left Mali in the 1970s and worked in the shadows their whole lives. Their dads were blue-collar workers and both died from work-related causes. Adama's father was a painter on local construction sites. His career disintegrated when he fell from a scaffold and became handicapped; he died shortly after taking early retirement. Amédy's father worked in a factory and died just before reaching a retirement he would never enjoy, three years before his son's spectacular death. Their mothers were both cleaners. Adama's stopped working once her older children were able to support the family. Amédy's mother worked on and off; keeping a good home took up most of her time. Adama grew up in a family of nine children, with seven boys and two girls sharing the apartment's bedrooms. Amédy was the seventh child, and only boy, in a family of 10 in which nearly all the girls enjoyed upward mobility. The smell of groundnut stew and fonio fritters was a reminder of the path from Mali to Grigny. For the two boys, as for so many others, France's twentieth-century political history came to a dead stop in 2002, their first election year as eligible voters. That April, Jean-Marie Le Pen's National Front made it to the second round of the presidential election. The media were aghast. In the runoff, one man stood in the way of the far right's path to power, and he swept the election with 82 percent of the vote. His name was Jacques Chirac.

This bleak outlook was darkened further by rising local tensions in Grigny. The unemployment rate exploded, as did rents in much of the private housing stock. Grigny became a favorite source of supply for Parisian drug users thanks to a highway running through the town. Serving Adama's and Amédy's neighborhoods on either side, the road allowed motorists to get from Paris to Grigny in 20 minutes during the traffic-free late-night hours. The drug trade took root, bringing a welcome rise in the price of merchandise.

Late 1996 witnessed an episode that would leave deep marks. Rivalry between youths from Grigny and those from a neighboring town exploded: a scuffle over honor led to a punitive raid involving around 60 boys. It ended with the murder of a young man from the rival gang. Apartment buildings were surrounded, the start of a long police investigation that would deeply affect families' daily lives. Witnesses contradicted each other and accusations piled up, shattering neighborhood solidarity. The town's young people all came under suspicion of having participated in the murder or, at a minimum, being complicit in it. Two were sentenced to 6 years and 12 years in prison, but the real verdict was the atmosphere of suspicion and silence that followed. Foued, a longtime social worker close to many of the young people involved in this episode, sees it as a deep rupture, a foundational event whose repercussions can still be felt today. For the "kids," like Adama and Amédy, the killing made a deep impression. It showed one possible way of settling problems – of existing in the world – and the silence of their elders left the act with an unchallenged aura of legitimacy. Inside the neighborhood, a climate of silence and taboo prevailed; outside it, unqualified condemnation reigned: two forms of denial about what had actually happened. Fantasies and fears about the neighborhood's young people proliferated; they, in turn, realized that such fears could be a resource, to be mobilized when needed. The "grown-ups," nearly all of whom had gravitated around those at the center of the drama, were left discredited and shamed. It weakened their roles as authority figures – a void Foued saw as an unprecedented breach in the process of neighborhood socialization. Killing and dying prematurely were now thinkable prospects. The list of victims would grow. This local event was part of a broader logic: the *routinization of fear* regarding boys in the *cités*. Youth became a threat, neighborhood goings-on became political, politics became repressive.[11] Fear spread, too, among those adults whose job it was to stay in touch with the young, and later it would chime with the debates surrounding the 2007 presidential election. After a term as interior minister, Nicolas Sarkozy won that vote on a promise to "clean up the scum with a power washer." "Tough talk," in practice, meant all toughness and no talking.

It took Amédy and Adama only a few years to advance from petty crime to serious delinquency. Each started high school on a vocational track but quit before the baccalaureate exam. Outside the neighborhood, Amédy became known for muggings and armed robberies. These earned him a series of convictions and a reputation, both with the police and on the streets. Among local boys involved in the underground economy, those of Amédy's generation praise his toughness and tactical intelligence, while older ones are more equivocal. He's sometimes described as a "hired gun," a person you could turn to when someone had failed to hold up their side of a deal. He knew how to handle weapons and how to use physical violence, and he was able to surround himself with boys sufficiently beholden to him that he could direct operations remotely. He was clearly not one to balk at "getting his hands dirty" – a line not everyone would cross. Within the neighborhood, he was also known for his kindness and discretion. He was one of the many boys who, entering the lobby of an apartment building, would carry mothers' shopping bags and kid around with neighbors. His illicit dealings didn't keep him from developing lasting friendships – including with Adama, two years his junior.

Adama was never really part of Amédy's crew, but for a few years he, too, did his share of "hits." At age 19, inevitably, he "went down": caught in the act in the middle of a hold-up. Time in prison had quite different effects on the two friends. Amédy described "the hole" as "the greatest fucking school for crime."[12] For Adama, by contrast, it marked the start of his gradual withdrawal from delinquency. Ultimately he would go back to school, obtaining a professional certificate and a job at a youth center in another outer-city town. Like Hassan a decade earlier, his work is more than just a job: it's a "huge personal struggle," a sort of redemption. The two friends' divergent careers never occasioned the slightest quarrel between them. The jokes, the adventures, the rounds of video games that Adama shared with "Dolly," as Amédy was called by his Grigny mates, could never be swept away by their contrasting livelihoods.

... and an "old-timer"

Hassan is 44. He was present at the pivotal moment when this teenage friendship was cemented. But although he was one of the few "grown-ups" in Grigny who stayed in touch with Adama's and Amédy's generation, Hassan didn't experience the 1996 events firsthand. He'd been living in Lille, completing his training as a software engineer, and only returned to Grigny three years after the disturbances. Affable and fun-loving, Hassan has never been involved in crime. With his knack for knowing the right thing to say, it's easy to forget the fact that he arrived in France relatively recently. He left the Kabyle mountains of Algeria at the age of 11, fleeing a country where his family could no longer stay. They had openly supported the National Liberation Front and paid for it in blood. His maternal grandfather was murdered along with several men from the village; like Tarik, Hassan remembers atrocities committed on his doorstep. When he first arrived, Hassan didn't yet speak French. Of his first contact with Paris he recalls a "strong smell of burning wood" as he got off the plane, a memory still sharp in his mind, though he can no longer smell it. His parents, Bouzid and Dounia, revered education. Consequently, Hassan, like his sister and two younger brothers, inherited an intellectual appetite and political consciousness seldom encountered in the neighborhood. Before returning to Algeria to marry, Dounia had been sent to France to finish her studies. Though her own education was stymied, she retained a love of reading and passed on her unquenched desire for learning to her children. She never got to witness their professional success: she died of a serious chronic illness at the age of 40. The family were ardent users of the local library. Of Bouzid, Hassan recalls how serious he was – immersed in a copy of Macchiavelli's *The Prince*, surrounded by piles of books on industrial and metallurgical techniques, an obsession of his. Bouzid became a skilled worker, employed in several factories belonging to a large conglomerate in the Paris suburbs. A trade union activist and inveterate reader of *L'Humanité*, the French Communist Party newspaper, Bouzid would rail against the world's injustices to his children.

Hassan's decision to return to Grigny probably owed something to this paternal political commitment. The city hired him as a social worker, putting his computer savvy to work as part of a small staff that crisscrossed the streets of the neighborhood. For several years, he spent time with young people who seldom encountered adults on a daily basis. More and more of them, like Amédy and Adama, would disappear behind bars for extended periods. Hassan tried, by his presence, to "plug the leak," to "short this circuit that the kids couldn't escape from." Jacques Chirac's ascent to the presidency in 2002 sounded the death knell of this "huge struggle": his team was dismantled by the local government. Haunted by a fear of getting bogged down, Hassan stepped back from involvement in the neighborhood and started a computer training and service business. His early interest in the Internet and "big data" ensured him a degree of success. He often traveled for work and his professional reputation rose.

The first time he agreed to see me, I found his new offices on the outskirts of Grigny, overlooking the town; piles of cardboard boxes bore witness to a promising expansion. There's something symbolic about this position of watchful proximity. The address is not a Grigny address – a point in its favor when it comes to attracting clients. And while Hassan still keeps his distance, he continues to watch, as if unable to fully abandon all those lives heading toward what he describes, in an oxymoronic phrase, as "fine messes."

Conflicting loyalties, recognition of debts

As the friendship between Amédy and Adama illustrates, loyalty always involves a delicate balancing act: faithfulness to one's prior commitments, on the one hand; respecting the rules of honor and integrity, on the other. As a clinical family therapist in the 1970s, the Hungarian-American psychiatrist Ivan Boszormenyi-Nagy explored the nature of "conflicts of loyalty" between children and parents.[13] At that time, therapeutic practice mainly dealt with individual psyches and pathologies. In contrast, when Boszormenyi-Nagy encountered lasting personal connections that were challenged by competing relationships, he instead focused on the initial circumstances that had surrounded their formation. Feelings of loyalty, he discovered, never exist without tension or conflict. Fidelity to a commitment is valued only when there's a choice of other possible commitments. Social life takes the form of new encounters that test the strength of established connections. Prior loyalties are always threatened by potential new loyalties. This risk is precisely what makes them so precious. If such conflicts are to be managed, there has to be confidence in the reciprocity and fairness of the relationship. Context becomes fundamental: determining attitudes and expectations, ordaining what will be seen as loyalty and what as betrayal. In the absence of dialogue or accommodation, expectations are likely to clash; they are never self-explanatory. For Boszormenyi-Nagy, this was where therapy could be useful, by making demands explicit and reminding each side of the context and circumstances that first gave rise to the bond. For when such conflicts go unresolved, it's hard to maintain feelings of belonging in a close-knit group – and the self-confidence that comes with them.

A factory of conflicting loyalties

From this point of view, the context of the *cités* is like a *factory of conflicting loyalties* for these boys. Between the behavior expected of a boy by his father, mother, brothers, sisters, teachers, "big brothers," social workers, educators, police, schoolmates, neighborhood friends, gang friends, business partners, or girls, and the behavior he thinks he owes them, lies a web of potential betrayals. If we then add a historical context in which working-class status, immigration, and place of residence have never been more stigmatized, we can see how remaining faithful to one's roots involves conflicting imperatives. The most obvious of these is the relationship with the neighborhood, poised between affection and disparagement. To do right by the neighborhood that brought you up means escaping it without betraying it – twin obligations whose fulfillment is likely to prove impossible.

Such conflicts can only be resolved at ground level: judging them from above is impossible. What we value, whom we value, what keeps us going – these all flow from some context, some situation, for which no formal reasoning can substitute. For example, one might assume that Adama's feelings toward Amédy must have changed profoundly as a result of his deep commitment to being a youth coordinator. "Dolly," after all, embodied everything Adama tries to combat, day in and day out. For Adama's youngsters, Amédy is a cautionary tale. After the January 2015 attacks, "Amédy Coulibaly" became a symbol for the enemy. To endorse the Hyper Cacher killings would be unthinkable.The few kids who dare to proclaim "*Je suis Amédy*" are confused by Adama. He provokes heated debates. His mission as an educator is at stake. Since Amédy chose death, repudiating him costs little. Yet, despite everything, mention of his death brings a surge of unfailing loyalty, as it did one day in June 2016, at a barbecue hastily organized to celebrate the baccalaureate results, which had been announced that morning. The newly minted graduates – more girls than boys, as usual – bustled around the kitchenette of one of the town's youth centers, stationing themselves in front of the salads and cakes. As master of ceremonies, Adama took care of the grilling on the sidewalk. Standing around with a few of his generation's "old-timers," he told stories from his youth. The thick smoke kept passersby away; they would return once the smell of grilled meat wafted up.

Adama: With Amédy, we didn't go to the same elementary school but we'd meet up after school, just stuff you do with a group, like going to the mall. You know, we'd be together. And all the guys who were with us will talk about Amédy the same way I do, with the same delicacy, the same tone. It's emotional … Amédy wasn't just some guy, he was important for us. Again, I'm not going to get into what he did, I'm not going to talk to you about … [*silence*]

FT: Ok … I understand what you mean ….

Adama: Because people will say, it [the attack] was good or bad, but I can't talk about that. For me, Amédy was special, he was epic. A great person, *wallah*. He did it [the attack]. We're not going to talk about that, but separate from that, he was a great person. He was always there to help his fellow man.

FT: So for you, that's what should be remembered about Amédy, that he was "great," "epic"?

Adama: Yeah. Really, really great. A good guy. A guy who helped his fellow man, like you wouldn't believe! And then, you know, there are secrets.

FT: Things you can't say?

Adama: I mean, these are old stories from when we were kids. He was an upstanding guy. A good guy. A good companion.

FT: So you didn't feel any hatred toward him after what happened? I've heard people in the neighborhood take different positions. There are some people who say what he did was a betrayal. You didn't experience it that way?

Adama: No. It wasn't a betrayal. He didn't betray anything. He did what he had to do, that's it. Anybody who talks about betrayal

> didn't go through what Amédy went through, and what I went through with him. They can't understand. He didn't betray anything at all! Now, I'm sad for the families, for all the people who died. But I would say that's between them and him. Between him and me, it's something else.

To reject Amédy would force Adama to deny an important part of his past, but also an important part of what drives him now. When discussing memories of their friendship, Adama invokes a number of bedrock values: solidarity ("a good companion"), integrity ("an upstanding guy"), morality ("a good guy"), generosity ("he was always there to help his fellow man"), virility. The memories are "something special" and "epic" because these values still resonate. They guided his career change after prison and gave meaning to his uncertain path back to school. In a sense, it was in the name of what he shared with Amédy that he became a youth coordinator. His return to the neighborhood was like a putting to rights: he became a respectable elder in service to the younger generation. To deny their bond would amount to a betrayal of this calling, and a betrayal of his affection for Grigny. Still, he has to separate the "companion" from the "jihadist." There can be no equivalence between Dolly and "Abu Bassir Abdallah al-Ifriq," Amédy's final *nom de guerre*, which he declared on video. Adama is unable to name the acts his friend perpetrated (the words "attack," "murders," "killings," are unsayable) and refuses to judge the reasons behind them. There's "them and him," on the one hand; "him and me" on the other. This dividing line crystallizes his opposition to those who call Amédy a traitor to the neighborhood. He senses that these "other people" I mentioned in our conversation never "went through the same things" as him and Amédy. They belong to Hassan's generation. For them, Amédy was a "kid," one of many. His hostage-taking embodied the failure of their unspoken mission: keeping the kids in line, to give the town a better image. Amédy did know how to give back – as he once did on a trip to the south of France organized by one of the town's youth centers when he was still in high school. Happy to take advantage of the sun and the beach, he left the organizers with memories of a "really well-behaved and responsible" boy: seeing to it that the curfew was respected, making sure the dishwashing and housekeeping got done. With the attack, Amédy failed to give back what he had received. Or perhaps what he meant by it was that he hadn't received enough. Either way, his posthumous presence stands at odds with what the grown-ups have to be. Thus, Amédy betrayed them.

Getting closer

As the anthropologist Marcel Mauss explained in *The Gift*, to live with others is to exchange: behind the "spirit of the thing given" hides a three-fold obligation to give, to receive, and to give back. Whether it's a piece of advice, a joke, a gesture of politeness, or the surrender of an object, every exchange is undertaken within a circle of relationships: "To refuse to give, to fail to invite, just as to refuse to accept, is tantamount to declaring war; it is to reject the bond of alliance and commonality."[14] Collective life rests on a set of personal debts and obligations that create a situation of unspoken interdependencies. What makes these interdependencies difficult to see is that giving back right away would be inconceivable as it would mean refusing to receive. It's the momentary forgetting of what one owes that causes bonds to grow strong: the nature of the gift is to oblige the receiver eventually. As Adama's mourning shows, this invisible social fabric, with its distant acknowledgment of debts, is what grounds the morals of the stories people tell themselves, much more than grand abstract principles (it is forbidden to kill, it is good to teach young people, etc.). Conflicts of loyalty and acknowledgment of debts are what gradually bring into being the values that come to define the boundaries of the sacred. They make those values real, they connect the meaning of human actions with flesh-and-blood creatures. Discord over Amédy arises between Adama and some of the "grown-ups" only because they agree on the essentials. It's not surprising that those grown-ups most deeply invested in organized community life – that is, those who are most like Adama in their daily lives – are the ones who show the greatest venom toward someone who, for Adama, remains an "amazing" person. Dolly is an intermediary; like many others, he acts as a conductor of personal debts and loyalties.

These acknowledgments of debts and conflicts of loyalties require keeping up appearances. They demand that Adama dismiss the significance of "Abu Bassir Abdallah al-Ifriq," for example. Preserving appearances and statuses is more important than making some impossible reckoning. There can never be a hard-and-fast contract. Form is at least as important as substance. What the grown-ups required of Amédy was never that he achieve success legally, or even clean up his act. Such a demand would be unrealistic in a town where a quarter of the labor force is unemployed. The "*grand frères*" don't see themselves as saviors; at best, they are buffers. The moral debt is minimal: a modicum of discretion, even if that requires disappearing from view. The neighborhood isn't a place where everyone knows everything. Some things are known to all, but others aren't meant to leave the confines of a small group. The *cités* are more of a rumor mill than a panopticon. When Amédy would go off to prison or come under suspicion of having taken part in some unscrupulous score-settling, he wasn't seen as a traitor – provided some degree of discretion was maintained. Only a grandstander would detach himself from his social roots. With the Hyper Cacher killings, Amédy broke an unspoken rule uniting successive generations of boys: keep up appearances, save face, give back without making a big show of it.

"A white fence-post in a black forest"

Conflicting loyalties and acknowledged debts don't always stay within the narrow confines of the neighborhood – as I experienced with Marley. The chances of our meeting were slight. What brought us together was the unlikely journey of a book.

The delinquent and the sociologist

It all started with Yasmina, a former student of mine at university who went on to become an economics and social sciences teacher living in Grigny. When I showed up to an event at a local cultural center one evening, I was surprised to run into her in the packed hall. A young Grigny local was presenting his first short film that evening, made with the help of a grant from FEMIS, the prestigious European film and TV institute. The event was joyous, the film exciting. The atmosphere was one of celebration for a neighborhood "success story." Most of the audience were young college students, drawn from the neighborhood's "minority of the best."[15] Conversations in the lobby were full of hope for the future. Between slices of pie, I told Yasmina what had brought me to Grigny and she gave me contact information for a boy who would "interest" me. Marley was an old friend of hers from junior high, someone she'd always been fond of. But he'd "turned out badly." It emerged that about a year earlier, the two of them had gotten back in touch because of me: Yasmina had read my first book, *Des capuches et des hommes*, and she'd thought of Marley. She felt it gave her a better understanding of what had happened to him, and afterward she got in touch and lent him the book. As amused and flattered as I was by this story, I was even more "interested" in her offer to act as go-between. Cell phones did the rest: I left the auditorium knowing that Marley would meet with me in the coming days.

The next day I went to another event – a nighttime barbecue on a concrete terrace to celebrate the June weather and the end of the Ramadan fast. I'd been invited by one of Adama's brothers, Abderrahmane, who had organized the event, and I arrived with Abdou, with whom I'd spent the afternoon. A former rapper in his forties, Abdou is now a well-known boxing trainer, neighborhood activist, and local social worker. The little terrace was packed. Other than Abdou and Abderrahmane I didn't know anybody there, but clearly, with these two figures introducing me, I couldn't be such a bad guy. I was treated with benign indifference. When Abdou and Abderrahmane had social obligations to attend to, I found myself alone: the only white person on the terrace, the only vegetarian not eating the halal merguez perfuming the air. Marley was observing me with amusement; he told me a few weeks later that I looked like "a white fence-post in a black forest, standing around like an idiot, not knowing what to do with his hands." He put a stop to the spectacle before it went on too long. Guessing who I was, he came over to introduce himself. At that point, my book became a conduit with multiple meanings.

The power of the book

First, it was a mark of distinction, which says a lot about what intellectual achievement means in French society. When a surprised Abdou and Abderrahmane came over to find out how we knew each other, Marley was rather proud to announce that he'd read my book. They looked on incredulously as he relished his small victory, which landed like an unexpected uppercut: "What, you didn't know I read books? Dude, go away and let me talk to the sociologist!" Second, it formed a point of connection, lending our dialogue immeasurable, almost self-sufficient, value: the need to understand. The first question Marley asked me came down to a single word: "Why?" Why would I want to write a book about "normal stuff from everyday life," about "regular people like us"? When I answered that I was trying to get a better understanding of behaviors I found intriguing and which, for me, were far from "normal," he flashed a grimace of confirmation:

> You're totally right; it took me a while to get that, 'cause at first I thought, this book doesn't say anything! It's just normal life. So I

> stopped reading, since I already know all about it. And then I thought about Yasmina, 'cause she's from the neighborhood but she never understood my life. She couldn't understand why I left school and didn't do what she did. I understood that she couldn't understand. And when I understood that she'd finally understood, I thought: "*ouech*, actually this isn't bad," so I read the whole thing. And then I realized something: that it's the neighborhood that made me ... like that.

The act of reading had opened up an unlikely sphere of understanding (a word Marley repeated several times) in which the connections between us were more important than what divided us. It allowed Marley temporarily to make his own meaning of the forces that conditioned his life ("it's the neighborhood that made me ... like that") and created a framework for a good-natured dialogue, since our discussion was socially "off-field."[16] The book became an invitation. We went off and stationed ourselves between the grill and an abandoned pavilion. Marley presented his life in a jumble. We were interrupted from time to time as guys came over to greet him with a dap or tease him with a cutting jibe. I would get a polite glance or a mechanical handshake: though welcome, I still remained a stranger that evening. And yet the book forged an immediate bond between us. After each visitor walked off, Marley would launch into a little sociological commentary, just for me. For example, when he admonished Saïfi for working out too much, the latter, wedged into a tight-fitting Bayern Munich T-shirt, replied mildly that "staying in shape" was important since "you can never be too ripped, man." But as soon as Saïfi was gone, Marley delivered his acid judgment: "See, it's the neighborhood that made him like that – except with him, he doesn't know!"

Our conversation stretched on, with two interruptions from Marley: first to "settle some business" when a car pulled up to get his attention, then to say hi to a small clutch of boys on their way to the final prayer of the day, draped in long djellabas that showed their street clothes underneath. Despite the festive atmosphere and his friendly tone, I struggled to process Marley's stark outlook on the future. He kept repeating that "this is all gonna end badly," that there were too many "scores to settle," too many "hits to take and to dish out." One phrase in particular struck me the most, perhaps because it was so hard to accept that a first encounter could be a prelude to an ending: "For me, it's gonna be death, in five years, I'm sure of it ... I'll be dead, there's no other way out."

Rebels without a cause, or a cause without rebels?

The image of the fighter, the language of war, and the imperative of combat all ricochet through Marley's words. They broadcast what is clearly a rebellion in embryo. Yet they struggle to articulate anything resembling an objective, even as a muted desire for revolt pushes all else aside – including the final countdown.

Combat, confusion, and compensation

Marley didn't seem shaken by this certainty of his premature death. The judgment he sketched of his time on earth was satisfactory: "I don't think I've wasted my time, and I've seen a lot of crazy shit. I've lived, you know? So if it ends soon, that's just how it is." At first sight, one could see this as a mark of the endlessly ridiculed nihilism of a generation full of rebels without a cause. And yet, when I sought to discover why he saw no other way out, Marley stuck to a dry accounting of the facts. He laid out a series of specific causes and inexorable consequences: this unresolved business deal, that ongoing personal conflict, and so on. These facts revealed the contradictions of his situation as an entrepreneur in the underground economy. It's full-time work, and though Marley is unable to cash in on it, it makes him feel like he's in command of events. Every day brings the prospect of new "hits" and "schemes." Marley isn't a specialist in one particular task or a specific line of work. He operates on the basis of whatever opportunities present themselves to him. He makes enough money to support himself and enjoy a local reputation, but he has no job security or guaranteed income to fall back on. His work is in tune with the times: he's always chasing after a new project, moving from job to job without any line of continuity. He's his own boss, in a constant "project of freedom."[17] In the sphere of illegal activity, such long-term precarity piles up more and more baggage that can never be cleared away. The boys sum it up in a pithy formula: "blood debts are money debts."

This sense of insecurity echoes a heightened awareness of the world's injustices: the certainty of being dominated coexists alongside uncertainty about what grand narrative could explain the situation. Marley's habituation to violence results in a self-reflection mingled with confusion; plans for the future being shaped with fatalistic resignation. As we tackled the various possible ways of dying, the Islamist question almost logically poked its way into our conversation.

FT: Have you ever been tempted to go to Syria?

Marley: You're crazy, people who do that are nuts. It's totally ineffective ...

FT: Why?

Marley: Well, when they go to Syria it's to kill Jews, right?

FT: Uh ... no, I don't think so! Really Marley, I've never heard that. You're way off.

Marley: Well, I don't really know, I'm sure you're right; I don't actually care about any of that stuff, and I don't want to go out on a limb since I'm not sure of myself, I don't know much about geopolitics. But I thought when people go to Syria it was to kill Jews, or to get justice somehow. But in that case, what's the point – if you want to kill Jews or rich people, you just go to a bank in Paris and blow yourself up.

FT: So, what do you think about what Amédy Coulibaly did?

Marley: I mean, he went crazy. He screwed up. I didn't really know the guy, but you know, he didn't even think of blowing up a bank or bumping off rich people. A Jewish supermarket – what's the point? And then we're the ones who pay for it.

Marley seemed to understand Amédy's gesture, but offered no mitigating circumstances for his act, or even any particular respect for a person to whom he personally owed nothing. He expressed no sympathy for jihadists, whom he saw as "nuts," but he did endorse the political dimension of their actions. In fact, it was on this very point that Marley disparaged them (they're bad strategists), even as he admitted to being ignorant of the Syrian situation, which he misrepresented with racist prejudice, tinged with conspiracism. My doubts about the connection he drew between "the Jews" and "Syria" injected no tension into the conversation. The tone of our dialogue was such that Marley could almost admit that it was purely cosmetic, and he gave me credit without devaluing himself ("I'm sure you're right"; "I don't know much about geopolitics"). But from this conflation, one obvious point emerged: the legitimacy of a struggle against obscene inequality ("us" and "rich people") and the demand for radical restitution that it implies ("bump off rich people"). It's as if there were indeed some sort of just cause to support, but a lack of words to identify the oppressor, to pinpoint the terrain of struggle, and to orient the meaning of such a rebellion – hence the hazy aura around such figures as "the Jew," "the banker," or "Syria," which serve to embody the sentiment.

The class free-for-all

In the era of the Industrial Revolution, Karl Marx imagined two scenarios for the proletariat: it could be a "class in itself," with objectively exploited workers who nevertheless remain unconscious of their common interests and let themselves be manipulated; or it could be a "class for itself," where workers picture their common interests and mobilize for the class struggle.[18] During the postwar boom, a third configuration took shape, in tandem with the spread of mass production and mass consumption. In Richard Hoggart's formulation, it took the form of an opposition between "them" and "us." The world was split in two, with a constellation of hostile bosses, decision-makers, and advanced degree-holders, on the one hand, and a self-enclosed group of the downtrodden and those close to them, on the other. The injustice and illegitimacy of the social order were taken as given: what the opposition between "them" and "us" accomplished was to make the feeling of being unable to "do much about the main elements in their situation" acceptable, to avoid the "tragic." Belonging to the "us" fostered a sense of self-worth and trust in one's fellows, easing the adjustment to life's unalterable hardships.[19] Today, none of these three scenarios – class unconsciousness, class consciousness, fatalistic dignity – can make sense of a situation that is more like a *class free-for-all*. Here, any shared understanding of a common subaltern condition is thwarted by the absence of a narrative about how the situation could be collectively overturned, as well as by a fragmented collective solidarity. It runs up against individual helplessness and a sentiment of absolute injustice. Death – whether that of "rich people" or of Marley – becomes the hyperbolic expression of these feelings.

The class free-for-all came into view later that evening. It was almost two in the morning. Bringing the night to a close, a group of men in their thirties was gathered around Abderrahmane and a water pipe. He was reminiscing, recalling stories from their teenage football team: the legendary goals, the clashes with rival teams, their rise to the top division, the zealous referees, the blustering coaches, and so on. The names of a few old players from the neighborhood with whom they'd lost touch were recalled with affection. One name in particular shattered the playful atmosphere: Bülent. At the mention of his name, Abderrahmane informed part of the group of his recent death in Syria, a fact confirmed by those "in the loop." Eyes were cast downward. No one wanted to get into a political argument or a substantive discussion. I already knew what Abderrahmane thought of those who went to Syria ("bullshit for assholes") from having talked with him about it a few days earlier. But that night, Bülent was just a player in the top team from the old days. Gripped by an excess of emotion, "Peace to his soul" was all Abderrahmane could say. The phrase was repeated with feeling by the small group of friends, as if the deeper causes of such a death, so absurd to an outside observer like myself, were taken as given – and, ultimately, not to be talked about. The tribute to the old teammate gave way to uneasy silence.

Around the *hookah*, in the cool night air, no one doubted that life is a struggle, that there is dignity in a soldier's death. Yet Bülent, like others, seemed to have rallied to the wrong banner. But could there be some other flag fluttering on the horizon? Abderrahmane dodged the question. As a good captain, he knew the important thing was to stay united through the virtues of team spirit: moving backward, together. The evening ended on an open question: what *were* the little-league team's colors back then?

* * *

Looking backward is, in fact, important. This class free-for-all, this factual and normative verdict that seems to have impressed itself on people's minds – where did it come from? What expectations, what beliefs, what sorts of men are produced by "the neighborhood" Marley speaks of? The word, uttered alternately with disgust and love, conceals a set of social imperatives, enduring relationships, and institutions – school, "business," prison, virility, and the police – that condition the daily lives of many working-class boys. They establish a certain way of interacting with the world, circumscribe the problems to be solved, define what is worth experiencing and supporting. They shape the political socialization of a whole swath of young French men on the margins of the city.

— 2 —

ON THE MARGINS OF THE CITY

seeing a sword
where the sculptor had, in all good faith, designed
a torch –
and not being altogether mistaken

Georges Perec, *Ellis Island*

Imprints of school

In France, education lies at the heart of political passions and debates, in affluent and working-class neighborhoods alike. Here, the right to individual emancipation collides with increasingly rigid patterns of class reproduction. On this point, we must avoid an anachronism: namely, the deeply rooted belief that working-class parents are disengaged from, and their children opposed to, the education system. The time when an "anti-school" culture existed – when boys forged a manly class solidarity by rejecting education – is over.[1] That culture belonged to an era when working-class pride, the dignity of manual labor, and full employment made rejecting state education an accepted way of claiming one's place in the world. The situation has been transformed by the devaluing of manual labor, the democratization of education, insecure work, and immigration. For the children of immigrants, the duty to succeed at school holds the family together. This promise is what redeems parents' sacrifices and, for sons, the social humiliation and physical suffering endured by their fathers. The children carry a mandate: a whole group's hopes for upward mobility – the possibility of symbolic restitution – can be read between the lines of each school assessment.

A badge of dignity and an unrequited love

When Radouane, Tarik, and Hassan passed the baccalaureate exam, their first thoughts went to their parents, in a precious moment of shared emotion. As for Adama and Marley, their failure to do so was almost a moral transgression, a bruise they wish they could erase. Years after quitting school they still brood over this regret: "not going further at school." This mandate isn't a part of family discussions, because it's not something to be discussed. Family life is usually built on a stifling of miseries and hopes. For parents who never went to school, their inability to master the thing they want most is more tolerable when not discussed. Only Hassan and Radouane had the benefit of detailed conversations at home about what they were learning at school: Bouzid, Dounia, and Latifa had prior experience with classrooms and books. For the others, school, though of the utmost importance, isn't fully imported into the family. Consonant with the parental project, and at odds with daily life, success at school is a *badge of dignity*, an emblem for gaining respect and proving one's value.[2]

The expectations are enormous, far too great to be met. For "good" and "bad" students alike, they yield a shared experience of discord and disappointment, exposing the distance between dreams of education and actual outcomes. In this sense, to go to school is to confront a reality principle, one often more difficult to overcome for boys than for girls. Those who do manage to achieve extensive education – Adama calls them "school kids" – constantly reevaluate their itineraries. These retrospective reexaminations force them to accept that, in a sense, they've been had.

Radouane finished his education at a private business school in Paris, where he earned a Master's in accounting. What might be seen as an improbable success, after a baccalaureate obtained by the skin of his teeth, now seems, at age 25, like a partial victory. Radouane focuses on the glass half empty. He regrets having gone to university, then to an "average business school." He would have preferred to attend one of the special preparatory programs for entry into one of France's elite *grandes écoles*: his business school was a second-rank establishment, more of a "scam" than an elite institution. He resents his teachers ("I wasn't the one who decided where I wanted to study, it was all down to chance, and teachers who didn't let me do what I wanted to"). The more he focuses on the education he received, the more he wishes he could do it over again in light of his current knowledge and skills. His criteria of excellence have gradually been redefined. Bitterness is always relative – measured through comparison, rather than by what's been gained.

For the "bad" students, the confrontation with reality is more immediately violent. Bad grades are penalties offering little respite; they dash hopes more quickly. In these cases, opposition to school becomes frontal. But despite how it looks, it's not a sign of disenchantment. However excessive, it is, rather, the mark of an *unrequited love*, as Marley hints when he looks back on his past as a student – 10 years after quitting school at 16, the minimum legal age.

Marley: I was a ... how do they say it? ... [*he mutters, searching for the right word*] ... "a problem child" ... Nah, that's not what it was ... [*pause*] ... "a child with behavior issues" [*laughs*]. I laugh now, but when I heard that when I was little, I thought: "What are these fuckers talking about?!"

FT: How old were you then?

Marley: I was little. Like, elementary school already. I got in a fight with my principal, yo. They put up a petition against me to kick me out. They were nuts!

FT: So you got kicked out?

Marley: They made me go to a special live-in school. My mother and the principal forced me. I said I didn't do anything.... It's true I'm quick to get mad, but I mean, bro, putting me in a boarding school with mentally handicapped kids – man, that wasn't my idea of fun!

FT: [*laughs*]

Marley: I can talk about it now, but before, I couldn't talk about it like this, I've gotten some distance on it. I fucked shit up like you wouldn't believe, I bullied everybody [*laughs*]. I liked to fight too much, I went too far. I beat up seventh graders, eighth graders, ninth graders – I was in sixth grade.... You know how it is when the teacher says "You're out, leave the classroom."

FT: And you wouldn't leave?

Marley: I wouldn't leave! I thought: "Why are you throwing me out, I'm here to learn! You throw me out 'cause I talked too much?" For me it was illogical. You throw your student out of class when he wants to learn! They think that shit's OK. They put me in a school for behavior problems, an ITEP. I don't even remember what that means 'cause none of us called it that.... Hold on ... [*he looks up the acronym on his smartphone*]. Here it is: "*Institut thérapeutique éducatif et pédagogique*" ["Therapeutic Educational and Instructional Institute"]. What is that? They're fucking crazy! Man did I hate that place! We called it "*l'Institut technique pour enfants précoces*" ["Technical Institute for Precocious Children"].

It's striking how much perspective Marley has managed to gain on his past (the discussion is playful, we laugh together several times) even as a tenacious bitterness remains (he searches for the right words, he rants, acts out several scenes for me). Ten years after the fact, verbal violence has replaced physical violence as a means of keeping such "illogic" at bay. The play on the institution's name captures the distance between the official and the unofficial: the "child with behavioral issues" becomes the "precocious child."

Faced with a monolithic and hostile world (the "crazy," "fuckers," "nuts"), Marley took refuge in an outward identity. For those who feel excluded, two alternatives offer immediate opportunities to contest the powers that be: the codes of the neighborhood and the precepts of Islam.

A furious desire for intelligence

In the classroom, playing the *cité* "bad boy" and upholding the codes of the street are ways of grasping at an alternative status.[3] Marley beat up older students and refused to obey the teachers, even to the point of going "too far." The more school seemed a lost cause, the more he had to gain from playing by the uncompromising rules of power, toughness, and independence – rules he began to learn when he started dealing and pickpocketing. Those were successes he could counterpose to his failure at school. The codes of the neighborhood are different from what Paul Willis described as the "shopfloor culture"[4] of working-class boys in the 1970s. "Shopfloor culture" could easily substitute for school culture because both shared the same key feature: they drew a link between present and future. Each was oriented to a set of future goals (earning a diploma, becoming a worker) that made the present more secure by investing the future with meaning. By contrast, the rules of the drug business are oriented solely to the immediate present: links between generations are looser, one "hit" follows another without adding up to anything more, uncertainty about the future prevails, as does the feeling of insecurity. It's an incomplete substitute, anchored in a fleeting present.*

* In the turn from student to delinquent, the issue of time is central. This discussion took place in the presence of Manda, Marley's new crewmate. The three of us were sitting around a parking lot, looking out over one of the rows of buildings of their housing project. Our conversation lingered on: it helped pass the time and reminded us of the time that had passed. Manda's background is similar to Marley's. Though he went on to a vocational program, he did not obtain the baccalaureate and left school at 18. Both

That's less the case when it comes to Islam, whose precepts do seek to establish some relationship with the timeless, with morality, tradition, immortality, and truth. Playing the Muslim is more reassuring at a symbolic level, but doesn't necessarily provide more structure. Religious practice is sporadic at this age – and, for those who practice it, less constraining than the rules and debts of "*le business.*" But in a country built on struggles over the meaning of secularism (*laïcité*), and which continues to be shaken by Islamist attacks, it's the best way to unnerve teachers and upend the classroom – a means of regaining control by putting teachers on the defensive. Just as "problem students" in Germany, for example, can sometimes espouse Nazism in class, it's an expression of pique more than a sign of firm adherence to a competing ideology.[5]

Opposition to the teacher as an individual is connected to the intimate experience of social contempt conveyed by a range of gestures, words, and looks, of which students from immigrant backgrounds are acutely conscious when at school. They must learn to move past these early wounds if they're not to end up quitting school "precociously," as Marley did. According to the sociologist Abdelmalek Sayad, these wounds result in an "unspoken indictment which they only articulate privately with trusted intimates, echoing the 'act of faith' that the ethos of meritocracy represents."[6] Since school is implicitly asked to undo an entire group's dishonor by raising the status of its children, school punishments are experienced as racist or Islamophobic accusations, as rejections of the group as a whole.

This disappointment exposes the fragility of a collective fantasy, and in the absence of words to make sense of it, the indictment most often takes place silently. It took Hassan years to move past it. He was a very good student in middle school. From a very young age, he'd been in the habit of reading a great deal ("our second home was the neighborhood library"). Unlike his classmates, when he was 16 he was sent to the district's upscale high school, which took in students from outside the Grigny *cités*, on the strength of his academic record. He experienced this move as a triumphant ascent. His expectations were quickly dashed, however. Without realizing it, he put his new teachers and classmates on a pedestal. Yet he soon found conversations between classes "lame and shallow," the teachers "condescending" and "not very smart," the classes "uninteresting." He felt both

stress how difficult it is to make money in *le business*, and in retrospect look back on school with regret. The feeling brought us closer that talkative afternoon, as an "ex-teacher" and "ex-dropouts."

"too good" for the school and "not good enough" for the people in it, as if his intellectual aspirations couldn't be realized within a social reality he found "sub-par." The incident that marked his loss of faith in the meritocratic story was when Julie, one of his classmates, told him jokingly that she'd worn a miniskirt to get a good grade on her history oral report. She'd wagered this method would pay off – and, according to Hassan, this proved to be the case, to his "disgust." Whether the incident actually happened that way matters little. The fact that Hassan believes it did is significant, however. He became disruptive, constantly challenging teachers, skipping classes, quitting school without obtaining the baccalaureate – an incomprehensible outcome for his family and middle-school teachers. He took the exam again the following year as an independent student. He just barely passed, and then went on to pursue higher education.

The contradiction between the sacredness of knowledge and the indecency that Julie's miniskirt represented for Hassan highlights just how much the intellectual experience of schooling matters. This is what Radouane is getting at when he criticizes the "phony business school with its two-bit classes" where he finished his studies. The point of school is to offer perspective on the world, to refashion these boys as thinking subjects. It should ordain a young mind to partake of the world of ideas and the verbal sparring that goes with command of intellectual life. For example, the boys have fully accepted the hierarchy that pits the "concrete spirit" of vocational education, geared toward lesser tasks, against the "abstract spirit" of general education, needed to achieve command of oneself and others – which they affirm.[7] But they haven't taken on board everything the French school system values. There is something *furious* about their desire for intelligence. It never follows the canons of the institution or the codes of those who already belong to it, like the teachers and their children. Hassan and Radouane best articulate this disjunction, since they went furthest in their studies. The desire has to be fulfilled immediately, in concrete reality and experience. Intellectual mastery is valuable when it focuses on daily life, when it affects the world in the here and now. Though formulated abstractly, it can't dispense with usefulness. It's an act of sublimation, a re-appropriation of the everyday. The masks have to fall away, life has to change. This unspoken demand for utility is often interpreted as a lack of taste or an inability to appreciate abstraction.The irony sometimes escapes the teacher – as it once did in class when Tarik, seated in the front row, kept asking me questions about the domino theory and the captive consumer in a situation of monopoly. This was seven years ago. I have a precise recollection of the mutual pleasure of this back-and-forth, the sharpness of his questions, our animated exchanges. Later I would realize that this moment of intellectual communion only happened because Tarik was trying to put into words the day-to-day operations of a thriving small business.

When hostilities end …

Although teachers in general symbolize social and intellectual rejection, there are regularly one or two teachers who represent exceptions that prove the rule. There is often the "one teacher" who, for a series of obscure reasons, manages to defuse the initial hostility, creating an opening for a partial reconciliation and a turn from mistrust to renewed trust. I haven't always been aware of it when I've been able to play this role – as I did with Tarik, who continues to address me as *vous*, to call me "*Monsieur*," and to send me his "thoughts" for International Teachers' Day, on October 5, an event whose existence I learned about from him. Thus the imprint of school goes both ways: reexamination as well as rejection. Its depth shows the extent to which all these boys are, deep down, "school kids" – as illustrated by Adama, when he looks back on his own trajectory.

> *Adama*: The kids in middle school would look at us and be jealous because we'd be out late, we'd hang out outside, we'd do stuff. They thought we were people they should be hanging out with, but we were into violence, crime, the wrong path. But you could sense this fascination …
>
> *FT*: You felt important?
>
> *Adama*: Yes, you've got to be somebody.… Sometimes I'd play around with it: we'd go to school just to tell stories about what we'd been doing the day before, the hijinks we got up to. … You know, I think I had potential … but I didn't use it wisely.… Anyway, I was doing other things.
>
> *FT*: Do you have any good memories, regardless?
>
> *Adama*: Yeah! There was French class, with a teacher who really got me. It was … the whole writing process, you know. I liked writing.… I didn't totally understand it.… She helped me improve that side of things, which I didn't understand at all and which, by the end, I started to appreciate. Telling stories.… That, I was good at [*laughs*]. I was a champion at that!
>
> *FT*: And that ended?
>
> *Adama*: Well after I stopped school, I went away for two years [*to prison*]. I did a technology program. But school helped me a lot to

gain perspective. I was often mad at them, but I think they did a good job with me …

FT: You mean, the teachers?

Adama: The teachers, the administrators, the whole faculty. They helped me a lot. They always put me in classes with people who didn't have my background at all. People who were first in their class.

FT: You liked that?

Adama: I didn't! But they realized that, little by little, it would open me up to ideas I never would have had otherwise. In retrospect I think, shit, I could have ended up getting the *bac* because of them.

FT: It opened your mind a bit?

Adama: Of course it opened me up, because the people in my class … now they're teachers! They've done amazing things: biologists, things like that [*laughs*]. Those dudes have gone far. I was poison, I scared them.… I noticed they'd often say to me: "We didn't think you were like that." Those words *came up all the time* … [*emphatically*]. I wasn't aware of the effect I had. Of course, I was almost a mental case. I mean, that's going far, but people had to watch out for me.… And people would tell me: "Hey, you're actually a cool guy, you have fun, you tell jokes," as if I was always angry. But really, if you didn't know me, it was natural to be afraid of me, you'd think I was just the worst little rat.… It helped me with self-improvement, you know. Working on myself, I would think: I shouldn't come off a certain way to them.

Despite having his education cut short by a prison term for robbery, Adama still has precious memories of school, as a promise ("I could have ended up getting the *bac*") and as a series of new departures, ultimately happy ones. These are indeed reexaminations, both intellectual ("the whole writing process" that made him a "champion") and social (experienced through his ability to get along with people who were "first in their class," who "went far" and saw him as something other than "poison"). Finding people who "got" him helped him shed his image as a "mental case"; he could then "get" himself via his own work of "self-improvement" and self-control. These reexaminations didn't bear fruit immediately, but they did offer glimmers of what has now become clear in the light of the present.

If there is one thing that unites these boys with their parents, it's the desire for achievement by proxy, to convert present effort into future success. That's already a goal for Tarik and Radouane, who envision nothing less than "the best private schools" for their hypothetical sons. For Adama, it's already a roadmap for his four-year-old daughter and his nine-month-old son:

> I want a first-class education for them, I want them to rub shoulders at school with people who'll help them in the future, who have nothing to do with their social background – even, like, a kid whose father is a diplomat or a minister! Because it's the connections you make at school that make it so you're OK in the future. They're the ones who'll make you something. . . .

It's as if the game always changes once you know the hidden rules.

The incompleteness of *le business*

Once Adama, Amédy, Tarik, and Marley started slipping steadily into crime, illegal activity replaced school almost symmetrically. The chief purpose of a diploma is to land a job. In this sense, the street doesn't push school aside so much as it picks up where school leaves off.

Making money

Marley made the turn after his first stay in a juvenile detention center in 2007, at age 16. He'd been enrolled in a bakery apprenticeship training program. His program had six months left. He'd already pictured himself working in the patisserie where he was employed on work-study. He was being paid, but from time to time took part in a few "hijinks" with neighborhood friends. He was arrested by police one afternoon on an RER commuter train while joining up with a group of friends who had just robbed passengers a few stations earlier. At the time, there was a lot of talk about repeated attacks by outer-city "RER gangs," which received national media attention and shocked the country. An active search for the perpetrators was underway. These attacks foreshadowed the more organized "*diligences du Far West*" ("Old West stagecoach") attacks, involving masked groups in the Essone region between 2013 and 2015. Marley was found guilty of the attack – which he denied – and went to prison for the first time, for several months. When he got out, he made peace with the end of his school career and a pastry-making future. He returned to "Far West" territory, filling the void left by his return to freedom. He opened up about it one afternoon while with Manda, a new member of his crew.

> *Marley*: Back then I'd get up in the morning like I was going to school. I'd pack my backpack with toys, a notebook ... and then I'd rob people. It was just an everyday thing for me, it was nuts. I preferred

being alone, that way there were no problems. I didn't need anybody's help to do a hit on someone. I'd see a guy who was all neat and proper – a guy like you – and I'd say: "Hey, gimme your phone!" I would do people my own age, 'cause I was young. I couldn't attack old people, out of respect. I liked to say stuff like [*in a menacing voice*]: "You know why I'm here!" [*laughs*]. What's crazy is that we robbed so many people, sometimes we'd come across the same people again [*laughs*]!

FT: You remembered them?

Marley: No, but they did! Off we'd go, robbing people from eight in the morning in all the stations. When we got to the Gare de Lyon, there were guys from the old country who would buy it all for 30 bucks and then sell it at a cellphone stand. We were young, we wanted money, we'd sell cheap when the stuff could go for 100 euros. I'd go home and then rob again. Sometimes I'd make four round-trips.

FT: Every day?

Marley: No, after a while the cops started to go undercover on the trains, things got hot. There were some dudes who got busted 'cause they went in groups. When you're in a group, they watch you. The cops wait for you around four in the afternoon or early in the morning when people are going to school. In my head, I was thinking an average wage is 1,200 euros. Divide that by 30 days. That's the amount I'd need per day to get my minimum wage.

FT: When you got that amount, you stopped?

Marley: Exactly. A lot of times I would do my whole week's work in one day. Then I'd stop. But they kept going – they killed it! They took it too far. They did atrocities, they beat dudes up for no reason, they bashed in people's heads, crazy shit. I'd knock somebody around real quick, but I knew they knew I was stronger than them ultimately.

FT: Did you ever get into fights?

Marley: A bunch of times! What I loved most was the good Samaritans [*laughs*]. I'd say [*angry*]: "You think you're a superhero? You want to protect people? Who do you think you are?" Oh yeah, I'd knock everybody around. I mean, I can't say I regret it, I had a lot of fun. It was a blast. If I'd lived in a rich neighborhood, I would've had a blast some other way: maybe some graffiti on a wall [*laughs*]!

These "stagecoach attacks" were a turning point. They were no longer occasional and recreational, like when Radouane stole GPSs on the weekends; they'd become routine work. The work had the air of a craft (with its own techniques, risks, achievements, accomplishments) and a profession (with its expertise, wage, expectations, constraints, ethical codes, and limits). The way it mirrored school is striking (the backpack, the notebook, the daily schedules; the "school kids" his own age who became targets, in a reversal of roles), as is the reference to the low-wage labor market, for which school is intended (the goal is to secure a regular minimum wage, not to get "bonuses"). Marley "loved" it as long as he made sure certain limits were respected: he would "knock somebody around real quick," sparing "old people." He worked alone to ensure security (he was never caught in the act by police). He evaluated the risks, the gains, and the permanence of the job – unlike those who operated in groups and "killed" the customer base, and the job along with it. The calculations were promising: in one week, he could make what his mother earned in a month.

Being part of a crew

Marley experienced his entry into *le business* in terms of choice and independence. But to last in the profession, working alone is unthinkable. It's impossible to set oneself up in it without collective support, without a small, close-knit crew worthy of trust and secrets. Each participant sees himself as a free agent, working by the task and on his own account, but able to work with the crew. A model crewmate has four main qualities: technical competence; the ability to defend the group (against the police and rival crews); discretion (being able to keep a secret is what guarantees a successful hit and the crew's source of profit); and loyalty. He's a partner and accomplice, always being asked to prove his loyalty and acknowledge debts. A prison spell will reveal how cohesive a crew is. When one or several crewmates get locked up, it tests the loyalty of all. Those who go down mustn't "squeal" their partners' names; in exchange, the partners repay the debt by helping the prisoner to "commissary," providing a wage based on the sentence, the circumstances, and the member's job performance.

This formula applies in all cases but its interpretation can cause friction, especially when a rookie has failed on the job. That was the situation Marley's brother found himself in. Caleb usually avoids illegal activity, but he recently let himself get "caught up" in an enticing burglary scheme. The "easy hit" failed. Caleb was held responsible when the scheme's initiator, Nazredine, got sent to prison. Lacking a crew or experience, he was forced to pay what was owed. Out of family loyalty, Marley intervened to negotiate the price of silence downward (several hundred euros per month, which came out of Caleb's pay as a trucker). In a stormy face-to-face meeting after Nazredine's release, he and Marley fell out when the former demanded extra "damages and interest" (several tens of thousands of euros). Marley rails against Caleb ("You call that a big brother?") and the damage he suffered as a result of the screwup. By playing without a crew, Caleb had implicated Marley in a new cycle of debts that seem far from being settled.

Honoring debts and being able to keep a secret make it possible to join a crew ... and to leave one. When Chang was about 18, he went down for a robbery he'd committed with Amédy. He was caught by police, while Amédy managed to hide. Chang was careful not to implicate his friend, taking full responsibility for the theft. In return, Amédy made sure Chang was comfortable in prison. When Chang got out and quit the recently formed crew, Amédy didn't raise the slightest objection. Chang would not betray him: he had proved the great value of his silence. As Georg Simmel notes, "The sociological significance of the secret, its practical measure, and the mode of its workings must be found in the capacity or the inclination of the initiated to keep the secret to himself, or in his resistance or weakness relative to the temptation to betrayal."[8] In a sense, Chang earned his freedom. Now living abroad, he's become an internationally recognized artist in the hip-hop world.

Tarik, too, had to maintain his crew's secrecy when he decided to quit dealing after a close brush with a prison term. At his level of involvement, there was no way to leave all at once. Tarik headed a "semi-wholesale business." Before he could "retire," he had to prepare his crewmates to take over the franchise and reassure his suppliers and customers, who, by the very nature of the trade, were more powerful than him. He set up a plan to put his business partners in direct connection with one another, while he gradually reduced his presence so they could build trust. He then made his retirement official while still responding to the usual inquiries, hoping one day to be rid of them. Crew secrets – those shared with or kept from everyone – are temporary. Before a robbery is carried out, only the robbers will know the target, the place, and the timing. But once the mission is accomplished, rumors circulate, which strengthens loyalties. Reputation is probably worth at least as much as material gain, though for anyone who hopes to last in the trade, these two objectives are in tension with each other.

The stability of a crew is fragile. The desire to leave it and its gravitational pull are both constants. From this point of view, crew secrecy ensures the group's cohesion and its hold over its members. As Georg Simmel again stresses, "The secret society counterbalances the factor of isolation, which is characteristic of every secret, through the fact that it is indeed a society."[9] Secrecy is the sociological cement of loyalty. To betray, therefore, is to destroy the crew. When he was released from his fourth prison sentence, Marley felt the debts he was owed were not really being honored, that his crew had "changed too much." His crewmates had started doing drugs and drinking regularly, spending more time hanging around the neighborhood and financing their own consumption than working. Marley broke with a crew that no longer really was one. Too visible, too noisy, it had lost what had given it its integrity. After "searching" for a long period of time, he joined up with Manda. United by a similar educational past (Manda had been in a vocational program, was expelled from three high schools, and never took the baccalaureate exam), they were soon on the "same wavelength." They spent hours talking, playing out scenarios, calculating their shares of the hypothetical loot. It wasn't by chance that Marley introduced me to Manda. For this duo in embryo, it would have been inappropriate for me to keep seeing Marley without also meeting him. Their crew is as much a vehicle of resignation as of hope. While Marley and Manda still dream of a "payday" (they'd like to invest in some real estate, to open a restaurant), they regret being unable to capitalize on their past, after almost ten years of "just getting by." They still think about the educational degrees that might have allowed them to find honest work. Manda moves back and forth between "hits" and legitimate temp jobs, which he always lands through connections. The last one involved him replacing his father as a janitor in a contractor company specializing in the management of bank safes.

If a crew does end up dissolving, loyalties and debts from the past can be reactivated at any moment. Though Adama's crew has long been "out of service," he confides to me in a mixture of dread and excitement that it's still possible some future event that lands an old crewmate in trouble could lead to its being re-formed. If the situation demands it, a single call would get everyone back in action, "like in the old days," without a thought for the consequences. Everyone has to do what must be done because that's what is done. That is the price to pay. This hypothetical imperative is the crew's moral cement. It's based on a *private morality* between crewmates who have chosen each other "till death do us part," but it carries no imperative weight beyond this circle. In the eyes of family, other friends, girlfriends, social workers, or the few teachers who "got" them, such obligations are immoral and thus not spoken of. A crew can never assert the kind of moral superiority that might invest its secrecy with deeper meaning, as most secret societies do. It is an incomplete secret society. It can sustain a feeling of cohesion only by inverting or concealing the stigma of its amorality. It establishes temporary reputations, without producing lasting honor.

Unlike many other objects of emotional commitment, *le business* is unable to boast of any universal code of ethics. In it, one can earn money and respect, but never points for morality. Crime is a temporary job, intended to be given up. A necessity devoid of virtue, it is a *task-profession*, aiming to accomplish narrowly defined tasks and serve specific interests, as opposed to a *calling** based on the idea that "fulfilment of duty in worldly affairs [is] the highest form which the moral activity of the individual could assume."[10] In *le business*, there is no such thing as a calling. Apart from limited recognition within a small universe of gangsters, there is no pride in "confessing" to have stolen or sold drugs. To enrich oneself through crime is *haram*, led by weakness in the face of *sheitan*.† Invoking the Koran would be "hypocritical"; it would add the stain of insolence to the sins already committed. As Tarik put it at a time when he was still fully involved in such work, "I'll really be a practicing Muslim the day I've got clean hands." The money earned is dirty and remains so for a long time – which explains the penchant for extravagantly "blowing" extra cash, discarding it rather than hoarding it.

Getting one's hands dirty

Money is dirty not only because it's dishonestly earned. Over time, it also involves getting "dirty hands" – an expression that refers to doing bodily harm to another person beyond what's reasonable, inflicting disproportionate pain. Someone who "gets their hands dirty" too often is suspected of enjoying the immorality of their acts – for example, those who, in Marley's words, did "crazy shit" on the RER trains. Such behavior is seen as being more about perversity than necessity. Exactly what qualifies as "getting one's hands dirty" is a moving target; it depends on whom one asks. When everyone is tainted by the stain, it's easier to condemn competitors than to reveal one's own dirty deeds.[11] On this subject, discretion, fear, and shame prevail. Only rarely do Marley, Tarik, and Adama lead me onto this intimate terrain, except in veiled terms. Probably it would create too much mutual obligation: they would be revealing secrets they would rather wash away; I would have access to inappropriate information. For Tarik and Adama, who officially are no longer in the game, the

* *Translator's note*: The term "task-profession" is conceptually paired with "*mission-profession*," which is the standard French translation of Weber's concept of "calling" (*Beruf*) – that is, a profession guided by a higher moral purpose.

† *Haram* refers to the sphere of impurity and sin; *sheitan* refers to the devil.

subject is practically out of bounds. It evokes a past they are trying to put behind them. With Marley, fragments of such "dirty work" appear sporadically. Despite his condemnation of the "atrocities" committed by some crews on the RER, his own "beatings" have their murky aspects. He's also told me about a few people he "more or less left for dead," for "blood debts." I did not learn much more.

Is it even possible to be part of *le business* over an extended period without getting dirty hands? Unsurprisingly, it's Amédy – the only boy I can't ask for his own version of events – whose "dirty" episodes I heard the most about, like the violent punishments he inflicted on certain debtors to make an example of them or keep their associates silent. Yet quite often I heard descriptions of a boy who was loyal to his friends – "a decent, upright guy" with "such a big heart," who "didn't bully the weak"; a person who came to the aid of "others." For these people, one didn't need to be Amédy's partner to enjoy his protection, attention, or affection. These two portraits are not contradictory, and in the end it matters little whether or not his highly publicized death might have led my interlocutors to exaggerate in one direction or the other. For these are the two sides of the *paradox of* le business *as task-profession*. The deeper a crewmember sinks into a life of crime, the further he divorces his primary activity from the rest of his social life – hiding what he excels at – and the scarcer the opportunities become for him to gain self-esteem and respect from others. The better he gets, the less good he is. *Le business* is a curious social machine. It produces clandestinity, profit, and solidarity within insecurity and instability.

Common criminals

Financial reward is a function of the risk taken – prison. According to Tarik, a prison sentence is a "tax" that everyone tries to evade but which, for anyone who lasts in the profession, will have to be paid sooner or later.

To the "university" next door ... and back

Tarik just barely escaped incarceration when some of his crewmates went down, thanks to a favor granted him by the police officer in charge of his case. Moved by his handicap, the officer made it clear that he'd "blown his last chance" and had to get out. This was a compassionate warning that was never offered to the "able-bodied," like

Marley, Amédy, and Adama. All of them went to Fleury-Mérogis, the largest prison in Europe, only five kilometers from their homes.

Erving Goffman and Michel Foucault demonstrate the dual nature of the prison. As an institution, it's both inwardly focused *and* subordinated to the outside world. Goffman describes how, as a "total institution," it forces the inmates to redefine their identities through humiliating rules that have to be mastered in order to evade them at the margins. It creates specific behaviors, new ways of seeing and navigating the world, and new ways of seeing oneself. Foucault, for his part, has shown how incarceration helps maintain social control in a mass society, with "surveillance" eclipsing "punishment." Prison is a world in itself and unto itself. It instills its daily routines, gives meaning to past experiences, and serves as a reminder of what the legitimate social order rests on.[12]

It's also an interlude that stamps biographies with a before, a during, and an after. Spending time with Marley, Adama, and Amédy doesn't allow one to study "prison life" so much as to observe the banality of a recurring life experience. It's a training ground and an almost obligatory rite of passage for some boys. It is not simply a period of confinement. When a segment of society's youth regularly goes to prison, comes out, and goes back, its walls are no longer sealed off. These round-trips result from the historic transformation of its social function – confirmed by the explosion of the number of inmates in a society where inequality has advanced as the welfare state retreats and unemployment persists. Its leitmotif can be summarized as "punishing the poor," back and forth.[13] In this respect, rhetoric about the government's softness on crime reflects a collective obsession more than an objective reality. Today, a young person starting out on a criminal career risks imprisonment for minor offenses earlier than his elders did, with a high probability of recidivism. Since the 2000s, repeated incarceration has become the norm for a whole segment of youth. The prison statistics are unambiguous: they reveal a homogeneous world filled with poor young men, with immigrant backgrounds and low levels of education, serving short, repeated sentences.[14] The prisons house a narrow world within a narrow world. Confined to a single social station and a single task-profession, it deepens the marginalization of a population made up of small, partial secret societies with their own private morality.

At Fleury-Mérogis, the normalization of incarceration is unmistakable. The prison administration long filled the various wings of its buildings according to the inmates' *département* (local region) of origin, which meant they shared a common experience of the outside world. This geographic mode of organization flowed from an insight about the problems posed by carceral overpopulation: to contain conflict, mutual acquaintance can act as a lubricant. Inside the corrections facility, Adama, Amédy, or Marley found not just a familiar social milieu, but also relationships from the neighborhood, a network of individual debts, reputations to defend, resources that could immediately be put to use. A young prisoner from the *cités* is rarely in total seclusion. He's known and recognized by people a lot like himself, who come and go. When he arrives, he imports his past from the outside. When he leaves, he exports his past as a prisoner. He cultivates a network, tricks, skills. He earns his stripes and his credentials. In Grigny, the parallel with school is lost on no one; consequently, an ironic term is often used when referring to prison: "the university."

Marley belongs to the swelling ranks of this new generation of "graduates of the big house." He served his first sentence at 18 and returned on average every two years, for spells of several months. The first time he "went down" it was for involvement in a "stagecoach attack" that he said he didn't commit; the second time, he was caught "squatting" in an empty apartment with some of his crew (their occupation was reclassified as a burglary attempt, despite the lack of any goods to steal); the third time, he went in for a series of traffic offenses going back several years; the fourth time, he was convicted of "affronting a law enforcement officer" (this was in fact a physical attack on a police officer, to which I will return). Added to these were periods of surveillance via electronic bracelet, which he's now lost count of; the "university" is also known for its distance-learning program. As Marley explained to me one Sunday afternoon as we sat in his local kebab joint, the restrictions on his movement are a now-familiar existential nuisance:

> Prison didn't do anything to me, it's just normal. It gives you a chance to meet people and make lots of contacts with people who'll help you make money. But it's also a drag, 'cause it's like death – there's absolutely nothing else to do, other than lifting weights, praying, reading, or jerking off.

Softening the blow of this feast-or-famine experience ("it's just normal") is only possible under two conditions, which Marley has so far met: knowing "bosses," either in prison or on the outside, who can ensure his protection; and serving only short sentences. For those who spend "four seasons in the hole," as Adama and Amédy did, the imprint goes deeper.

"Four seasons" in the hole

Amédy was a regular in prison (he was sentenced six times). It started when he was 17. Enrolled in a vocational high school, he was sentenced to one month in prison, though he "swore" – even long afterward, and to his crewmates – that he was innocent of the charges. That first stay in Fleury, where he didn't yet know anyone, "terrorized" him, as he repeated countless times to his friends. To his mind, it was more an arbitrary confinement than a punishment. It cemented a nascent criminal career and instilled in him a conviction: "might as well be punished for something I actually did." His tumultuous relationship with the criminal justice system reached a turning point a few months later, on a Sunday morning in September 2000, when he and at least four friends stole three motorbikes from a parking garage in a neighboring town. As they loaded these objects of adolescent desire into the back of the van, the police arrived on the scene. The officers opened fire to stop the vehicle. Ali, a 19-year-old blond and blue-eyed boy of Algerian origin, was at the wheel. He died instantly, hit in the stomach by three bullets fired by a young police officer. Amédy, holed up in the back of the van, listened as his best friend died on the spot. He screamed with rage, slamming his head against the wall of the cargo hold that stood between him and Ali's body. Two accomplices escaped on motorbikes, with another fleeing on foot. Handcuffed and immobilized, positioned between Ali's body and the officers – who must have been in a state of shock – Amédy spent several hours in the parking garage waiting for the arrival of a medical examiner and police reinforcements. The police-shooting case went to court after two weeks, where it was dismissed by a judge. Amédy was sentenced to six months in prison for theft. The on-scene investigation took place without him, or Ali's family, leading to a nearly 10-year long legal battle. The dismissal of the case settled nothing. Back in the neighborhood, the young thieves shed no light on the matter. Out of loyalty, Amédy sought refuge in silence. As the only person convicted, he bore the culpability for his friend's death. To a few close friends, but never in group conversations, he would regularly repeat that he would "get revenge for Ali" – a boy whom he continued to describe, years after the affair, as one of the "only friends who never betrayed me." No one really paid for what happened that night. Neither he, nor his accomplices, nor the police. Amédy said little about the death; it remained, like so many other things, unspoken – especially since "everyone" in the neighborhood "knew" what he had gone through in the parking lot. But close friends of Ali in whom he confided – in a ritual invocation that sustained the memory of their friendship – have no doubt: after that senseless death, Amédy lived with the shame of having survived him, and an unquenched thirst for justice.

In the meantime, his thirst for money remained. Amédy racked up "hits," gradually gave up school, robbed a few stores. To boys of his generation, he became a "*gros braco.*"* His exploits were well known – like when he miraculously escaped a car accident during a highway chase and then showed up to class for good measure. They were often spectacular, like his motorbike expedition with two accomplices in which he held up a bank in Orléans (for a 25,000 euro score) and two establishments in Paris, all in the same day, while still a minor – an adventure marked by multiple injuries, and for which he would later be convicted. After the age of 19, the convictions multiplied: two sentences of three and four years in 2001 ("aggravated thefts"); a year in 2002 ("aggravated theft and possession of stolen goods"); six years in 2004 ("armed robbery"); three years in 2005 ("aggravated theft, possession of stolen goods, and the use of false license plates"); 18 months in 2007 ("drug trafficking"). These routine round-trips linked the prison to the city, as if the borders supposedly separating them had lost all meaning. As he explained in 2004, in a long anonymous interview given to a national daily newspaper:

> When they tell you you're going to prison, there's nothing to feel. You can cry, you can bang your head against the wall, you're going anyway. There's violence from the guards. But they're not all bad, some of them just ask to do their jobs, no more, no less. Because they know that since you're from the same neighborhood, you'll go to the same supermarkets. They think they might run into you on the outside. I've run into some in town. I'm not saying it makes me happy to see the guards, but I can't be ungrateful. They respected me in prison, I respect them.[15]

After 2009, he showed signs of stabilizing: a job with Coca-Cola and another at a fitness club. He even had his photo taken in a white T-shirt at the presidential palace, during a meeting on youth employment organized by Nicolas Sarkozy, an event that was much discussed after Amédy's death. ("Meeting him in person was impressive – whether you like him or not he's still the president," he told *Le Parisien*.)[16] In July 2009, he married Hayat Boumeddiene in

* A "*braco*" is a slang term referring to a holdup or, by extension, someone who carries out holdups.

a religious ceremony, went traveling with her, and left the neighborhood. The couple settled about 20 kilometers from Grigny, with a cat.

During a long prison stay in 2005, Amédy became friendly with Djamel Beghal, who was serving a 10-year sentence for planning an attack against the US Embassy in Paris on behalf of the GIA. Beghal seemed to become a spiritual guide for Amédy, as he did for Chérif Kouachi, the younger brother in the duo behind the *Charlie Hebdo* killings, whom Amédy also met briefly at the same time. Upon his release in 2009, Beghal was placed under house arrest in southern France. Amédy visited him almost once a month, on at least two occasions with Hayat. There, Hayat practiced handling a crossbow, a scene captured in a now-famous image. These bucolic interludes served as a stepping stone. Beghal went back to prison in 2010 on a five-year sentence, this time for planning the prison escape of a GIA terrorist – Smaïn Aït Ali Belkacem, one of the explosives experts behind the 1995 attacks on Paris commuter trains.* Two hundred and forty Kalashnikov bullets were found at his home. Amédy was convicted of acting as a middleman in the supply network. He was released from Villepinte a few months before his sentence was due to finish, for "nearly exemplary" behavior, as the Justice Ministry noted. He remained under surveillance with an electronic bracelet. He enrolled in two training programs, the titles of which, in retrospect, seem to sum up his obsessions: "sales" and "first aid." Seven months after he regained his freedom, January 2015 arrived. With hindsight, his "radicalization" seems as if it followed an almost linear path: a trauma; a series of short sentences; meeting a mentor and future accomplice during a long sentence; tactically practicing *taqiya*† with a soulmate; an initial failed attack linked to jihadist terrorism; another prison sentence, served quietly; finally, taking concrete action.

If this sequence of steps seems logical, it's because it's largely the product of an external reconstruction – a sort of "biographical illusion," in which the past is ordered in light of the present by imputing an inexorable direction to Amédy's life.[17] A more synchronic examination of the "four-seasons" prison stay where Amédy met Djamel Beghal paints a more nuanced picture than one of a sudden rupture or "personality change" followed by redemption via violent religion at the feet of a charismatic mentor – of whom he in fact saw very little; Beghal was in solitary confinement. Indeed, religion held

* In 1995, France experienced a wave of attacks carried out by members of the GIA, including two attacks in Paris on RER B and C commuter trains.

† *Taqiya* refers to hiding one's faith in a hostile environment to avoid persecution.

a marginal place in Amédy's daily prison life. Praying and reading the Koran were not how he killed his time or made his life better. He spent far more time figuring out the best ways to "commissary" (to consume goods from the prison store), doing pull-ups or lifting weights, cooking (makeshift stoves and a lack of utensils made food preparation in the cells time-consuming), playing on his PlayStation, watching TV, or hanging out with the prisoners, in an institution where everything cost three times as much as on the outside.

In the second zone

Along with direct testimony from his friends and from Eric de Sardan* – one of his lawyers, whom I met – four unusual sources offer a picture of what these years might have been like for Amédy. First, there are boys who, over the course of this extended period, served short prison sentences and briefly had contact with him. While no one wanted to speak directly on the subject, my presence in the neighborhood and the flow of inmates into and out of prison made it possible to piece together anecdotes and unexpected bits of information. Then there's the long pseudonymous interview published in 2004, noted above, which was conducted as part of a documentary for a national daily newspaper. There's also the hidden-camera film that Amédy himself produced and directed while in prison – using the moniker "Hugo" for the occasion – along with his cellmate, Karim. Over several months, they filmed their daily lives in Fleury with a pocket camera. These banned images led to two films: *Fleury, les images interdites*, broadcast nationally on television in 2008, and *Reality-Taule*, produced as a youth education film by a nonprofit group. In addition to these self-shot scenes, the film led to Amédy linking up with a number of people who worked with him in a semi-professional context, and with whom I was able to speak. Finally, there is written testimony from Karim, who gave an account of this adventure in a book published by a local neighborhood organization.[18] In it, Karim described his relationship, as a rookie serving his first sentence (he had landed a year-and-a-half after a series of violent robberies), with a more experienced childhood friend who ensured his protection and initiation: Amédy.

What immediately shines through is the profound sense of injustice Amédy harbored. Though rarely punished for contraband or violent

* A pseudonym.

behavior, he was constantly in the guards' sights. He was often moved out of his cell for organizing "shutdowns" – that is, refusing to return from the prison yard or go back to his cell, as a form of protest. He was convinced that, like "all cops," the building warden "hated my guts." Amédy loathed their periodic meetings, where he "made my life miserable." Yet, during the prison time he spent with Karim, he kept a low profile. He was never sent to solitary confinement; he earned a certificate in computing. He took part in a prisoner reentry program whose end-goal was to obtain a sentencing adjustment, which in his case could be estimated at three months, based on information from the prisoners' handbook and the facts of his case. According to Karim, the 10-day adjustment he ended up receiving (out of a 14-month sentence) reinforced his conviction: "That's where he discovered the true face of the justice system: the dirty tricks, the dishonesty, the bad faith."[19] Karim explains:

> In any case, Hugo [Amédy] felt he couldn't have any other life, that sooner or later he'd end up getting a life sentence because of his environment, the *cité* where he grew up, the fact that politicians bash *la banlieue* unless it's for some slapdash urban renovation to help the construction industry, etc. He was so blasé he sometimes seemed pessimistic or fatalistic. Sometimes, before getting released, he would tell the other prisoners that he'd be back. And since he's not all talk, he kept his word. Several times.[20]

After being denied permission to attend his father's funeral in Mali, during his second long sentence, it sealed his feelings of powerlessness and persecution. Sentencing adjustments and furloughs are not simply material benefits; they also represent recognition of a possibility and a promise: a change of direction. In the cell, Karim watched this resignation grow. He attributes it to a numbness that he himself, as a novice, clearly hadn't yet been able to cultivate. Amédy, by contrast, seemed able to articulate it very clearly. Karim describes this as follows:

> Hugo bashed the justice system, 'cause it doesn't exist. As he explained it to me, you can only be afraid of something that exists.... He was convinced we couldn't expect anything from them, after seeing the representatives of this justice system and this government lie and bluff. They don't have much compassion or heart, and the fact that Hugo had already been fired on by a police officer when he had no reason to use his weapon didn't help him see things differently. If you fall down enough times, it stops hurting. If you go to prison enough times, you don't even feel that panic you felt when you went into your cell the first

time. Little by little, you become immune to certain emotions like fear and apprehension.[21]

When this feeling of being trapped – in a cell, in a neighborhood, in a life situation – becomes the norm, it generates a sense of inertia. If your fate is already sealed, you might as well try to embrace the impending avalanche. Anything connected to the justice system seemed to follow an immutable, pre-written script, as illustrated by Georges Sauveur, Amédy's lawyer in the trial that led to his second long prison term:

> He displayed a kind of distance from the trial. He seemed relaxed, he came to the hearing almost smiling, though he realized the seriousness of the charges. He was one of those offenders who've accepted the idea of appearing before a judge and being detained in prison as just another step in their lives. He never mentioned to me, his lawyer, any facts other than what already appeared in the case file. He knew right away what he was going to say to the judge.[22]

Persevering in one's task-profession offers meaning, plans for the future. Amédy had planted himself in the *second zone*, a world in which all of one's relationships and shared understandings sanction living life at a remove – in and through illicit behavior. The second zone ratified his belonging to a group of individuals who knew they lived apart. The game that unites them creates a divide – between them, on the one hand, and those who aren't part of it, on the other. It pens them in, it fosters insularity. Rightly or wrongly, being rooted in the second zone enacts the impossibility of leaving the criminal world. Denizens of the zone, sharing similar backgrounds and nagged by the same sense of incompleteness, contend with each other in a mixture of rivalry and mutual aid. Introspection – the only means by which one's intelligence or skills can avert moral degeneration – is replaced by action. The second zone is a way for someone to reconcile themselves, unthinkingly, to having "dirty hands" and private moralities. Within this space, abilities and commitments that remain shameful elsewhere can receive recognition. In describing the "banality of evil," Hannah Arendt noted that "refusing to think" makes it possible to detach oneself from any moral intentionality by overvaluing know-how, an attitude closer to mediocrity and routine than to malevolence. There is something of this automaticity of practice in the second zone.[23] Motivated by economic profit, it is rooted in a contemporary ideal: being self-sufficient. In this sense, the second zone is to the class free-for-all what the "class in itself" is to the "class for itself." It expresses a common condition, shared difficulties and dissatisfactions, without ever investing them with collective significance. In the second zone, the struggle is never waged in the name of a group or a higher principle. A soldier in *le business* fights for no one but himself.

Cultivating these criminal practices undoubtedly produces results. Thus, the filming of the hidden-camera video was based entirely on habits Amédy had acquired while becoming a "*braco*." Amédy was the organizing force behind the film. He knew all the tricks for bringing the necessary equipment in and smuggling it out, and he knew exactly which scenes to film. His instructions for editing the film were based on a political standpoint: "showing that it really is hell and you go crazy in there." Intimately familiar with the premises, he could mark out the blind spots in the courtyard, the cell, and the showers where "dirty work" was done with forks and other sharp objects. As Karim puts it:

> The first day of filming in our cell, Hugo [Amédy] said everything was being done a little too anarchically. He explained that we had to structure what we wanted to do. We didn't know it yet, since we didn't know the word "anarchic," but his idea was to organize the work and lay out a plan for the filming.[24]

Amédy managed a team of five people, compensating each according to his needs and degree of participation. He made Karim his partner and didn't hesitate to fire those who failed to do their jobs – like Ali, the cameraman, who forgot to wake up for a long-planned exterior shot. He became a producer and director on the job, trading on skills he'd long cultivated: the art of clandestinity and secrecy (through a technique of shuttling the raw footage to multiple prisoners' cells, each unaware of the chain of connections between them); an ability to adapt (essential for recharging batteries using a radio set or filming with half-charged batteries); subordinating means to ends (using the rectum of the prisoner with the largest hindquarters to bring the camera in from the visitors' room); tenacity and methodical rigor (every minute of filming was the result of several hours of preparation); patience (even in the face of physical suffering when he broke a rib and continued to film without painkillers for a week); risk management (he jettisoned his first camera in the toilets, despite its cost, and didn't hesitate to retrieve a sock containing a memory card from a wall covered with barbed wire); a taste for panache; and an ability to negotiate. For example, he broke off his talks with the TV stations, conducted over the phone from his cell, when he realized that the offered price amounted to what he could earn in a single morning of robbery and wouldn't even pay the lawyers' fees for his five crewmembers in case of failure. While all these strengths made Amédy, in Karim's eyes, a "boss of the prison," this status was still relative. To the neighborhood's oldest professionals in *le business* – many of whom harbor a tender affection for Amédy, which makes discussions on the subject painful – he remained a "small-time holdup man." He wasn't really considered an expert. ("If you're good, you don't spend almost a third of your life in prison. Either you stop before that or you become more discreet," one of them told me.) His intelligence was acknowledged, but it wasn't enough to make him a "leader," as Damien Brossier, one of his first lawyers, explains.[25] He was still on the same track: a mid-level businessman, treading water – a situation that couldn't last.

To go further, Amédy had two options: make more money or help someone else. Hunger for money confirms a sort of personal election, in dollars-and-cents terms. It's an ostentatious and conformist celebration of individual success. In contrast, altruism involves looking beyond oneself, a critique of the ambient materialism; it's a movement toward the Other and the stranger. These two balancing poles – *materialistic accumulation* and *altruistic deprivation* (as noted above, "sales" and "first aid" were the words used in his final attempt at obtaining employment credentials) – come up again and again among those who knew him well when they try to summarize his character. ("Someone who really liked money, who always wanted more cash, and at the same time was always attentive to others, willing to help," one of them mentioned to me; "an obliging person," his neighbors say.) These two poles aren't mutually exclusive. They lie at the heart of the paradox of *le business* as task-profession – precisely the paradox that the second zone tends to eliminate. The hidden-camera film resembled a sort of failed synthesis, as illustrated by the response of one of Amédy's collaborators to the problems encountered in negotiating with the TV networks:

> Amédy would say, it's fine to play Che Guevara, but we're not gonna give this to the TV people for nothing. They're gonna get ratings and money, and for us it's free! We're not volunteers, we're the ones taking all the risks. So yeah, part of it was about speaking out, that was mainly why we did it, but at a certain point, when there's money at stake, there's money at stake.

Perhaps the one object that best embodied this back-and-forth was Amédy's PlayStation. He officially "commissaried" it – bill in hand

– for 320 euros. He organized tournaments in his cell and let Karim and a few others use it. Playing it is about crushing the opponent for one's own glory, and also about sharing moments of joy with a companion. It's a way of escaping, of measuring oneself against another by challenging him. The PlayStation is of this world and outside it. As Karim stresses, the game console is also a way to get back into the digital flow of the outside world while trapped within a barren universe: "A game console isn't just a way to pass the time, it's almost vital when the hours, the minutes, the days, and the weeks that go by take on an altogether different value."[26] Its confiscation by the prison administration during a move to a different cell was thus all the more bitterly resented.

This was the context in which Amédy met Djamel Beghal. Before he was an individual or a preacher, Beghal took the form of a faceless voice. He spent almost all his time in solitary confinement and in theory could have no contact with any other prisoners. However, for a time, his cell could communicate with Amédy's through the ventilation openings. Requests from prisoners in solitary, communicated via air ducts, represent genuine appeals for those keenly aware of the privilege of not being in their place – as Karim explains, in discussing his and Amédy's conversations with Farid, another inmate imprisoned for terrorism:

> For people in solitary, it's one of the few links with the outside. I mean the outside of the cell, not of the prison, of course. When someone is up there, you always have to respond when you can. Because everyone knows that solitary is where people take the biggest hit to their morale, and people commit suicide more often. So with Hugo [Amédy], we asked him what he wanted and we decided we'd do what we could to get things brought to him so he'd be warm. Hugo knew all the "*auxis*"* here, so it would definitely be easy.[27]

Indeed, Amédy's initial feelings toward Beghal were of pity, rather than piety. Amédy was moved by his isolation, his inability to "commissary," his poverty. His spiritual struggle gradually made him seem bigger. He put Amédy in mind of his own incompleteness. Little by little, Beghal's determination, force of character, and theological knowledge impressed him. They compelled respect especially because their soldierly qualities echoed those of *le business* as task-profession, while transcending the indecency of

* An "*auxi*" is the inmate responsible for a floor of the prison, the *auxiliaire*.

salvation-through-material-accumulation in favor of a higher form of "first aid." While the affinity was obvious, it did not result in any sudden devout religious practice or jihad as a political objective. Terrorism represented one possible form of defiance among many small, daily acts of resistance. Hints of this appear explicitly in the film's raw footage. Amédy addresses the issue in the same terms as the struggle against jammed showerheads, the morning meal in the canteen, or the winter cold. What was key was the gesture of public denunciation, as in a scene (deleted in editing) in which Amédy informs Karim that they're going to film Aziz, "someone special." Convicted of terrorism, Aziz recounts his arrest and confrontation with an antiterrorist judge. He delivers a message in Arabic, in the hope that Amédy might manage to transmit the images to the Al Jazeera TV network. Encounters with "radicals" were only one possible kind of encounter, among others. Amédy still seemed far from having missionary plans. In any case, that's what he declares to the camera:

> To earn my stripes here I had to fight early on, I've been here a year and now when I walk in the courtyard, I walk with killers, murderers, international traffickers [...], I shook hands this afternoon in the yard with a guy who did an attack. I'm not saying I'm going to get into that stuff, but I know a bunch of them. Yeah.

This concluding word – yeah – is not innocuous. It describes a situation in the present moment that cannot be summarized owing to its complexity. Abdou, an older neighborhood boy with a Master's degree who knew Amédy well outside the context of crime, concluded with the same word:

> Amédy would say all the time: "What's the point of prison?" If you think prison isolates people from part of society for a time, then it should keep going, don't change it! But if you think that when people get out they're better than they were when they went in, it's the opposite: they'll be worse, and they'll do worse. And in some sense, that's what he did. Prison led him to little crimes – to this one, then to this one, then this one.... To spend time with those kinds of people.... And, yeah – that's why I say it's a waste, because he wasn't a bad guy. He wasn't someone bad. And since he was someone who wanted to help people, surely it would have been easier to get him into religion, or ask him to do things that would make him an accomplice. It could start with just keeping an eye on things, you know, like a gradual process.... So, yeah.

A "little cat among the lions"

The way an individual gets caught up in "university" life can take different directions. Adama went down for a holdup just after his 18th birthday. He got two years. His past resembled that of his friend Amédy. But he experienced his incarceration as a turnaround: an extraction from the second zone. Three key factors were at play here. First, Adama wasn't living with a feeling of injustice as intense as Amédy's. Other possibilities remained thinkable. His experience in school, for example, proved that without demeaning himself, he could take on other roles than being a *cité* "bad boy." In addition, he was surrounded by visitors who held out the prospect of a different future for him: his mother and family, but also two social workers, Foued and Monique – whom he called his "godparents." They established a connection with him at a time when he was invested in opposition to authority. ("Things didn't start off on the right foot with Foued – early on we ended up scrapping, but fortunately he's got that sociologist quality, that intelligent side that can process things; he understood our pain and helped us work to become men.") These visitors'-room relationships transformed how he viewed the outside world: he could now see it as an opening rather than a confining force. Finally – and this is perhaps the most important point, though a rarity – Adama was safe. When he arrived, he didn't have to fight to mark his territory or assert his position. He was one of the youngest of a group of brothers who were respected both in the *cité* and in prison. Both inside and outside, his big brothers and their fellow crewmembers were always around; provided he behaved appropriately, this made him practically "untouchable." The experts he relied on in prison were different from those whom Amédy met, or even from what Amédy represented for Karim. More than peers or enigmatic models, they were "*grands frères*" whose role was *precisely* to ensure that he followed the "straight and narrow path." On the inside, they carried out a socializing function that complemented that of Monique and Foued. It started the night of his arrest, during processing at the police station, when he ran into Jackson, a "grown-up" who, like him, had just gotten pinched for another holdup the same night. When Jackson – a big bear of a man in his forties who specialized in "debt recovery" – related the story to me, a bitter frown made clear how much he experienced Adama's arrest as a double punishment:

> I was thinking, "I'll be all right." But then when I saw little Adama, I almost wanted to cry. It was awful to see him in the same shit.

Just before his departure for Fleury, Jackson, from the height of his broad shoulders, ordered Adama never to do it again. Facing the "enormous fear" that comes with the first days of prison, Adama received an ambiguous welcome from the neighborhood "grown-ups." Highly protective of him, they also felt hurt by his being there. ("The tone was, look, we're really mad, but you're with us now, nothing's going to happen to you.") He was also given moral support and money by his brothers on the outside. He could see the difference between him and the other prisoners his age, as he explained to me in his office one morning:

Adama: You have to understand, I wasn't in complete anguish. When you realize on the first day that nothing can happen to you – that nothing's going to happen to you – you can look to the future. Because you're not directly confronted with the hard side of things. I was the little cat among the lions. You see what I mean? Not the cat they want to tear to pieces, but the cat who's got nothing to do with this place. We're going to protect him, we're going to cover for him, we're going to feed him, we're going to build him up until he's a man. Not in the sense of becoming a big gangster; he's gonna be a man, with values, a good mental state. He's going to try to think, to make the right decisions. So, when I was in there, I saw how people handled their conflicts. I learned all that stuff. I watched the big gangsters who did too many drugs, the guys who did crazy shutdowns, the guys who did terrorism, 'cause you're in there with Corsicans, Basques.... You had that whole mix. So you learn. Prison is a book, you read everyone's lives. You watch it all. And then you take what you want to take. But what comes out of it is that these are all committed guys!

FT: Committed guys?

Adama: Committed, yeah. When they decided to do something, they would do it. They're all committed guys who've got nothing but their word. If tomorrow they want to smoke you, they'll smoke you.

In Fleury, Adama was beholden. He was receiving – much, and often – without being able immediately to give back. That generosity shifted the lines of debts and loyalties. Though the "little cat" wasn't able to directly give back to the "lions" protecting him, he also sought to cultivate this "sociologist quality." Because he was emotionally safe, he could open himself up and learn. He absorbed what he could from this cross-fertilization of lives and conflicts, and put into practice what he likened to a new form of altruism. It was his way of being loyal to his *grands frères*, of appreciating what it meant to look beyond oneself, to others, who'll be beholden in their turn.

He looked out for a "poor white guy who had nothing to do with us" – Pierre, who'd gone down for selling drugs. Adama came across him in the visitors' room. He noticed he never went out, "for fear of the guys from the *cités*." Adama introduced him to the rules of what to do when outside the cell, realizing he was able to offer concrete help to someone else. A new cycle of recognizing debts was born. In return, when Pierre got out of prison, he wrote to Adama and sent him money for the commissary.

When he got out, Adama sought to build on this new "commitment" he'd learned in prison, where all that counts is one's "word." But this intention would have remained a pious hope had Monique and Foued not given it an institutional outlet by enrolling Adama in a training program. He prepared for exams in social work and youth coordination at a moment when there happened to be an open call for applications, thus opening a career path for him. This wasn't a new departure for him. His plans to become a youth coordinator were an echo of the "revelation" he'd had in prison. He had moved from task-profession to calling. I still remember the exact moment when he first talked with me about his time in prison – a late afternoon in July, as he leaned against the hood of his saloon. At the time, there were too many details I was still unaware of to understand the meaning of this troubling word: "revelation." Why did Adama speak of prison as others do of religion, when nearly everyone else I spoke to would have answered with a silence laden with subtext, or a verbal violence of uncontrolled rage? I didn't yet understand that behind these differences stood the same existential angst, the same mystique of altruism. Adama had a singular experience of this while in prison, like a "little cat among the lions." Our impromptu discussion in the sun concluded with a "committed" verdict:

> I met guys who had nothing and gave me everything. These were dudes who didn't know me and looked after me like you wouldn't believe. They were major good guys. Real men. Real fucking men.

Adama turned up the volume, rolled up his tinted windows, and prepared to drive off. And now I realized: the second zone means men's business.

Masculine machines

Be a "real fucking man." Win respect and recognition for your manliness. This nearly constant imperative is hardly limited to boys from the *cité*: one only needs to look at the sphere of politics and elections.[28] Nor is this an offhand analogy. Pierre Bourdieu pointed out that

> a "real" man is someone who feels the need to rise to the challenge of the opportunities available to him to increase his honor by pursuing glory and distinction in the public sphere. [...]. Like honor – or shame, its reverse side, which we know, in contrast to guilt, is felt *before others* – manliness must be validated by other men, in its reality as actual or potential violence, and certified by recognition of membership of the group of "real men."[29]

"Real men"

Both in the streets and in *le business*, this public recognition is asserted above all through a strong body. Physical capacities are a sign of moral qualities. They function as indicators of loyalty – "hard against pain" ("*dur au mal*"), as the common French expression goes. A hard body and a hard demeanor often reflect the hardness of life: the scarcer material resources are, the more they tend to find expression in a physical brutality that seeks to fend off social violence and deprivation, yet in the process helps sustain it.[30]

In the *cités*, though male reputations can be established via football, bodybuilding is probably more key. Radouane, Tarik, Marley, Adama, Amédy, and Hassan all share a concern with increasing their muscle mass. Tarik's handicap doesn't stop him from "keeping in shape" in the bedroom he shares with Marie, his girlfriend: dumbbells and a weightlifting set take up most of the room. We often end up bantering about the latest developments in the size of his arms. Adama and Hassan have "lost a bit" with age and less free time, but they still reap the benefits of past vigor. Adama played rugby at a high level. Hassan long practiced Thai boxing and wrestling. They still show it – prominent shoulders, for example – and still hope to "get back to it." Their muscles, and the knowledge that they can be put to use in a fight, make up for any physical characteristics that could detract from their virility, like not being "tall." While Amédy was known for being short, it's his waist size that comes up first in conversation. Everyone I spoke to recalled the girth of his trunk, which the hostage-taking probably accentuated. It relegates memories of the rest of his appearance to second rank.

Building muscle differs from other forms of exercise in that it isn't really meant for public display. In this respect, it represents an exception. Football's popularity brings boys together around stories that can be shared, exaggerated, or twisted. Football is joked about, but never bodybuilding – as Marley's knowing smile hinted the evening we first met, when he made fun of Saïfi's "pecs" behind his back.[31] The pursuit of muscles is a "solitary pilgrimage," in the words of former bodybuilder Samuel Fussell. In describing a hypnotic immersion in a rigoristic activity governed by the self-administration of the "three Ds" (dedication, determination, discipline), he shows that building muscle is more an existential procession than a pastime.[32] The boys work out at home when they can. Marley, for example, installed a series of suspension weights in his living room, between the couch and the TV. When they do go to a gym or a group "street workout," each focuses on his own specific exercises. What prevails is the pleasure of being alone together, of sharing a communal performance of self-expansion. Only the results are intended for public view. The process, built on strain and privation, is a pathway, seldom a spectacle. In the training sessions I witnessed, no one was watching others as they succeeded or failed at their weights. The personal challenge is preeminent. Each individual gives his all, hits his day's limits, in a quasi-religious atmosphere of communion and devotion. Building muscle inscribes the prevailing class free-for-all in the body. The shared aspect of this individual struggle says a great deal about a common condition. For tests of strength are also exercises in transformation, paths to redemption, and a "de-spiritualization of asceticism" in which one has to re-create oneself every day, becoming one's best enemy.[33]

For a long time Radouane was a chubby teenager, a physical characteristic that matched his playful personality. After high school, he immersed himself in his workouts – I hardly recognized him after several months had gone by without our meeting. This impressive muscle building was part of a proactive change of direction in his life. In becoming a university student, he turned his back on illegality, on "neighborhood scrapes." This U-turn was a part of an ascetic rationalization of his use of time. Body and soul, he plunged into his studies, his weights, and Islam. He metered his time and maximized his activity. His systematic approach bore fruit. His grades climbed. He piled up diplomas (bachelor's, Master's, business school). His body dried up, then expanded. His theological knowledge thickened. For him, bodybuilding wasn't accompanied by any penchant for exhibiting the fruits of his labor – apart from a few selfies on social media. He rarely wears tight-fitting T-shirts – perhaps because, with his diplomas, his body isn't pure "labor power," as Karl Marx might say. Often, protruding muscles are turned to profit. But not with him. Sometimes they're the only asset with any labor-market value: a proper accumulation of muscle mass can safeguard a job as a security guard or a bouncer. Hassan has long worked in security to make ends meet, though also out of political conviction. He organized security for pro-Palestinian demonstrations and briefly worked as a bodyguard for Dieudonné.

Body sculpting can also be a way to leave one's social class without betraying it. Radouane now eats "healthy, *comme les bourgeois.*" He sees a nutritionist. We often talk about our respective diets. His attitude toward food is an early sign of his gaining distance from his parents. He marks his territory in the family fridge, associating the "fat" in some of its foods with "*les prolétaires.*" His body is chiseled, rationalized, aestheticized, not made by and for work. Bodybuilding is part of an ascent toward something that seems higher. It's a way of "becoming a real man."

A man's constant quest for the truth of his gender expresses the whole "hidden anxiety" of masculinity, a struggle against a diffuse sensation of vulnerability.[34] According to Loïc Wacquant, weightlifting conjures a "complete *masculine cosmogony* that promises to allay [a man's] innermost anxieties by funneling all his vital energies into the construction of the virile carapace of muscles."[35] In this respect, it's not fundamentally different from the desire for material possessions. It's an effort to improve everyday life through material accumulation, following a logic of maximization and profitability – though the apparent simplicity of the body in motion no doubt makes an expansion of the flesh seem less vulgar than the stockpiling of objects. But there's always a risk of this quest becoming senseless – hence the regular breaks bodybuilders take. The mere result is malleable physiques that change as periods of "letting go" follow periods of intense "working out."

The "right woman"

In seeking to dispel this anxiety, the quest for the "right woman" takes pride of place. Through the ideal of the monogamous heterosexual couple, the boys can hope to let their guard down temporarily, by having a woman who would also have them, while still remaining "real men." The ideal woman embodies a desire to let go without confessing weakness. For not all women are the same: there are "the good ones" – those one can have sex with and brag about it – and "the right one" – with whom one seeks to start a family and about whom one doesn't talk. The boys talk endlessly about the former, sometimes in surreal and pornographic terms. The latter are an exalted taboo. When romantic loyalty is involved, discretion and modesty prevail, even prudery – "this shyness about bringing sex to the conscious and 'sensible' level"[36] despite the ubiquity of crude sexual banter. The couple is a privileged preserve, inaccessible to crewmates. It makes whole the incompleteness of life within *le business* and its secret societies.

Marley and Manda know almost nothing about each other's girlfriends. The last time Marley was in prison, Manda helped support his crewmate by having things delivered to him once a week, without ever coordinating with "Marley's girl," though he suspects she was also helping him out. Indeed, she was the only person who went to see him in the visitors' room. Everyone knows who the girlfriends are, but they barely exist outside the couple. This distance is regarded as a mark of modesty and respect. It's also a way to avert the seeds of future conflicting loyalties, since in the long run girlfriends inevitably risk jeopardizing the crew. Future wives just aren't allowed inside.

Too much cross-contact can lead to serious conflict, as was the case with Adama and Fayawé. They first started going out when they were 19 and Adama was on furlough from prison. She was the little sister of one of his crewmates. His four-seasons sentence and the couple's brief history led to a breakup. When he got out, the crew fell apart over unsettled debts (those who'd supported Adama versus those who had been notable by their absence), conflicting loyalties ("With us, going out with your mate's sister just isn't done," as Adama confirmed to me), and a need for personal renewal ("I was leaving prison, there was too much dirty business, too much death in me," he told me). The period of score-settling lasted several months. Physical confrontations escalated until they reached a final threat, gun in hand. That signaled the end of hostilities. Fayawé's brother is now the uncle of the couple's children, a situation that is "not easy, at all," Adama admits. He shares with Fayawé what sociologist Olivier Schwartz has called a "space of assurance". It circumscribes the "sphere that is one's own, because it is nearby," acting to "restore a sense of presence" whereby "needs can be fulfilled, want can be warded off, distance abolished."[37] It suspends, for a while, the burden of certain social obligations. Exclusive and elective, it made it possible for Adama to be more "cat" than "lion," to envision himself outside the neighborhood, which he and Fayawé left together.

Tarik and Marie inhabit this sphere as well. They met during a hospital stay when Marie, a nurse's aide, was assigned to care for Tarik. An intimacy that felt like self-discovery was forged from a subtle interplay of distance and closeness (the handicapped boy versus the slightly older caregiver; the "non-practicing Muslim" Arab boy versus the white Christian girl with an older sister who converted to Islam 15 years earlier; the young delinquent on his way out of the game versus a future father-in-law retired from the organized crime scene in Marseille).

That the search for a shared authenticity should be expressed in the language of religion is hardly surprising. Tarik and Marie debate Islam on a daily basis. Marie converted "after much thought and reflection, but without knowing all about it." She learned from Tarik, who, she says, "educated me in the subject."[38] This desire to be a good couple is expressed through little everyday gestures (cooking, shopping, the morning routine). Its sacred side can be seen in a brief phrase that brings them together every time it's uttered: "It's *sunnah** to do that." Islam's crystallizing role took a quite different direction in the couple that Amédy and Hayat formed. They met each other in 2007 through a friend and fellow inmate of Amédy's. At the start of their relationship, they were both "getting interested in Islam at the same time" in the hope of finding "balance."[39] Hayat isn't from the neighborhood; she's from the eastern suburbs. After losing her mother, she passed through several host families and an adolescence punctuated by conflicts with the police. Her idyll with Amédy led to a religious wedding and a honeymoon in the Dominican Republic in 2009; the year before, they had traveled to Malaysia – a trip interrupted the following year by Amédy's imprisonment for complicity in terrorism. Then Hayat lost her job as a checkout clerk after deciding to wear a full-face veil. In January 2015, she left France for Syria while her husband undertook his martyrdom operation. Few in the neighborhood could tell me much about the life of a couple whose low profile surprised the public when it was reported in the press, though in light of many boys' romantic lives, such as invisibility was entirely normal. It embodies a precious, almost secret, goal. The wait is often long. Radouane and Hassan refused to have any "non-serious" girlfriends. They preferred to bide their time for a few years, reading surahs (chapters) from the Koran, in order to meet the "right woman" – their own. To Amédy's friends, Hayat had all the trappings of "the right one," a woman who would allow him to settle down and focus on their new life together.

* The *sunnah* refers to the entirety of the Prophet's words, actions, and judgments.

Police, death, and hatred: a political trinity

Confrontations with the police are perhaps the ultimate testing ground for a masculinity whose constant determination to assert itself ends up revealing its own fragility. Indeed, the same nightly scene is replayed around the few blocks of the neighborhood where drugs have become ubiquitous – men versus men.

Orders of battle

From afar, young white police officers in blue Robocop outfits eye crews of dealers – black or Arab for the most part – stationed near an "oven."* From a closer distance, they stare at people passing by or hanging around to kill time. A deceptive calm always prevails before the storm that one side or the other will, perhaps, set off. Will it be the police who intervene – through a long series of identity checks on young people already known to them, or a sudden raid to catch dealers in the act? Or will a rival crewmember spark hostilities by tossing projectiles from the roof of the building? During the few agitated evenings I witnessed, I hung back, positioned halfway between the police forces and the incriminated "oven," talking with an acquaintance. Ignored by the security forces (I was part of the scenery without really blending in) and tolerated by crews who saw me shaking hands, I never understood why the confrontation was initiated by one side rather than the other. Only one thing was certain: each explosion replaces boredom with battle. It puts a stop to the endless waiting that structures most of the officers' and the young people's work.[40] There was nothing left now but to assume the manly posture of hunter or hunted and maintain the role of combatant – even of warrior, if helicopters and armored trucks were to get involved.

While such scenes are relatively rare over the course of a given year, they remain chronic. In some neighborhoods of Grigny and in many towns in Seine-Saint-Denis, they've become familiar. This atmosphere of combat magnifies an everyday animosity, turning it into an insistent hatred. That hatred saturates a recurring interaction – the identity check – and the dread that it might degenerate at any moment. Police stops inspire a feeling whose repercussions for a teenager aren't hard to imagine: a sense of culpability for merely existing, and for being

* An "oven" is a place where drugs are sold, most often a stairwell, watched over by lookouts.

from where he's from. When it plays out in public, it swiftly gives way to another emotion: shame. Nearly all the boys I know from the *cités*, whether or not they're involved in *le business*, have experienced these little moments of humiliation, when forgetting your papers is enough for them to end up at the police station or when certain insulting phrases continually resonate in their heads. Only Tarik is protected by his wheelchair. Sometimes two stigmas can neutralize each other. There's only one way to completely guard against it: not leaving the house. This hatred is felt by everyone, even the "quietest" boys, for whom these identity checks seem all the more violently arbitrary. In the words of Pedro, an educator in Grigny, "The police leave indelible marks that can never really be erased." And the police don't always distinguish between educators and their flock. In Grigny, they don't hesitate to patrol near youth centers, seen as dens of criminal suspects. Adama was recently subjected to an aggressive identity check in front of "his young people." Such episodes send the message that some educators are less legitimate than others.

Taking the pulse of hatred

To take the pulse of the hatred, consider a common scene. It's late one summer night, and Marley finds himself in a car with his girlfriend, Priscilla, at the wheel. They are driving home a male friend, who sits in the backseat. Priscilla doesn't have a license. Marley is explaining to her how to operate the car. At a red light, a police car pulls up behind them. Priscilla panics and stalls. The officers get out of their vehicle. Marley instructs Priscilla to move to the passenger seat and squirms his way behind the wheel. The officers probably see this suspicious movement. They stand ready to intervene. They approach the front of the vehicle, with its tinted window – which they proceed to break. According to Marley, this is what happened next:

> There was glass everywhere, they were in fucking cowboy mode. I got out and said to the cop: "Why did you break my window, you piece of shit? I'm going to fuck your mother you fucking piece of shit! Go ahead, hit me!" So yeah, I was flipping my shit, and I knew I was already going to get an "insulting an officer" charge. But we were right in the middle of the neighborhood, there was nothing they could do. They were standing there, hesitating. So I said to him: "Keep your mouth shut, get off my ass, you piece of shit! Just let me calm down, then we can talk!" I started walking, I was thinking, right next to the car. The cops are standing there, there's three of them, just looking at each other. They don't really know what to do. One of them decided to be the hero. He went

> over to question my mate in the back. I was facing the other two cops, they were looking at me. I kept going: "What are you going to do? Are you crazy? Breaking my window, you piece of shit, how do you think I'm gonna react, you fucking asshole?" At that point, a cop pushes me. Now I know I'm gonna get "insulting a cop" and "resisting arrest," so I knew I was going to prison. He thought I was going to come at him to land a punch – and then I saw him coming to give me one. I took a step back. He put his whole body into it – like, trying to put everything into one big punch. I just took a step back. He was in front of me, winding up. And bam! He just wiped out, on the ground – bam! His jeans ripped – a huge rip! [*laughs*] At that point he was on the ground in front of me. Now there were two of them on my mate, they didn't manage to get his papers. I see the guy on the ground. I just think, if I bash his head in a few times, he'll be out. You know, I was still mature enough that at that point, I backed off. I walked around the car, didn't touch him. And then he starts following me on all fours! I think to myself, "Fine, what's the point, I'm dead, I'm screwed." I saw my mate and a cop falling on the ground in front of the car. I was so full of rage, I gave the cop this big penalty kick. His face went like this – bam! KO, knockout. I ran through the neighborhood and hid. You know how crazy that was?

This scene is a good illustration of the mechanics of escalation. The situation began with a young woman's traffic violation and ended in a violent attack by two boys who ended up in prison. Before the situation was even underway, the officers were already primed for confrontation (shattering the window "in cowboy mode"), Marley was already primed for counterattack (the barrage of insults and disrespect, "flipping my shit"). The tragic ambiguity of the stop ("we were right in the middle of the neighborhood, there was nothing they could do" versus "I'm dead, I'm screwed") appeared in a sham fight that ended with a punitive pummeling (the "penalty kick" and "KO, knockout"). At no point did Marley seem to feel remorse. He enjoyed revisiting the scene as he recounted it to me several years later. The only thought he had when seeing the officer on the ground was to knock him out, and he was unable to stifle the impulse once he saw his mate, also on the ground. It's possible Marley was exaggerating (though the confrontation, filmed by surveillance cameras, was documented and led to an arrest warrant). But, whatever the facts, his feelings were unambiguous. For they really were feelings of hatred, a morbid impulse that ended in an attack and an escape. Encountering police while going about one's business – even for those only guilty of being there, as is most often the case – triggers a reflex: to run, filled with rage. Even if it means running toward one's own death. That is what happened with Zyed Benna and Bouna Traoré, who were electrocuted by a transformer in a power plant at ages 15 and 17, respectively, while trying to hide to avoid a police stop in Montfermeil on October 27, 2005. Those two deaths would trigger a wave of urban violence throughout the country.

Total rioting

What we've become accustomed to calling a "riot" is, above all, a revolt. It's not by chance that police brutality is always the trigger. The deaths of Zyed and Bouna in 2005 reawakened local memories of the tragic deaths that run through the history of every neighborhood. The echoes of those deaths bring back traumas that some boys try to suppress through a desire to come to blows. Only a small number of such boys act out the role of rioter. The youngest might be 14 or 15 years old. After 30, it's rare to see a "grown-up" enter the ring. The boys on the front lines are those who spend the most time outdoors and those on the bottom rungs of *le business*. They're the most exposed to the police: that's what makes the battle so fierce. Before they settled down, Amédy and Adama took part in the Grigny riots. The idea of avenging their mate Ali was never far from their minds. Marley also saw combat, but at 26 he's grown tired of it. Tarik, Radouane, and Hassan always stayed away from such nights, which they saw as losing battles, getting their friends hurt and making the situation worse for residents.

The riot crystallizes a relentless state of war against the police that makes death a tangible presence, without the police always realizing it. A majority of boys are deeply convinced that at any moment they or their loved ones could meet the same fate as Zyed, Bouna, or Ali. The disproportionate number of premature deaths in working-class neighborhoods suggests they're not entirely wrong. In ascending order, such deaths involve victims of the police, victims of score-settling in *le business*, and victims of drug overdoses, whose isolation renders them invisible. Amédy heard Ali die a few meters away from him. Like Adama, he mourned several crewmates who died as a result of rivalries on the job. Among his acquaintances, Tarik can count six who disappeared without explanation, now probably lining the "bottom of the Seine," and two tetraplegics, paralyzed by bullets in their spines. To this macabre reckoning one could add his stillborn twin brother, a younger sister who died in childbirth, and memories of decapitated heads in his Algerian village at the height of the terror. These boys have also had to confront the fear of their own deaths, having escaped several "accidents on the job" that could have been fatal.[41] Identity checks and prison are also small forms of social death. Their weight can be felt in the atmosphere. Finally, there are those, more numerous, who are simply victims of their social condition – who die owing to work or the harshness of daily life. Life expectancy is never distributed randomly across the social chessboard.[42] The fathers of Amédy and Adama died prematurely (the latter also lost a brother in a traffic accident). The health of Tarik's and of Hassan's father is a worry. Radouane's father has been a near-invalid since his retirement. All these boys live with what Amar Henni calls "the normalization of death."[43] Growing up, death is a problem and a possibility that one quickly learns to live with.

Rioting is also a way of warding off fate, adding pleasure, excitement, and play to the ambient tone of suffering and humiliation. It's a festive occasion that becomes a spectacle when boys see themselves reflected through the eyes of others and learn from those more experienced than themselves. Such moments of socialization and group celebration are unpredictable, and thus seductive. Improvisation heightens the feeling of freedom and jubilation generated by a fleeting role-reversal in the game of hunter and hunted. There is no plan, no strategy – just an effervescence that celebrates pride in belonging and moments outside the everyday. Whenever I mention these moments with former rioters, a panoply of tragicomic memories floods to the surface. And despite unanimous condemnation of "youthful foolishness," there's always a sense of "a good time had by all," blending carefree vitality with the promise of long-ago defiance. The spectacle of fires also represents a singular transfiguration of the everyday. They illuminate the gray of the neighborhood. This is remarked on in the heat of the moment, behind improvised barricades or, nowadays, via video feeds that disappear as soon as they go viral. Indeed, the powerful aesthetic of rebellious pyromania ensures a media coverage that intensifies symbolic struggles around the political meaning of such nights of upheaval.[44] Setting fires and throwing stones are ways of capturing attention, fueled by the desire to be seen and to be recognized, to define the media agenda for a brief moment. If the riots of 2005 spread, it was in part because they suddenly hit the front pages of the world press, as rioters used this new visibility to test out a feeling of social dignity and a once unthinkable degree of influence over events. As a former rioter mentioned to me, "What changed was the attention, 'cause we had no idea it was going to come out in the papers. [. . .] Before that, if a guy did a hold-up and it made the papers, we'd all say what an idiot! But with this, people were talking about us everywhere, all the time!"* Those who engage in the "hottest" actions are, indeed, the youngest participants in *le business*. But the violence of the riot is different from that of the task-professions. By exploding the imperative of secrecy, it sketches the contours of a collective seeking to leave traces of its own existence. It expresses a more general revolt that, through physical confrontation, engenders a capacity for action, captures an audience, an ability to influence. This short-lived trench warfare is to the class free-for-all what the class struggle is to class consciousness: a sudden, brutal laying bare of political injustice. The *scenario of the grand battle* thus appears. It instills the possibility of achieving collective interests, the notion of soldierly dignity in combat, even though the common cause has no name. Thoroughly political, the hatred of police recalls Clausewitz's thesis: war is indeed the continuation of politics by other means.[45]

Such means raise the question of limits. On July 19, 2016, in Beaumont-sur-Oise, Adama Traoré was celebrating his birthday: he was 24 years old. When he saw three *gendarmes* stop his brother and girlfriend, he fled. Chased all the way home, he resisted and found himself pinned to the ground, frozen in place by the weight of three officers, preventing him from breathing. He died of asphyxiation not long afterward, in the police vehicle transporting him to the station. On October 8, 2016, on the outskirts of Grigny, a group of 12 or so boys aged 15 to 17 attacked a police car with Molotov cocktails. Two officers, a woman and a man, were seriously burned. For several days, they hovered between life and death. On February 2, 2017, in Aulnay-sous-Bois, Théo, 22, was subjected to a police stop that ended in 60 days during which he was unable to work and the indictment of one of the officers for rape with a nightstick. For more than a month, confrontations between youth and police spread throughout the country. Amid this commotion, on February 23, 2017, three young jewelry thieves were chased by police. They took up positions in Grigny where, in the middle of the neighborhood, they fired on the officers with a sawn-off hunting rifle.

* * *

The *class free-for-all* on the margins of the city isn't the product of an anomic universe closed off to the outside world – what some call the

* The young people who rebelled in 2005 did not know what the 1983 *Marche pour l'égalité et contre le racisme* represented. Their joy in setting the news agenda for the first time cannot be understood without looking back on the history of their political socialization.

"jungle of the ghetto." Nor does it flow from any nihilistic individualism. On the contrary, it results from a constellation of *recognized debts* and *conflicting loyalties* which, little by little, bring into being a social world and a *private morality* where each individual exists by virtue of others.

An *unrequited love* of republican education creates an ambivalent attitude toward knowledge and the social recognition it confers, a tangle of respect and disrespect. It feeds a *furious desire for intelligence* that struggles for recognition from society and has little chance of being satisfied by obtaining honorable work. This thwarting is experienced as a betrayal of family hopes. *Le business* as task-profession offers relief and prospects: to earn money; to feel manly; to be part of a crew. But all solidarity in *le business* is temporary. It's almost impossible to go the distance when such commitments require violating elementary rules of morality ("*dirty hands*"), hiding the skills and excellence one has acquired, and seeing oneself more and more as a *fighter*, unbound by the laws of God or man.

This stance of combat and confrontation impels a demand for immediate restitution and ultimate redemption. It is the final endpoint of the *class free-for-all*, translated into action. *Le business* as task-profession produces an emptiness and a deep sense of fatigue, physical and psychological. It is embodied in a paradox: the more one is good (at *le business*) the less one is good (morally). The outside world is filled with reminders of every kind that social legitimacy cannot be found this way – and repeated experience of stigmatization and discrimination guarantees, as if such a guarantee were needed, that the message is received. The routine movements in and out of prison, the normalization of death, and the contradictions of masculinity (a combination of strength and anxiety) carve into body and mind a situation that more and more resembles a *dead-end*, fueling feelings of absolute injustice. Such circumstances are sufficient to place a person squarely in the *second zone*.

To have any hope of leaving it, there are two paths: *materialistic accumulation* and *altruistic deprivation*. These aren't specific to outcast urban neighborhoods, which are merely peripheral products of contemporary capitalism. Materialistic accumulation is a form of conformism, the assertion of full ownership over one's things and one's body. Altruistic deprivation is experienced in the little moral accommodations that everyone tries to make, insofar as possible. These shift existing lines of indebtedness and loyalty: having given without being quite obligated to do so, one gains permission to receive. They most often involve the creation of a private domain and comfort zone, notably embodied in the feminine ideal, and, more prosaically, in the promise of couplehood.

Both of these paths are precarious. Their uncertainty, at bottom, is that of the Western democracies since they started struggling to offer any collective project for the future, and since the continuation of capitalism began to seem a chimera in the face of a planet that is also tired. What makes it especially tragic on the margins of the cities is that, there, awareness of one's own finitude and the fragility of earthly existence is particularly acute. In this sense, materialist accumulation and altruistic deprivation are not what Max Weber called "paths to salvation."[46] The shortcomings of politics, the economy, and the education system, along with disdain for artistic creation, make it difficult to frame beliefs or ideas suited to the world's contradictions. What then remains is a religion rooted in the historical pathways of immigration and decolonization: Islam.

We must now try to understand what Marley, Tarik, Radouane, Adama, Amédy, and Hassan have made of it. And what it has made of them.

— 3 —

RECONVERSIONS

Well you may throw your rock and hide your hand
Workin' in the dark against your fellow man
But as sure as God made black and white
What's down in the dark will be brought to the light

"God's Gonna Cut You Down"
traditional folk song

Being or becoming Muslim? The "community" illusion

The "return" to Islam by the "bad seeds" of the West is commonly seen as an immersion into a familiar universe: the "community." As the sociologist Ferdinand Tönnies showed in the late nineteenth century, the word betrays nostalgia for a particular form of sociability, where human connections are experienced through similarity – in contact with shared spaces, experiences, and memories. They're fortified by trusting interpersonal relationships, passed on through tradition, and experienced as submission to group imperatives. "Community" is contrasted with "society," which rests on fleeting, impersonal, explicit, and self-interested connections. Society liberates individuals from purely local particularisms, even as it rekindles the anguish of individualism: "We go out into *Gesellschaft* ['civil society'] as if into a foreign land."[1]

From this point of view, religious communities appear an especially integrating force, in that they bring human beings together not because of what they have or what they are, but because of what they believe. This notion lies at the heart of the Muslim religion, with the *Umma* denoting the pivotal moment when the very first believers rejected clan-like organizations to join a new, single community of faith. It supposedly takes concrete form in unconditional solidarity among all Muslims – extending even to the creation of an Islamic nation.* Among non-Muslims, the "Muslim community" elicits varied sentiments. On one side, tolerant multiculturalism lauds its dignity and seeks to grant recognition to its faithful "representatives"; on the other side, those imbued with republican distrust are spurred to put up defenses against the "communalist" threat.

The power of a symbolic option

In the era of the Industrial Revolution, Tönnies stressed the importance of proximity in neighborhood relationships: communities were villages. Starting in the 1990s, a new political option labeled "Islam" took root locally in working-class neighborhoods and had a lasting effect on these relationships. This option thrived on the decline of many socializing institutions; on the disillusionment of immigrant children, for whom achieving political power began to seem impossible in spite of all their activist work on the ground; on the sense of injustice fostered by continuing social segregation and economic inequality; and on a growing demand for more professionalization within a faith that was then quite unstructured. This option arose not so much from a desire to live apart from society as from a demand for symbolic recognition, equality, and participation in public life, in the here and now.[2] Geopolitical tensions tended to amplify its resonance: for some, the bleak prospects facing the "Muslim community" came to seem like a universal condition, leveling the specificities of the French case. To their eyes, as capitalism internationalized and dematerialized, a new Muslim insularity was emerging, between stigmatized neighborhoods and the imaginary of a deterritorialized global Islamic village.

In this context, the "community" is said to serve as a refuge, as demoralized young people often put it. This can be seen quite clearly among those who leave for Syria or Iraq.[3] Radouane tells me the same thing when we talk about the role of faith in his life – as we did one winter evening while discussing his future in the artificial heat of his car, the setting of choice for our conversations.

* The *Umma* evokes the image of a mother (*Umm*) as well as attachment to a community of Muslims connected more by their faith than by their family, national, or political attachments.

FT: Are you more optimistic or pessimistic about the future?
Radouane: Here? Pessimistic. It isn't possible to live here in France. For a Muslim who wants to practice his faith 100 percent, it won't be possible.
FT: You feel like you're sort of making a compromise ...
Radouane: Well yeah, you can't practice your religion.... Here's something that sucks: my work contract is going to expire. You see my beard? If a Frenchman has a beard the same length it's fine! Well, it won't be fine for me, 'cause they'll think, he's Muslim, he does the daily prayers, etc. With me looking like an Arab.... You see what I mean, it sucks! Even, like, a Muslim girl who wears the veil – she can't go to a job interview like that. Some of them make concessions and take off their veil when they're at work, even though what they're doing is crazy. They know very well that what they're doing is terrible, unfortunately. But there's nothing they can do. It's either that or they don't work. They don't make any money and can't be independent.
FT: That's hard for you to deal with?
Radouane: The way I see it, we're Muslim, we're a community. An *Umma*. When one member of the community isn't doing well, it hurts. See, when you're sick, when part of your body is sick, then your whole body's sick. Well it's the same for the community. And right now the community is doing really badly. And it's divided, too! You've got one sect that says this, another sect over there that says that ... I mean, even with my father, we don't agree. It's not good.

Despite the *Umma*'s organic unity, the "Muslim community" is more an idealized fantasy than a reality. Radouane acknowledges its fragility, which flows as much from internal divisions ("sects") as from hostility from the outside (beards worn by the Muslim "we" versus those of "French" hipsters). These "disagreements" testify to a simple fact: the heterogeneity of the Muslim population.

The about-turn and the spectacle of rupture

Although all the boys invoke family tradition or a return to origins when they embrace Islam, the desire for community is a label, more than anything. What lies behind it is an imagined narrative of a long collective history.[4] Within families, it often appears as a pious hope. The gap between religion as practiced by the parents and that embraced by the children shows how far two different social worlds set them apart. For the parents, it's an ancient practice, often more cultural than religious, carried out discreetly. Islam was imported from the countries of their birth to a secular republic that only belatedly discovered the existence of a large Muslim population on its soil.

For the most devout, faith flows from repeated readings of verses and surahs in an Algerian, Moroccan, Tunisian, Malian, or Senegalese context. It conveys snippets of a national history that has come to a close. For the sons, Islam holds the allure of renewal, a spiritual quest, fidelity to an inexpressible authenticity.

Whenever these two Islams meet, almost inevitably they face off. Allah becomes the name of a generation divide forged by history. Mohamed worried when his son Tarik started decorating his flat with the words of the Prophet. Though Mohamed is a believer, any kind of ostentation remains suspect in his eyes; it brings back the painful past of murderous GIA raids in his home village. Bouzid clashes with his son Hassan when he hears the latter make increasingly emphatic theological arguments. To the organic intellectual and trade union activist Bouzid, what Hassan views as a written catechism looks more like a repudiation. Radouane keeps his discussions with Chérif to a minimum, to avoid conflict. With his father in the hospital for serious back and bladder problems, now is the time to assume the responsibilities of an only son.

Mothers often serve as intermediaries in these testy dialogues, as the sons' involvement in Islam represents a quite concrete attempt to reconnect with their fathers. This is almost destined to fail: in relationships built on few words, saying the wrong thing is inevitable. There are more feelings than the Koran can express. How does it become possible to say "I love you" or "I'm sorry"? When it comes to recognizing paternal loyalty or filial debts, deeds are better than words – as when fathers and sons attend the same mosque on Friday evenings, for example. This may have been the meaning behind Amédy and Hayat's religious wedding. The ceremony took place without the bride, in the presence of Amédy's father and an imam, in what seems like a thoroughly masculine way of honoring a mutual bond. The depth of such family sentiments can be measured by the silence that attends extreme situations: Amédy's father remaining mute as he listens to the umpteenth defense strategy presented by his son's lawyer. The pain of an imprisoned son, kept from his father's funeral in Mali. Amédy was willing to use religion to weaken the symbolic power that his sisters increasingly assumed: accusing them of insufficient piety, of disrespecting their origins. As they achieved a success that eluded him, and as the oldest sister began to assume a parental role,* the Muslim religion

* To illustrate, again from Eric de Sardan's viewpoint: "I would see his older sister, who was working, who'd pulled through, and she was sick of going to see the lawyer. [...].

allowed him to assert a kind of superiority – to shift the locus of disgrace.*

These contradictory desires – taking control, re-forging a bond – lead to the first step in the *about-turn*. In this step, religious reconversion is reduced to a *spectacle of rupture*. This is something the oldest are best positioned to speak about, since they've already moved on. That's true of Hassan: now past 40, he remembers a feeling of "excessive exaltation." The usual distinction between "converts" and those of "Muslim origin" is, in this sense, misleading. The about-turn is more obvious for those raised in a Christian environment, but it's the same turnaround and the same show. It can be seen in something as simple as the décor of a living room, as with Marley: hanging on the family walls are colorful scenes from the Bible and the life of Jesus, typical of West Indian Protestant homes. Here, faith is put on display, in color and holograms – a stark contrast with the pocket Koran resting soberly on his bed.

A floating political imaginary

By connecting personal life to the public sphere, these spectacular about-turns become political. This is because such individual gestures, often excessive, happen repeatedly. Their impact spreads by force of numbers; they spur intense debate, for or against. The imaginary of the "Muslim" label imbues the class free-for-all with a set of shared ideals and identities. Islam gives a name to a collective cause, one that's sensed but remains unidentified. Its unifying power is all the greater because it floats free of all context. Already in the 1980s, Abdelmalek Sayad observed how Islam tends to become "the last remaining medium or the last remaining national reference to which

She was sick of her brother's behavior, she would have liked to stop taking care of him, but couldn't help herself, I think. Either on her own, or because of family pressure. And they did have to pay fees. [...] In my recollection, I don't think it was really his friends who were paying, it was more his family. Probably both the father and the sister." People close to him also reported that his status as only son affected their father–son relationship. Amédy's repeated prison stays undermined the head-of-family status that would have fallen to him, making him, in his father's eyes, a "*loumbouré*" (a good-for-nothing, in Soninke dialect).

* Here is how Eric de Sardan described Amédy's father in a January 2017 interview: "He was a very modest man, very simple. [...] He gave the impression of being dependable, good-natured, very affable, very friendly, modest. He was what you might picture as the image of a first-generation immigrant worker. Honest, modest, at ease with himself. He was devastated by his son's behavior. He could not understand his son's behavior. He didn't have a protective attitude about it, he wasn't saying, 'it's not his fault, it's the police ...' You get that sort of thing very often, but in this case not at all."

French 'immigrant' groups can still cling [...] because, at least in the case of immigrants, it is more and more often decontextualized and 'de-nationalized' [...] and beyond the religious aspect itself, it seems to serve [...] as a way of proclaiming [...] one's belonging to the underdeveloped world."[5] The ubiquity of the theme of *Hegira* ("emigration," as embodied by the departure of Muhammad's companions from Mecca) no doubt strengthens this evocative power. By sacralizing the courage involved in leaving their country, it ennobles the family's act of emigration. But once the context and subtext are gone, Islam increasingly comes to resemble the lowest common denominator of a dominated population, rather than the idiom of a fully self-conscious community. This "exculturation" extracts Islam from any cultural context – in a society which, for its part, is no longer sure what it thinks about religion.[6] It enshrines what Olivier Roy calls the "loss of religious authority."[7] Thus unmoored, faith is asserted as an expression of individual choice, regenerated, rationalized, self-assured. The about-turn is a paradoxical attempt at individual empowerment. As a result, "with the help of a different 'generation' of emigrants, a 'shameful Islam' – hidden, eliminated, and eliminating itself from the public square and public commitments – was replaced by an avowed and declared Islam, which asserted itself religiously, of course, but also, beyond religious assertion – and perhaps more centrally – it asserted itself culturally and politically; in short, a militant Islam."[8] Thus, the prevailing economy of social positions generates a politics of faith, readily replacing faith in politics.

A few months after our long conversation in his car – where he ranted about how "the community is doing really badly," as we sat across the street from a supermarket – I met up with Radouane in the passenger seat of his old Peugeot. We pulled up to his flat. Neighbors stopped by to shake hands at regular intervals. One of them, an "uncle from Tunisia," handed him a large *sarouel* (the traditional baggy trousers worn in many Muslim countries), which immediately became the object of boyish banter: its principal advantage is to let you pray without the nuisance of getting your "parts" squeezed. Comfort was a topic on Radouane's mind. He had just returned from Saudi Arabia, where he'd undertaken one of the five pillars of Islam: the *hajj* (the pilgrimage to Mecca). Nineteen days of intense spiritual activity (Radouane went from the mosque to the hotel and back again without making a single tourist outing), and profitable as well (the trip was organized by an agency for the sum of 5,000 euros). On the *hajj*, the ideal of the *Umma* becomes palpable, swept along by the energy of several million people. After pitching a tent on the

Mina plain, the high point of the outing arrives: the day of Arafat.* The pilgrims then migrate to Mouzdalifa, "an empty expanse where you sleep under the stars." But instead of the religious effervescence he'd expected, Radouane was seized by a feeling of discomfort and disgust. This, however, didn't detract from the grandeur of the experience, or from the prestige of the host country.

Radouane: Saudi Arabia is a good country. Really, in terms of organization, the pilgrimage was perfect. There was nothing to criticize. It's not easy to handle 2 million people. Imagine if 2 million people came to France tomorrow, or La Courneuve! It was really well run, there was nothing to criticize. We didn't lack for anything.

FT: It's funny you say that, because just now you were telling me you didn't really like dealing with the other countries ...

Radouane: It's not that I didn't like it, it's just that's how those people are. Where they're from, that's how they live – they shove, they don't care. That's their way of life. You know, when you go to China, people spit on the ground. Where they're from, that's normal. It's natural. Except it's really gross! It's disgusting, you feel bad for them. You think, these people have nothing in their heads. They don't realize how they live. You've got the whole planet coming to this holy land. It's not easy ...

FT: Do you think the Koran ought to help them understand how to live better?

Radouane: You know, they're supposed to follow it. They shouldn't spit. But look, who follows the Koran to the letter? That's why I say that, compared to other communities, the French have good manners. People don't shove, they make an effort. Things work well here!

Radouane didn't travel with friends. It was practically a secret. ("I got my ticket, I didn't tell anyone anything, I did my thing, and I left, without making a big show of it, because it isn't good to do that.") He made friends on the trip, and stays in touch with them – those boys have become his "brothers." They're from all over France, all customers of the same travel agency. ("We French kept to ourselves.") The pilgrimage aside, the change of geographical setting shifted the meaning of declared solidarities. In Medina, the well-mannered "we" became "France" ("the French" versus "the other communities")

* This is the second day of the *hajj*. In the early morning, the pilgrims take off from the Mina plain and head to Mount Arafat, situated about 20 kilometers from Mecca. It was on this hill that the Prophet delivered his farewell sermon and where the main sermon of the *hajj* is delivered today.

in an expression of nationalism ("we have good manners") and paternalism (he "feels bad" for these "other ways of life") that could be heartily endorsed by the same political parties that would see in Radouane the end of "*la France éternelle.*" It's all a matter of context. The "Muslim community" doesn't exist in and of itself, not even "for or against France." Islam from below is rooted in ever-shifting histories and personal geographies; Islam from above floats in a void of first principles.*

Every narrative of faith celebrates the vivid moment when the "lightswitch flipped on." This moment is experienced as a revelation, signaling the "true" moment of entry into Islam. Certain life events become foundational, invested with meaning: for Marley and Adama, a prison stay; for Radouane, going to university and a romantic disappointment; for Hassan, his return to Grigny and the start of his career as an entrepreneur; for Amédy, meeting Hayat after being released from prison.† Beyond self-proclaimed membership in the *Umma*, what matters is the declaration each person makes to himself and to others, revealing his deepest convictions to the world. Vindictive orations, punctuated by shouts of "*Allah Akbar!*," reveal the naïveté of recent initiates, who smother their new-found faith with clumsy declarations of love. They annoy guys like Tarik and Hassan, who were raised in the religion from an early date. As Pierre Bourdieu notes, such public affirmations speak to a promise of transformation: "The official social world is what puts things out into the open so that they are visible to all, as opposed to things that are in a hidden state, closed off, focused inward, in small, clandestine groups."[9] Such boys *become* Muslims, rather than simply being Muslims, and they make that fact known. Islam is not a "space of assurance," nor does it pertain to any fixed community. It's an *act of officialization*. In the face of individual shame and guilt, coming to religion acts as a token of loyalty ("This is where I'm from"), a certificate of singularity ("This is what I am"), and a floating political imaginary ("We are what we believe and we believe in what we are").

* In debates on "religious nationalism," three distinct visions of the *Umma* emerge: one positing a pre-constituted nationalism, one that plays out a new anticolonial nationalism, and a non-territorial trans-nationalism.

† If we believe Hayat's depositions to police in the investigation carried out in 2010.

The Koran: reading and sharing

Often described as a religion of the book, Islam imparts value by means of a sacred object: the Koran. It is striking how much this book responds to the need and desire for understanding.

Critical re-intellectualization

Reading the Koran is an act that fills the imprint left by schooling. More than anything, it resembles a powerful experience of *critical re-intellectualization*. Religious texts constantly stress the "clarity" of "uncomplicated" language that leaves the "purity" of the divine message inscribed on the "faithful tablet" perfectly intact. The Prophet appears as an educator: by making the complex accessible while never simplifying it, he addresses each when he speaks to all. The book's organization into verses, surahs, and hadiths (the sayings of the Prophet) allows brief, fragmented forays into the text. For those not accustomed to reading much, being able to set the text down at any time defuses fear of the written word. Partial knowledge of the Prophet's story provides a set of guideposts; these offer protection from humiliation in the face of what are sometimes incomprehensible printed pages. This autodidactic re-intellectualization also occurs through the acquisition of a second language, Arabic. For Adama and Marley, that discovery became a goal. For those who already speak the language, it serves to rehabilitate a delegitimized bilingualism – whether merely hoped-for, halting, or solid. It's a clear finger in the eye to the education system, which values a selective bilingualism (French and English, and to a lesser extent German and Spanish) and distrusts the use of Arabic, suspected of signaling a "lack of integration." Since language lies at the heart of subjectivity and emotion, it's not hard to imagine how this disfavor stokes feelings of injustice. Moving back and forth between French and Arabic is a way of shaking up daily life and can help recover a sense of history.

How much a person reads depends on his or her preexisting level of comfort with the written word. Unsurprisingly, Hassan, Tarik, and Radouane read the most. They were on academic tracks in high school and went furthest in higher education. They also speak Arabic. Hassan is the most meticulous reader, clearly a result of the many hours he spent at the library with his mother. Radouane reads only a little, but does so every day. He strives to ensure that his faith, like his life expectancy, will last for the long haul:

> I read three or four pages per day. That way you don't get put off of it. It's to keep up my longevity, um ... I mean, my endurance, sorry ... Slowly but surely – that way your brain takes it all in, you don't get put off, you like it.

He makes do with a few supplementary books, such as *The Book of the Oneness of God* by Muhammad ibn Abd al-Wahhab, a founding figure of the eighteenth-century Salafist movement. Adama skims more than he reads; he's still marked by his school experiences. ("Me and books, it's complicated. I take it at my own speed.") Marley says he stopped "halfway through" the Koran.

On the one hand, this book – to put it mildly – doesn't get a good press in the republican education system. On the other hand, it's a bestseller. Becoming a reader of the Koran means adhering to the standards of legitimate cultural capital and intellectual excellence espoused by the school system, even while turning one's back on it. It's a way of re-appropriating the imprint left by the school experience. In Marley's living room, to the right of the television, stands a little bookshelf. There, opposite a series of suspension weights, one can find the few books that really matter. "Useless" books end up in the trash. My first book spent some time on the shelf, until Marley lent it to someone else. He proudly showed me the cover of his latest acquisition – *A Guide to Kittens* – as well as the price tag, as if he wanted to signal it wasn't stolen. As a social object, the book remains sacred. The fact that I "write books" has never been a damper on our relationship: quite the contrary. Marley's purchase of the *Guide to Kittens* is a sign of the importance he attaches to his "little furball"; he wants "the best" for it.

To some degree, reading the Koran also involves a performance for his friends' benefit, a way of playing the organic intellectual. Arguments with friends are sometimes settled with citations from a discreetly circulated text, in a manner reminiscent of a certain Little Red Book from a different era. Arguments from authority, or in bad faith, are common, as are staunch opinions about some particular surah, delivered by someone who clearly hasn't read it. Having personal experience with academic seminars and public debates, I can't say there's anything unique about this. Amédy seemed to consistently shy away from this game: I've never met anyone who could recall having a religious discussion with him.

Koranic gifts and counter-gifts

Just as amateur writers mimic professional writers while also seeking to set themselves apart, so too does this layman's engagement with accredited practices help salve lingering wounds. It readjusts the gap between disappointed hopes, unrealized aspirations, and precarious social positions in the present.[10] The Koran is of greatest help when it's shared; hence, it creates connections. Indeed, it's an object that circulates. Radouane owns four of them: two in French (the first was given to him by the "aunt of a friend in Morocco," the second was his own personal purchase, consecrating his commitment to the faith) and two in Arabic (the first was given to him by "the guy who taught me how to read Arabic," the second by "a brother from the mosque who doesn't know how to read Arabic"). These *gifts of Korans* obey a codified logic, as Marley explains.

FT: Where's your Koran?

Marley: I don't even have my Koran anymore ... I gave it to a little dude, Faty.

FT: Oh, you gave it away?

Marley: Yeah, because he wanted to reconvert, there was stuff he wanted to know. I brought it to him so he could pray right. I told him: "Take it, do what you want with it."

FT: You lent it to him?

Marley: I just gave it to him, I'll buy another one. You know, when someone's given you a Koran, and then somebody wants to come to Islam, you need to give too, it's important.

FT: Somebody gave you one?

Marley: I'd gone to prison. My sister sent it to me, I read it there and lent it to a guy in another cell. That son of a bitch, when he got out he didn't bring it back to me, that motherfucker. Next time I see him, I'm gonna fuck him up [*upset*]. That was my first Koran and I'll never get it back. I lent it to him, it wasn't a gift.

FT: Because it was given to you by your sister?

Marley: Nah, it's because of the guy I asked to give it to me. He's the reason I reconverted. Moussa – he's lived here a long time. He kept it in his glove compartment, in his car. In Arabic/French. When he gave it to me, I could tell he didn't want to. But he did, 'cause he figured if I was asking for it, it wasn't for no reason. He figured I wanted to learn something, that it was for religion. That Koran never left my place. But I lent it to that piece of shit – who's already Muslim! He's already Muslim, which means he already knows shit. It's not like this was a guy who didn't know anything and wanted to learn. That motherfucker, he didn't tell me the truth.

The circulation of Korans reflects the structure of debts and loyalties at a given moment in time. Giving a Koran is a way to pay back what one has received, by indebting a novice who may receive it only if he makes an explicit request. It was costly for Moussa to give away an object that probably had great sentimental value. But because Marley wanted to "learn" and "convert" – and Moussa had once been in the same situation – he was obliged to give it up. The difference between Faty and the "piece of shit" (also a "motherfucker" and a "son of a bitch") is clear. Marley was happy to give his Koran to the former. Doing so followed a logic of gift/counter-gift between expert and novice: giving, receiving, giving back in order to pass on. The "piece of shit," by contrast, acted unfairly. He was already a practicing Muslim, yet incurred a debt: he "didn't tell the truth." He broke the chain between himself and Marley, as well as the more symbolic chain linking him to those who "reconvert." Marley is prepared to "fuck him up." An ordinary Koran is lent; a Koran for *reconversion* is given. Marley's brutal words testify to the importance of this anthropological rule. As Marcel Mauss notes, "The gift is thus something that must be given, that must be received, and that is, at the same time, dangerous to accept."[11] It creates obligation and dependence – through suggestion, never coercion: Marley made it clear to Moussa that he had no choice but to give him his book; his message to Faty was "do what you want with it." The "reconvert" feels he has the upper hand. By agreeing, the giver, for his part, finds a "mutual validation of belief" that confirms him in his own decision.[12] Ultimately, each has convinced the other that the latter has chosen "his" Islam.

Such acts of giving are neither decreed nor described. If Marley harbors so much hate for the "motherfucker," it's because he lacks the words to describe what seems to him a betrayal. The silence surrounding such exchanges stands at odds with grand normative imperatives; the latter are always too explicit to be fully heard. These gifts and counter-gifts of Korans gain their power from the halo of silence that surrounds them. As Maurice Godelier explains, the sacred creates an opacity that masks the connections among men. It preserves social life by rendering it unconscious of its own workings. The sacred is an "anchor for fixing the identities of societies and individuals in time": the "enigma of the gift" is the archetype of this.[13] Its value is all the greater in capitalist societies because, there, calculation stands at the heart of social relations; such societies thus no longer need gift-giving to reproduce themselves. Gift-giving, by becoming a mere residue, has also become an ideal, so that it "operates in the imaginary as the last refuge of a solidarity, of an open-handedness which is supposed to have characterized other eras in the evolution of humankind."[14] These Koranic exchanges belong to this imaginary of the possible. They pave the way for altruistic deprivation, for self-sacrifice. Here lies the "motherfucker's" sacrilege: his theft reintroduced self-interest and calculation where previously there had been none. He shattered the utopia of a mysterious fraternity.

It's thus unsurprising that Korans circulate beyond the circle of the self-proclaimed *Umma*. Fraternal feelings arise chiefly from specific histories, rather than from floating political imaginaries. They're about exchange, not spectacle. Amédy gave a Koran to his final lawyer, which he dedicated in honor of the latter's "kindness" – a book she has conscientiously kept. This, surely, was less about proselytism than a mark of respect and gratitude, which only a gift of the "Book" could express.

Re-aestheticizing the world

The enigma of the "Book" is not merely an intellectual experience or a social anchor point. It's also a spiritual and aesthetic experience. It makes sense by affecting the senses. In reading or hearing certain chants, all experience the same encounter with beauty, but few manage to describe it. The verdict usually comes in three unchanging words: "It's so beautiful!" Here, Hassan is an exception. On this subject, he chooses his words with extreme precision:

Hassan: Back then I would observe Eid and Ramadan, but it was nothing. I would ask myself questions of a spiritual nature. The world is not beautiful. Why is it like this? What am I going to do if I don't find it beautiful? At first, I was into literature, philosophy. I read, I thought it was all really beautiful, but I didn't grasp the substance, the content.

FT: What authors did you read?

Hassan: There was Voltaire. There was also Kant, who I liked a lot. Descartes, a little, but at the time I wasn't really into the logical stuff. At a certain point, I wanted to get into Nietzsche but I found that a little too hard-core for me [*laughs*]. I was getting less and less into philosophy. So these are questions that stuck with me. When I was 26, I had some friends who started giving me books and the Koran, to see what I thought. I started reading, but what kept me from diving into it at the time was a philosophical issue: an eye for an eye. If you keep going around and around, the blood never stops. That was something impossible to accept.

FT: And you accept it now?

Hassan: Yeah, I accepted it. Because, in a sense, the law of retaliation is clearly stated in the Koran. But it's also possible to forgive. And that really hit me, because I realized that you had the possibility of forgiving, and that it was morally superior. That was a sort of reconciliation with religion. I'd been basing myself on ignorance, that's all.

FT: That liberated you?

Hassan: Well yeah, because the first thing it does is it takes away superstition. And then, when it came to philosophy, I had gotten rid of anything that smacked of aestheticism. The notion of beauty, and all that.... It was pure reason that interested me, if you like. That was a distortion. In the Koran, there's a sublimation of the concept of reason, but also of aesthetics. And that impressed me, I wasn't expecting that. As a concept, in terms of beauty, I found that powerful. And I don't mean the translation! If you go into the texts in Arabic, the aesthetics are awesome! The aesthetic concept is extremely present in the Arabic. There's a reconciliation with logic for those who don't consider themselves intellectuals. And there's also the reconciliation with beauty. For example, there are landscapes, it speaks in metaphors. There's reconciliation for anyone who thinks: "Hey, the arts, all that stuff, that's not for me." Affect is really important. When people come back to religion, there's a real rush of beauty. When you're in it, you're submerged by new sensations. At a certain point, you want to break with everything you did, everything you were before. In other words, you want a metamorphosis for yourself.

This "reconciliation" between intellect and beauty is not trivial. In daily life, the feeling of injustice combines with the neighborhood's image of ugliness and meanness – a recurrent complaint when things aren't going well. The dearth of artistic activity and manual creativity, the lack of attention to emotion at school – such things are not unrelated to aesthetic sensations suddenly becoming "awesome." In contrast to a "reconciliation with logic" that proceeds through calculation and balance, the experience of "reconciliation with beauty" contains within it the indeterminate, the indescribable, the mysterious, the excessive – in short, transcendence. This re-aestheticization of the world is the emotional engine of reconversion ("you're submerged," "you want a metamorphosis for yourself"). Its power makes one want to share it, to "convert" others, too. It reinforces the enigma of the gift.

It's here that the book as object takes on its full dimensions. By allowing individuals to communicate, little by little, in silence, and from afar, it can be shared without being contaminated. It's given because of all the things it says that cannot be summarized, since beauty remains irreducible. Salman Rushdie, the writer against whom the Ayatollah Khomeini launched a *fatwa* in 1989 for having dared to imagine the life of Muhammad in *The Satanic Verses*,[15] knows this power of the printed word all too well. In his telling, this becomes the moment when reader and writer – one could also say giver and receiver – "merge, through the medium of the text, to become a collective being that both writes as it reads and reads as it writes."[16] Hassan said just that, in three words: "rush of beauty."

In the here and now: getting better

These "new sensations" are less the sign of a final "reconciliation" than the portent of a new departure. After the about-turn – where religious conversion is about ringing declarations – comes *reconversion*, which leads to a reordering, reorganizing, and re-appropriation of one's life. In Islam, this is given a name: reform (*islah*). The process unfolds over a lifetime – or "longevity," in Radouane's slip of the tongue. That lapse is a reminder that becoming religious is a way of confronting the existential anguish of death, a cross between deliverance and rebirth. Max Weber showed that paths to religious salvation are embodied in daily life in "purely ritual activities and ceremonies," but also in "social achievements" and "self-perfection."[17] What a person does for others and him- or herself, what he or she becomes socially, matters at least as much as scrupulous observance of religious rites.

A bookkeeping of guilt and merit

At this point, systemizing one's behavior is key. Since reconversion involves a drastic change of direction, anyone will realize the path he or she's embarking on will be dotted with imperfections and hesitations. Intermittent reading of the Koran salves this guilty feeling. Moving ahead "step-by-step," as Adama put it, is a way to protect oneself from the chasm between what one is required to do and what one actually does. In this fragmented approach to the sacred, the "ethic of good works" takes the lead:

> Every action, whether virtuous or wicked action, can be evaluated singly and credited to the individual's account positively or negatively for the requirement of salvation. [...] Each individual as the carrier of one's own action possesses ethical standards only tenuously; s/he may turn out to be a weaker or a stronger creature in the face of temptation, according to the internal or external situation.[18]

This "very precise bookkeeping [...] of the guilt and merit of individual actions"[19] particularly suits boys seeking redemption, absolution from "dirty work," in order to "go legit." Minutely doling out concern for others, as against concern for oneself, is an acceptable compromise between materialistic accumulation and altruistic deprivation. It makes it easier to stick to the psychologically costly process of exit, becoming a generous reservoir of points for good morality. Looking after one's *hassanate** becomes the best way to avoid "hell," an outcome feared by all. This quest for morality points inspires "reformed" day-to-day behaviors, as Marie and Tarik jovially demonstrated one evening over dinner at their flat.

Marie: When I was Christian, I would go to catechism. But in day-to-day life there was no behavior to strive for. Whereas with this, it's really elaborate. It's about daily behaviors. In the morning, when you wake up you have to wash your face three times, wash your mouth three times. It's hygiene for daily life. [...] For example, before, when I brushed my hair I would throw away the hairs. Now, I burn them, or throw them in the toilet. That way they don't get everywhere [*laughs*]. You never know! [*laughs*]

FT: But what do you do with them? [*laughs*]

Marie: Nothing, I throw them away! [*laughs*] But I'm not leaving them in the trash anymore where you can see them.

Tarik: There are lots of little day-to-day things you do. Like, throwing out bread, that's a sin! Refusing to give someone something to eat, that's a sin! Whatever their religion is, if you don't help them, it's a sin!

Marie: Your behavior gets better.

Tarik: It's the behavior of the Prophet, as we say.

FT: You actually live a better life?

Marie: Exactly, that's right. I was already into helping people. I'm a nurse's assistant after all! This gives me a little bit more.

Tarik: Spitting on the ground is a sin! And there's global warming, too!

Marie: I never throw anything on the ground, but I did before [*laughs*]. I hate that. Also, when I finish my food, there's nothing left on the plate. I sop it up until it's finished. Every time, Tarik will tell me it's *sunnah* [in line with the teachings of the Prophet] to do that. It's not good to leave even a crumb of bread on the plate!

FT: Well, I already do that, but I'm not Muslim! [*laughs*]

Tarik: Really? Well, with us it's written down! It gives us good points! [*laughs*]

* The *hassanate* refers to the number of good deeds required to enter heaven.

This systematization of self-perfection takes place through routines and rituals. They draw a line of demarcation between past impurity and the purity to come (cleanliness, hygiene, helping others, respecting the environment, etc.). The somewhat childlike parallel between the *hassanate* and getting good points in the classroom is unsettling, as is the parallel between Tarik's description of a "good Muslim" and the "good student" that he tried to become: following written and spoken instructions to the letter; expecting observance of both form and substance; results recorded in a precise system of grading; success leading to a move to a higher level, and so on. But here, re-intellectualization yields knowledge at a practical level, which can be mobilized immediately – from "hairs" to "clean plates." It follows a never-ending path toward the possibility of advancement. As a result, it permits a reevaluation of one's place in the world: an engine of learning for those furthest from the norms of the school system.

For oneself and others: brushes with purity

Observing religious rituals undoubtedly raises one's score in the *hassanate*, but it matters less than the purification of day-to-day behavior. Tarik doesn't pray every day and attends mosque episodically. Marley is a bit more conscientious. Adama prays five times a day and goes to mosque on Friday evenings "when he can." Amédy could also be seen there wearing traditional attire, but wasn't a regular. Friends of his saw him there as late as two weeks before the attacks. Hassan carries out his five prayers and attends mosque when his schedule as a business owner permits.[20]

Only Radouane abjures all flexibility in this regard. To say he follows a schedule religiously would be an understatement. For the last two years, his every working day has adhered to the same formula: wake up at 4 a.m. for his morning routine; breakfast; read the Koran; 5:20 a.m. prayer at the mosque, where he encounters only "old people"; he starts his work day in Paris at 9 a.m., where he can pray in a special staff area; back to his neighborhood for a workout at the end of the day; a final prayer at 10:10 p.m. at the mosque. In addition to all this, there are two days of fasting, Monday and Thursday. Beyond the ceremonial aspects, these efforts at "reform" of his behavior and body testify to the close interrelationship between his faith, his masculinity, and the mantras of self-improvement. His muscle-building sessions are sandwiched between prayers. They also resonate with his sexual and emotional experiences. Radouane recounts going through a flirtatious period after receiving the baccalaureate ("I went out a little, I had one or two girls"), followed by a relationship that didn't last ("It went badly, we weren't right for each other, I found her overwhelming") and a traumatic event ("I can't reveal my sins, I can't tell you exactly, but it had to do with a girl, I seriously regretted it, I was in a bad state – I thought, I can't do this again. So I got into religion"). A lover's quarrel? Prostitutes? Violence of a verbal, moral, physical, or sexual kind against an acquaintance? It was hard to read between the lines of his reticence, but his guilty expression left little doubt: remorse was involved in the reconversion of Radouane's free time ("Going out and hitting on girls and all that, it's not good"). In any event, Islam seems to help with his difficulties establishing relationships with the opposite sex. But the high cost of such a rigorous use of his time may eventually work against the "longevity" of his religious commitment. Since Radouane returned from his pilgrimage to Mecca, he hasn't managed to "get back on schedule with going to mosque" – which "isn't good for points."

Ultimately, this obsession with the *hassanate* is just an extension of the passion for meritocracy. The counting of points is based on a certainty that salvation is tied to individual merit. It diverges from the fatalistic working-class tradition of salvation by chance, "which restores absolute equality between the players" since "the winner can claim no superiority, whether in skill, intelligence, or money."[21] Indeed, the universal basis on which such reforms of individual behavior are justified ("to become better") muddles class divisions to some extent. An ethic of conviction – hang in there and stick to it – and commitment to a more virtuous world don't necessarily strengthen a group against its competitors. The notion of a unifying religion that promotes social harmony is a commonplace. It's regularly invoked to justify attending mosque: Radouane points to the intergenerational mixing that takes place there; Hassan to the fact that he can meet "professionals and managers" there.

But mealtimes are perhaps most telling. Eating together means sharing a meal, but also sharing time, pleasure, and beliefs. As for me, I've been a vegetarian for nearly 10 years. It's a relatively unusual practice in France, less common in working-class neighborhoods than in the most affluent districts. There have been many occasions when my diet might have put me in an awkward position. The "longevity" of a field study inevitably leads to socializing, which almost always leads to food: a meal at the kebab place, a snack at the Tunisian restaurant, dinner at home, a barbecue outside, a picnic in the park, and so on. Such moments would force me to reveal something that causes no stigma as long as it's hidden. Was I going to offend someone who'd invited me with the best intentions? Would I disclose an uncomfortable class marker and find myself snared in a clash of stereotypes – the "Parisian vegetarian bobo" versus the "kebab-eater from the *cité*"? Every time I had to pull my dietary habits out of the closet, a lengthy discussion would commence about my choices and how I justify them. Such conversations produced marked sympathy – on both form (now it was my turn to bite the bullet and justify myself) and substance. The most convincing arguments were the following: animal suffering, health concerns, and a refusal to participate in an obscene system of industrial exploitation; in short, my considered refusal to "get my hands dirty" and "participate in the system." As for my sticking to principles despite social pressure, I think it earned me deep respect. There's an obvious parallel with the symbolism of halal and Ramadan: both "they" and "I" put our values where our mouths are, even if that means finding ourselves isolated. We do so to put a little of the sacred – and therefore politics – on our plates. Despite our differences, we share the same invisible motive: to make the world seem, by means of our little individual reforms, a bit better.

Completing the truth and settling into the comfort of de-intellectualization

And then there's the substance, which takes the form of a knot. Both critical re-intellectualization and the re-aestheticization of the world serve a transcendent purpose: *completing the truth*. The life of Muhammad embodies a hope of drawing closer to such a completion. It's presented as the mirror image of a real life – or even of "real life." The narrative form of the story, in which one sees "oneself as another,"[22] is an effective response to doubts about the meaning of one's place in the world. Throughout the story, the perfection of his example is broken down into accessible episodes. Those with Christian parents, like Marley or Marie, stress how Islam – since it came after the Christian or Jewish revelations – seems like a fulfillment. It perfects the deeply rooted monotheism of their upbringings. As Marie put it:

> All of the prophets are perfect. But in Islam, there's Muhammad, too. And he's the last of the prophets. You can't believe in the prophets and then forget one! Everyone knows the Antichrist will come down, Jesus will come down – and then with Muhammad, it will be the end of history. That's a story that isn't in the other religions. It's a fulfillment. Following the behavior of the Prophet means going towards the truth.

Completing the truth comes as a relief to boys who are tired of the contradictions of their private moralities and the paradox of their illicit task-professions. But the amount of time it takes to "follow Muhammad" – theoretically infinite – cuts against the "awesome" exaltation that characterizes the beginning of each reconversion. The more time goes by, the more it tends to diminish and devalue one's being, sparking feelings diametrically opposed to the initial ardor. Fear and doubt always threaten to "stall the engine."

Adama: I'm afraid of the Koran, of course. For me, it's the book of truth. There's a lot of things that I do ... that I've done, that are ... how do I put it ...
FT: You are afraid of what you might discover? You prefer not to know, is that it?
Adama: I have to know. I want to know. But right now ... for now ... the engine is stalled. I'm required to know.... But I'm still in the learning stage and I want to be less ignorant of religion. But for now, I think that's where I am.
FT: Do you fear God?
Adama: I mean, I wouldn't be asking him for forgiveness five times a day if I wasn't afraid of him! [*laughs*] I'm not an ideal person, I've screwed up, and maybe I'll screw up again, you know, I'm not perfect....

Max Weber observed that because "the Koran was believed to have been divinely created, the contents of the scripture must be always validated as divinely inspired."[23] This is a weight one must learn to bear. The more one's theological knowledge grows, the more the imperfections and misunderstandings show through. As a result, day-to-day conduct always threatens to overwhelm the rest. To obey non-negotiable commands is calming, reassuring. It distances a person from his own deficiencies, to the point where "*fides implicita*"* is "[no] longer an actual personal acceptance of dogmas; rather, it is a declaration of confidence in and dedication to a prophet or to the authority of a structured institution. In this way, faith loses its intellectual character."[24] Gradually settling into the *comfort of de-intellectualization* is the psychological down-phase of every reconversion.

What space remains for the exercise of doubt, or what some call free will? Once again, it's Hassan who found the most precise way of describing this inner tension:

* This expression refers to a believer's disposition to subordinate his personal convictions to religious authorities and thus defer to standards they define for him.

> There's a moment in religion where there's a sort of struggle between established truths and doctrinal truths.

The "established truths" are the result of a personal confrontation with the texts, whereas the "doctrinal truths" are there to justify ritual practices. The former are the product of critical re-intellectualization; the latter, of the comfort of de-intellectualization. Each person must find the right balance.

But between these two phases, the purposes of faith remain the same: achieving contact with completed truth. This, according to Scott Atran, is one of the primary differences between science and religion: "Religions are morally absolute, however conceptually flexible and open-textured, whereas science endlessly pursues ever changing truth by strict and rigid means. Religion establishes truth to provide moral and social stability. Science sacrifices surety to discover truth's illusions. Religion abhors the competition for truth. Science can't live without it."[25] Belief in the existence of an ultimate truth is the cornerstone of the moral, emotional, and societal security that religious reconversion achieves. That's why, again according to Atran, "Religion survives science as it does secular ideology not because it is prior to, or more primitive than, science or secular reasoning, but because of what it affectively and collectively secures for people."[26] Nevertheless, today, both in TV studios and on the streets of the *cité*, this vestige of the past is subjected to pointed questioning. The comforts of de-intellectualization seem to have won out, bringing forth a twin threat: the "ignorance" and "intolerance" of the reconverted.

Beyond the here and now: being the best

The challenge of "longevity" runs up against the problem of virtuosity. Getting better is seldom enough when it's also possible to become *the* best, or when one is likely to find someone better than oneself.

Against others: the virtuoso

As Max Weber makes clear, "That people differ widely in their religious capacities was found to be true in every religion based on a systematic procedure of sanctification," so that "religious virtuosity, in addition to subjecting the natural drives to a systematic patterning of life, always leads to the control of relationships within communal life, the conventional virtues of which are inevitably un-heroic and utilitarian, and leads further to an altogether radical religious and ethical criticism."[27] Salvation through merit and good points involves measuring, judging, separating: in other words, casting some segment of one's peers into a realm of difference, like the Chinese spitters Radouane mentioned.

This universal tendency toward "fundamentalist intolerance of other 'species'."[28] which is simply the product of group belonging, finds itself strengthened here by three dynamics. First, there's the importance that the Islamic texts attach to *jahilya* (the pre-Islamic, polytheistic period predating the revelation, a state of culpable ignorance); to *kufr* (the infidelity and ingratitude involved in a refusal to believe); and to *jihad* (effort and struggle against adversity to reach the path of God). Then there's the excessive value placed on competition, which is fostered by capitalist society. From schooling to jobs, in sports and in public life, one has to be the best, and show it – reveling in an idealization of excellence. Finally, there's the form this competition takes on the urban margins: a valorization of the image of the fighter and the scenario of the grand battle within the second zone, whose contours grow increasingly narrow. These three dynamics – religious, economic, and social – are not causes in themselves. They crystallize a climate that spurs people to find confirmation of their own virtuosity in a rejection of "others." Despite what is sometimes claimed, this feeling of superiority has little to do with a clash between "Muslims" and "non-Muslims." Self-proclaimed groups matter less than the individual salvation of those who claim adherence to them – as shown by "the rising torment of being insufficiently Muslim," the "dread" of which "gives rise to the super-Muslim's obsession."[29] The ethnocentrism of the times is, to a large extent, a form of narcissism.

According to Olivier Roy, the breeding ground of this rejection is "holy ignorance," the product of an age in which "religion and culture part ways." In the context of globalization, decolonization, and social media, he argues, the experience of faith has become decontextualized, stripped of all "religious markers."[30] Given the individualistic logic of conversion, it's the spectacle of rupture and the desire for renewal that win out. The born-again convert is then at an impasse, since it's impossible to pass on the experience of rupture – the very experience to which it owes its existence. This leads Roy to argue that the problem of "globalized Islam" is mainly a product of autodidactism and a desire to stand out: "The sectarianism lies in the mindset, not in the ideas [...] one wishes to be a 'taliban' (student) and yet also to be an expert right away. But the final word is that ascribed to the expert: the real expert, who harkens to tradition; the autodidact does not invent, he mimics."[31] For him, virtuosity is a leitmotif and a pretense: it hides the comfort of de-intellectualization under the façade of an impatient claim to imagined excellence.

Though the spectacle of rupture and the about-turn are indeed foundational, there's a danger in viewing this initial phase as a permanent condition. Heightening this risk is the fact that such ruptures seek to be impressive and attention-grabbing. Thus, the propensity to perform displays of confrontation is probably the only characteristic that both Islamist attacks and slogans like "*Je ne suis pas Charlie*" have in common – though the latter seldom express unconditional support for terrorist action.[32] Whether through violence or free speech, each exists only in adversity. But permanent rupture is extremely costly, almost untenable. Maintaining such a posture to the exclusion of all else inevitably ends in a kind of self-extinction – in sacrifice or death. That was the path followed by Amédy or Bülent, but those cases remain exceptional. Endurance requires moving beyond performances and slogans, setting them aside in order to make something out of them.

The "caterpillar" and the "butterfly": reconverting and sticking to it

With the passage of time comes the work of gradually softening the about-turn. Living requires reconciling the purity of heaven with the rocky slope of one's own imperfect trajectory. It's for this reason that young Muslims speak of "*reconversion*" more than of conversion. It is not a linguistic error. The encounter with Allah is less a rupture than a directive, one that helps in envisioning the next step: namely, finding new uses for what one already has, moving ahead with the resources available, making something constructive from one's past mistakes, finding continuity. Blank slates exist only in speeches. Reconversion, by contrast, is about routinization, embedding the about-turn in the richness of the existing social world.

This requires some minimal effort toward inner peace and reconciliation with others, whether they seem "worse" or "better" than oneself. Hassan, being in his early forties, offers a glimpse of how this unfolds, as he did one fine summer afternoon when we found ourselves in a neighborhood tea shop. It was the height of Ramadan: a propitious time to look back on his "youth." Hassan insisted on buying me a coffee and two pastries despite my polite protests ("That's not OK, I can't watch you salivate while you're fasting!"), which were soon calmed by his affable manner and the faint odor of fresh cakes.

Hassan: When you have your first spiritual shock, you don't want to be the same person anymore. You experience a metamorphosis. You come out of your chrysalis, like a butterfly. You don't want to be a caterpillar anymore! But the truth is that a butterfly can be ugly! Every day I try to better myself and I don't always succeed. Sometimes I regress. It's about introspection: when I'm not so generous, the next day I'll try to be better.

FT: And this comes down to prayer?

Hassan: No, I mean in general. The goal I'd like to reach is every day, before going to bed. When people are able to sit down calmly, then you've got something other than an appeal to hatred.... In the beginning, I would have liked to be what I wanted. But at a certain point, you realize you're hurting one person, then another, with your certainties.... With that attitude, you push people away, even though these are people you've known a long time, childhood friends! One of them will come up and she'll greet you with a kiss on the cheek and you'll say, "Stop it, I'm done with you!" You start going to war because they're like this or like that. Same thing with family, sometimes you have a rough time, you're not in control, you're into the rush that comes with it. And so you hurt people, you wound them verbally.... That's what reform is for. It's something you build up over the long term.

FT: How did you come to this realization?

Hassan: Time. Because at first, you're into the purification part. You feel sort of exalted. You want to live like in the time of the Prophet. You know, that's the hardest form of Islam.

FT: That's something where you've changed?

Hassan: It's more about explaining to people, but without hurting them.

FT: You hang on to certain practices that you value?

Hassan: Yes. For example, if you ask me to go out to a club, I'll say no. I don't want to play the cop while you're drinking, but I'm saying we can sit down at the table and talk about all that. Once you take the time to explain, there's no problem. I'm not trying to hurt people, but I'm not dodging the question. I'll explain, I'll be pretty frank about it. There are women I work with and we're extremely friendly, we eat together, we laugh. Just now you said "You're doing Ramadan, I don't want to eat." But my practices are my own business. I'm not going to tell you: "Tsk, tsk, you're impure." I have my convictions, but I have nothing against you. I don't define myself in opposition to you. I define myself through a spiritual relationship that I have with God.

With the time it takes to create the conditions for dialogue (how do you "explain" your budding convictions to others without being excessive?), reconversion is only possible if it builds *on* the initial about-turn. The power of faith lies in the act of persistence, of fully accepting the initial commitment, holding steady ("not dodging the question"; "being frank"). What's central here is *perpetuating the act of officialization*. Those who've never known the repeated experience of social stigma would never guess at the political power of this mechanism of affirmation, this refusal to deny one's identity. Pierre Bourdieu described it in these terms:

> Moving from the unofficial, the clandestine, the shameful, the things that cannot be said out loud, things that must be hidden, to the official, constitutes a radical change, and I think one of the most powerful political effects is the effect of publication, *Öffentlichkeit*, that is, the action of making things open, making them clear, making them public, publishing, displaying. People who are invested in order, in law, the Right, etc., are those who can display themselves, display what they are, in a non-shameful way; who have the whole social order with them.[33]

Sticking to one's faith means managing to hold one's position. Unlike the exhausting paradox of *le business*, perpetuating the act of officialization, by acting as a revelation, brings calm: the sense of no longer feeling a gap between what I think, what I say, what I do, and how people see it all.

Holding on to one's faith also means holding on to values, by being able to articulate difference instead of fighting it ("I have nothing against you, I define myself through a spiritual relationship that I have with God"). Moments of potential conflict or emotional friction (the kiss on the cheek; the cakes during Ramadan) are also opportunities to put one's morality to the test. And because "it is in experiencing emotions that we reveal our own values to ourselves,"[34] they can become moments of reassurance. Sticking to one's faith by facing up to difference – even hostility – also means becoming aware of oneself and one's place. By refusing to kiss a woman on the cheek or eat a cake, while remaining "friendly," Hassan learned to put his values forward without imposing them. He feels a sense of coherence: social conventions are no longer experienced as compromises. I could see this feeling of peace in his eyes. Maybe because, by refusing to eat meat and fish in the country of beef bourguignon and bouillabaisse, I simply recognized it.

In a hazy light

Listening to Hassan's account, one can see how a "friendly" acceptance of difference came at the end of a long road that wasn't always smooth. What we call "tolerance" is part of a continuum of minute variations, made up of a whole series of options, possibilities, and limits that are less about grand higher principles than the social and historical conditions that make any "peaceful coexistence"[35] possible. These positions appear in a hazy light. Marley can't for a moment see himself going to Syria with the "nutcases," yet willingly accepts the proposition that "Jew = rich"; Adama devotes the bulk of his time to street education and "violence prevention" even as he understands, in the fullest sense of the term, Amédy's fall. On this scale, time remains the master variable. Here, religion grasps the continuum by its two radical extremes, each of which aims to aggrandize those who adhere to it.

On one side, there's the assertion of an uncompromising pacifism, standing beyond mere tolerance. Islam defines itself as the religion of a peace that must be defended at all costs. It aids in establishing contact with others even as it remains unbending in the face of those it judges to be malicious. These are Hassan's two faces: curious to meet those different from him, but prepared to have it out with the "intolerant" – like the handful of "condescending teachers" who once questioned how much time was actually put in by the neighborhood youths he took in as interns, insinuating that his company was a "sinecure for cousins"; he "chewed them out during the internship review meeting." They're Tarik's two faces, with his definition of "Islamism" as synonymous with universal peace ("Islam means peace and I'm 100 percent for peace: I'm a radical Islamist!") and also war against terror ("If I have a weapon in my hands, I see those guys and I'll smoke 'em on the spot, and believe me I'm a good shot; you have to take them down on the spot like dogs, that's all they deserve; the minute they start shooting, they're refusing dialogue").

On the other side, short of a resigned acceptance of difference, there's the scenario of the grand battle, in which armed struggle is seen as the ultimate realization of the class free-for-all. It marks off the concrete world of close-knit loyalties from an abstract universe of "the enemy." With Islam, it has a cause that can be named: the battle will be waged by and for religion. These are the two faces of Amédy or Bülent: attentive, generous, open to dialogue (even debate) with those close to them and ready to kill strangers for Daesh. They're the two faces of Radouane, an easy-going joker ready to go off to his death if need be:

> There's a council of experts in Saudi Arabia who follow the Koran and the *sunnah*, and if they say one day that it's time to take up arms, we'll make war like anybody else; when it's time to fight, the French or the Americans get on a plane and go – except they fight for the state, we fight for Allah.

While it might seem obvious that only those who have cultivated an intellectualized and contextualized approach to Islam would espouse an uncompromising pacifism, and that those with limited theological knowledge always risk manipulation by those with more expertise, knowledge and intellectualization are no protection against resorting to violence. Ideologists of hate have enough of a presence on the Internet, and studies of genocides are sufficiently clear on this point, to give pause: the ability to "compartmentalize" horror and morality can produce a mental fissure within utterly ordinary people that can't be reduced to mere manipulation.[36] When Radouane defers to a "council of experts" whose exact positions he struggles to explain to me, one should keep in mind that he's hardly the least informed (nor the most expert) individual in theological matters, and that his level of education puts him in the top 10 percent of the French population. As for Adama and Marley, though they don't read the Koran much and don't speak Arabic, they tend to embody a form of tolerance that rules out notions of battle – a matter of "respect" for the former and "resigned acceptance of difference" for the latter.[37]

Nor should we place more value on autodidacticism than makes sense: a novice's approach to the texts and rituals is also shaped by a whole range of relationships, mediations, and moments that orient his trajectory. These directly influence how religion is internalized. A person's relationship to prejudice can never be reduced to a sum of knowledge or ignorance. In his work on the authoritarian personality, Theodor Adorno noted, for example, that among "individuals or groups who take religion seriously," three characteristics systematically amplify the tendency toward ethnocentrism: religious observance out of social conformism, in which religion is "preserv[ed] in a noncommittal ideological form" (practiced in order to belong to a group, more than to work on one's personal failings); "religious subjectivism," which values authentic faith against religious institutions and "dispenses with any binding principles" (religion is practiced as a way to start a new life and get in touch with oneself, for the sake of immediate gratification); and "the disposition to view religion as a means instead of an end," esteeming it as "a particularly well advertised commodity, rather than for its real quality" (religion is practiced more for the sake of earning public esteem than out of moral obligation).[38] In sum, the more religion becomes a social convention, the more it tends to bring authoritarian attitudes. The less internalized, systematized, and unselfish a person's religious practice, the greater the risk that the quest to become the best in the eyes of God will involve crushing the Other.

The value of reconversion and the reconversion of values

Involvement in religion serves as a practical and symbolic route to finding one's place in the world. It celebrates the power of connection and attachments, particularly for boys seeking to leave their crew and *le business*. It's also a spiritual experience that reinvests lives burdened by material difficulties with grandeur, beauty, and morality. It attains its fullest value over the course of the long, slow time of reconversion.

The myth of the continuum vs. the myth of rupture

When the French republic's "bad seeds" come to religion, it's not a return – either *of* religion or *to* the community. This communalist illusion rests on a *myth of the continuum*. In such a world, everything would be solid, permanent, persistent, and alike. But that is an essentialist fantasy of coherence – a view shared by self-proclaimed prophets of a clash of civilizations, from the Trump administration to Daesh; from French-style *laïcisme* to young Muslims stuck in the initial act of the *about-turn* and the *spectacle of rupture*. It turns Islam into a label, a *floating political imaginary*. It's hardly surprising that many leading politicians and many supposedly depoliticized young Muslims in the *cité* share this same militant vision of the world. Whether they're in permanent campaign mode or the bloom of adolescence, both are in the grip of the immediate and the short-term. This way of seeing things animates the spirit of our age, creating confusion between words and acts, claims and representations, moments and people. Thus, the myth of the continuum has become a necessary fiction: instead of time for deliberation, it substitutes instantaneity and deeply held beliefs. The utopia of a better world already exists in embryo, it is almost here already, in the inner upheaval caused by *critical re-intellectualization*, the *re-aestheticization of the world*, and the promise of a *completion of truth*.

If we make allowance for time, however, we find that history – whether large-scale or small – is never frozen. The continuity of religious practice erodes once we begin to observe it. Religion is above all, as Danièle Hervieu-Léger writes, "in motion": yesterday's "observant" have become today's "pilgrims" and "converts."[39] The pilgrim's sociability and spirituality stem from a collection of practices: voluntary, malleable, individual, mobile, temporary, and exceptional. They make it possible for individuals to "reconstruct their own development by means of a narrative" in an "effort of biographical construction" that serves to "adjust their beliefs to the data of their own experience."[40] The faith of the convert becomes a vehicle to express his protest, his freedom of conscience, his authenticity, his singularity. The evangelist's text seems as if it were written just for him. It is a revelation of the true life – that in which one might become the best – and a reconversion to real life – the life that one has chosen. Adama, Amédy, Marley, Hassan, Tarik, and Radouane were not born Muslim. As pilgrims and converts, they became Muslim. To be more precise, Islam became the conduit of a desire for spirituality, intelligence, and autonomy. It's less a matter of heritage than of bricolage or adjustments. In a different context, this desire might have taken a different form: among the young South Koreans now converting to Buddhism, for example, the obsession with self-perfection oddly resembles the "rush of beauty" so well described by Hassan.[41]

But there's a risk of oversimplification, this time falling into the individualist illusion that drives the *myth of rupture*. In a world of constant conversion, everything would be liquid, dissimilar, changing, novel, discontinuous, fluid. There would be only individuals, in search of authenticity, lost to one extent or another in the capitalist jungle. Rupture would then be little more than the grave-digging of a nihilist generation. But human as atom, emptied of all social depth, doesn't exist, any more than does the community. The magic of the spectacle can persuade us of their respective existence, but not of what goes on behind the scenes – there we find a gradual effort to soften the rupture, to adapt to what exists already, to seek out continuities. As Loïc Le Pape points out,

> The discourse of converts thus stands in tension between two poles: that of acknowledging change, which is necessary to express the depth of their feelings, particularly vis-à-vis the host institution and their coreligionists. The second pole is that of continuity, which is

> expressed notably in relationships with family, acquaintances, friends' groups, etc., and which aims to present the convert's personality in terms of a continuity of choices and constancy in relationships with others.[42]

These two poles take shape in often conflicting narratives, alternately espousing "free choice" and fidelity to loyalties both past and present – and thus to the individuals, groups, and institutions that embody them.

The politics of the reconverted

Reconversion explores this extended retrospective examination of one's past, which everyone undertakes. It confronts the test of time, seeks to regain continuity by building on rupture. Pilgrims and converts are obliged to become "*reconverts*." Reconversion builds on, while reordering, the past, forging a link between the change of direction and the social meshwork of personal histories. It sketches the outlines of a concrete answer to an existential question: what does it mean to hold on?

Going the distance means learning to assert oneself, to confront difference, to put into words what one believes. It means realizing what one is holding onto, how one is holding on, and why one is doing so.[43] *Perpetuating the act of officialization* makes it possible to regain one's self-esteem, and sometimes the esteem of others. For going the distance also means achieving greater coherence, achieving the experiencing of a more systematic life in a world where everything seems relative and one must constantly invent oneself. The arithmetic of "good points" makes it possible to reconcile a certain idea of justice and merit with the need for reparation, through "longevity" and routine. In reconversion, we find both re-appropriation and deprivation, since not everything can be said, or even understood. Though values may benefit from being made explicit, what binds two people together does not. The opaque mystery of that bond is lodged in that most precious of objects: the Koran. It is read, lent, given, returned, in accordance with a set of little, hidden rules. The *enigma of Koranic gifts and counter-gifts* makes boys beholden to one another, outside the disenchanted realm of calculation. They create fellow-feeling, and, like a veil, they sustain that humanity and reciprocity without which life and togetherness have little meaning.

In this regard, reconversion through Islam is political. It says something about how the *cité* is organized. For the sociologist Patrick

Michel, it's no coincidence that a growing attraction to religion followed the collapse of communism in the Western democracies:

> Communism cannot be reduced to an ideology or a practice – it induced behaviors and attitudes, but also "states of belief" that underpinned those behaviors and attitudes, as well as the utopias that could fuel such states of belief; thus, all contemporary societies are left to cope not only with communism's collapse, but also with the disappearance of that super-reference to whose very existence communism was indispensable.[44]

But how to believe in a new collective utopia when democracy officiates without offering direction or guideposts? How to understand change and the path to come? Religious reconversion is a micro-response to a deficit of politics. Today, it probably less resembles the "opiate of the people" than a political language largely unconscious of itself.

It's within this knot that the tension between *critical re-intellectualization* and the *comfort of de-intellectualization* is resolved – a tension that's especially acute at a time when education has never mattered more. Between the concrete fact of a business degree and the notion of a martyr's death, it's Radouane who perhaps embodies this tension most spectacularly. It's not by chance that, as he looked me straight in the eye and reiterated the possibility of his "going off to war," our conversation veered to his "disgust for politics." For "France" also means "all these guys on the left and right who all think the same thing and don't give a shit about us." Radouane mixed up the names and parties. He railed against the "labor reform," which, for him, epitomized political injustice: "They send us cops to pass a law we don't even understand." As if the notion of earning respect through work were a hoax: a trick which, as it often does with Radouane, took the form of a slip of the tongue: the El Khomri bill was now the "el *connerie*" bill.*

Between the two extremes of a theoretical alternative sublimated by religion – uncompromising pacifism versus the scenario of the grand battle – let us now try to identify what, over the long run of reconversion, distinguishes the cement from the crack.

* The "El Khomri" law on "labor, the modernization of social dialogue, and secure careers," named after socialist Labor Minister Myriam El Khomri, was adopted on August 8, 2016, after several weeks of social contestation, by applying article 49.3 of the Constitution, resulting in the law's immediate enactment without a vote. "*Connerie*" is a rude term meaning, roughly, "bullshit" or "nonsense."

— 4 —

WAR AND PEACE

I'll tell you what freedom is to me: No fear!
Nina Simone, in Peter Rodis, *Nina: A Historical Perspective*

Turning 30: the verdict

As people's thirties approach, the social position they will occupy starts coming into focus; it gradually becomes clear that little room for maneuver remains. No longer exactly young (the 15–25 age grows more distant), they aren't exactly old, either (the over-60 group is still far away). There's a growing sense that the future is foreordained.[1] As inequality began rising in the 1980s, it became increasingly apparent that living standards were declining relative to earlier generations, eroding the typical view of a person's twenties as an age when everything still remains open, possible, thinkable. Belief in a "law of intergenerational progress" collapsed, leaving lasting scars and giving way to a period of "transitional socialization."[2]

Scars

The unspoken pact between immigrant children and their parents appeared ever more untenable, highlighting how the end of adolescence, as Donald Winnicott observed, resembles what sailors call the "doldrums" – that zone of inter-tropical convergence where hot and cold winds collide, confounding all the usual predictions of navigation.[3] Paul Nizan summed up this shift in *Aden, Arabie* when he wrote: "I was 20. I will let no one say it is the best time of life. Everything threatens a young man with ruin: love, ideas, the loss of his family, his entrance into the world of adults. It is hard to learn one's part in the world."[4]

Three scars matter most: entering the labor market, forming a couple, and moving into one's own home. The first years of employment resemble a kind of reckoning. School lies in the past. The wage sets the limits on daily life. To some degree, the future is already foretold by economic insecurity and the opportunities available. Extended couplehood reassures boys about their masculinity. It also bespeaks something more intimate about the project of building a domestic "comfort zone," confirming the possibility of embarking on a lifetime partnership – of transmitting something, rather than nothing, to the future, where children provide an additional source of hope. Moving into one's own home anchors the desire for autonomy within the boundaries of a concrete place, the first tangible marker of separation from parents, brothers, and, for those who leave, the neighborhood. At a time when housing prices are rising faster than wages, those who become homeowners and build bricks-and-mortar wealth stand out as unusual. These scars – work, family, home – combine to accelerate existing trajectories. As a result, individuals may hold one of two conflicting understandings of their life-course, in a "coherent series of steps" that connects their past and future:[5] the *meaningful path* and the *circular dead-end*.

Achieving a meaningful path means experiencing a sense of dignity by forging a coherent narrative of one's personal history, via a rehabilitation of the past, a confirmation of the present, and an anticipation of the future. Recognition of personal "successes" and acceptance of personal "failures" are fitted together in an acceptable compromise. Individuals reconstruct their personal biography, ordering and relating the parts to the whole. Doing so makes it possible to envision a better life by balancing increments of change and continuity to build an acceptable memory of the past – creating a sense that, like it or not, they are tracing a path through the world. Conversely, the circular dead-end results when a person is unable to embed his or her trajectory within a meaningful sense of time. It produces an imprisonment in the present moment. The eternal present makes it impossible to achieve a decentering of the self: there is no room either to reevaluate past situations or to project oneself into a foreseeable future. The paradox of *le business* renders the distinction between life's "successes" and "failures" indeterminate. The meaning of important life events continually changes from positive to negative and back again. They no longer function easily as symbolic landmarks. Acts of criminal violence are "successes" within the private morality of crewmates but "failures" outside this underground world. The same is true for academic, emotional, or professional "failures," which crewmembers turn into "successes" through disparagement. To minimize dissonance, crewmembers reassure themselves by persisting in behaviors condemned by an "outside" whose contours become increasingly blurred.[6] These "others" become ever more numerous as the walls around their small world thicken. Awareness of a hostile outside helps keep the second zone in existence. This dead-end takes the form of a circle from which there is no escape, whereas the meaningful path resembles a line that one would draw.

These are two ideal-typical representations of human time: each individual case involves a particular configuration tending toward one of these two poles in varying proportions.

Toward the meaningful path

As they entered their thirties, Adama, Tarik, and Hassan built their life projects on the basis of a solid meaningful path. When Adama got out of prison, his return to school helped him achieve a respectable distance from his most painful moments, underscored by a spectacular weight loss. In becoming a "lion," the "cat" grew thinner. He was covered by a decent package of social benefits and had freedom at work, which made up for the almost nonexistent opportunities to advance in his career. Fayawé enjoyed better prospects – a typical gender pattern. The couple embodies the meritocratic story that makes the *banlieue* more a flow of personal trajectories than a stock of problems. With white-collar positions in social work and the private sector, they represent upwardly mobile "little-middles."[7] Relative to their parents, they embody a degree of social success, one that's already being transferred to their two young children. Adama's turnaround can't be entirely put down to some republican fairytale – far from it. If he managed to hold up while in prison, it was as much thanks to his big brothers' status within *le business* as to Monique and Foued. Afterward, he was able to capitalize on his criminal past. He owes his status as a homeowner to the deferred repayment of a symbolic debt: Ceylan, a friend his age, became a real-estate agent after finishing school. They reconnected after having lost touch. Adama had once protected her brother Ozil's business from a rival crew's constant extortion. Ceylan presented him with a "golden opportunity": a canceled sale that needed a quick buyer, below the market price. Adama thought he'd "never be able to buy a house." He had enough money to make the down payment and the couple's situation allowed them to get a mortgage. His is the story of a statistically improbable rise to homeownership. The moral of the story is that Adama achieved the ideal that Western society has promoted since the 1970s – "homeownership for all!" – outside of market channels.

For Tarik, too, his exit from crime was centered on the couple. Marie made him promise to "cut out the nonsense." Between them, a kind of equilibrium settled in between what each gave to the other. Marie cared for Tarik and his disability; he, in turn, taught her Arabic and the basics of a religion that had intrigued her since her older sister converted to Islam. A close-knit relationship developed. From time to time, one of them will take me aside and ask me to arbitrate one of the little disputes they like to act out. Marie's job stability has given Tarik time to make a new start. While he doesn't own his apartment, he rents in a subsidized housing unit, renovated for the disabled. It is strikingly comfortable: newly repainted, equipped with gleaming furniture and the latest-model flatscreen TV. Despite his accounting degree, Tarik's disability has held him back in his job search. He's now thinking of starting a business. Like Adama, he has managed to save. He's currently looking to "buy a little place."

Both Adama and Tarik still deal with "loose ends," a recurring phrase hinting at the fact that one never gets out of *le business* as task-profession unscathed. Plowing the profits of crime into bricks and mortar makes it possible to turn a page, to tell oneself that from "dirty" deeds, "good" things can come. For those who try to leave the second zone, this is where Islam can soothe guilty feelings. Seeking entry/refuge in religion thus offers less a sense of identity than a way for someone who "got his hands dirty" to refashion himself into a moral being. Hassan seems to have opted for the demands of an intellectual and aesthetic immersion in Islam and an overinvestment in work rather than fulfillment through couplehood. Proud of his office, his projects, and his tax returns, he starts work early in the morning and finishes late in the evening. His nights are short. He looks to the future, which will likely involve him buying his business premises.

In the circular dead-end

In contrast, for Amédy and Marley, turning 30 looked more like the ending to a story. Up until his final incarceration in Villepinte, from 2010 to 2014, for involvement in terrorism, Amédy was clearly in a logic of escalation. He accumulated prison stays. His list of contacts expanded. His sense of injustice grew ever sharper – as confirmed by everyone who shared a cell with him. Between each round-trip, he piled up "hits." Rumors fly, but the evidence leaves little doubt. The more time went by, the more he persisted in what he knew – better and better – how to do: holdups, stolen goods, transporting illicit cargo, dealing out retribution. He made the most of a deeply rooted orientation, taking things a few steps further with each new job. The monetary ends justified the harshness of the means. In the second zone, not much difference remains between inside and outside. Amédy was involved in several score-settling missions in a little wood where rival crews sometimes clashed, and where police were not unknown. (Several boys are said to have been roughed up there and sent back to the neighborhood without clothes.) A number of times while in prison, he was tasked from the outside with reminding certain inmates of the debts they owed. Amédy appears to have issued as many orders as he received. For a long time, I thought he was in the top tier of the town's criminals. This erroneous notion was more a reflection of the tempo of my research as it progressed: the first boys I met had tended to work under him. I later got to know more dominant crewmembers who described someone less sure of his strength, but always appreciated. Maybe it was Eric de Sardan, his lawyer, who – having observed Amédy's criminal career over time and compared it to those of his other clients – gave the best account of his imprisonment within the second zone.

> Amédy had a great potential for violence. But nothing you could see on a day-to-day basis. There was an obvious sense of general violence, because when you yourself are capable of putting yourself in great danger, why not do the same to others? Imagine a holdup on motorbike, like the one he did. It's the most dangerous thing you could possibly do! He risked getting caught in a chase, of falling off at any moment! It was an adventure, a kind of escape forward. He hits a bank with his mate, then they go off and do more holdups. Punches are thrown. They get chased. Yet at the same time, there's a kind of resignation. When you visited him, he wasn't the sort who was begging or has you call his family 20 times. Legal proceedings are slow. Months go by when nothing happens. And he keeps to himself. You think, he must be having fun with his mates, he must be fine with being in prison. You almost get that impression from how he never complained. He never made demands, he never whined. There was nothing rebellious about him at all. With his lawyers he was always pleasant and smiling. He was into this sort of life of adventure, like an outlaw. By the end, he had totally broken with the kind of life his parents had wanted for him. For him, death was always present, maybe because of Ali [his friend who

> was shot down while Amédy was with him in 2000].... Maybe it was a part of his personality.... Maybe it was some boiling hatred that no one noticed.... Obviously a rejection of the system and the institutions. Maybe a fascination with a personality, since I always saw him more as a follower than a leader.... In the end, that gives a pretty consistent picture, no?

Marley, in blunter fashion, was expressing this same back-and-forth between "resignation" and "escape forward" when he foresaw his own death. One afternoon, as he led me to a no-man's-land to look for spent cartridges where he'd been doing target practice with a shotgun, I had an insight into what lay behind such words. Objectively, there weren't many exits. He had no diploma and no experience in legal employment – aside from his fraudulent management of a bankrupt company. That case was still pending. Marley had ignored the collection notices threatening legal action. He'd settled his dispute with the company officer in a *mano a mano* that ended with the restitution of his mother's pillaged savings. The damages were paid, but not the interest. More recently, a glimmer of hope had appeared. Marley invested the recovered savings in a black Mercedes; another boy joined him and bought a second vehicle. Manda became their employee. Could the *banlieue* dropout find salvation in an Uberized capitalism 2.0? They were now latter-day chauffeurs: employers and workers in a business where they imposed their own pace of work. They drove 10 hours per day, taking turns with the same vehicle. To the chagrin of the indebted taxi drivers, who could be their friends' parents, they crisscrossed Paris and its suburbs, ferrying hurried businessmen, families back from vacation, college students brimming with plans for the future. Manda was skeptical of the long-term prospects. But the rent was paid, the refrigerators were full, their time was occupied. The comeback didn't last long. Marley was convicted in the bankruptcy case. His disregard of the letters hurt his case. With a previous probation now violated, he got two years. This "four-seasons" sentence – his first – almost doomed our relationship. Marley broke it off by getting a message to me, a mixture of humility and bravado:

> It's not worth coming to see me anymore, I don't think you know where I am, there's nothing new to say, we've gone over it all, I'm living through the end of my story now, so we won't be seeing each other anytime soon.

When I found out about the situation – Manda and his lawyer informed me of what was going on – it seemed to disturb him. The word "prison" was never used in any of our subsequent exchanges: the mere fact that he knew that I knew was enough to change their tone. I suspect that's how I entered the increasingly narrow circle of his little world, now made up of the few people who came to visit him.

Between the meaningful path and the circular dead-end, there's a gray area. For Radouane, the "path" side involves his studies, his white-collar job, a wage higher than his parents'. The "dead-end" side includes his "phony" business school program, the bedroom he seems unable to leave, the lack of a girlfriend, his disgust with politics, his distress over friends who are "doing badly." His photos on social media alternate between the stylishness of a dynamic Paris office worker in a two-piece suit and the daredevil with tattooed biceps riding his motocross bike. His Facebook friend Momo summed up this duality in a comment on a video Radouane posted showing him sustaining a wheelie for dozens of seconds, as if defying fate: "Motocross master with a Master's degree! *Mashallah*,* bro!"

Toward a sociology of inner peace

Between the motocross master's dreams of adventure and the prudent arrangements of the Master's degree holder, we find the same anthropological enigma. How does one juggle infinite desires with a sense of limits? How does one manage to find a place for oneself? How do you determine who you are in the world?

Being safe

These small, constant efforts can never be made without some minimal level of material, emotional, moral, and social comfort. This is a necessary condition for undertaking the changes, adjustments, and perspective-taking needed to serenely assume a place in society. It means that so-called "physiological" needs and the need for security must be broadly satisfied. But it can't be reduced to a material issue. To feel safe, one must be able to envision a predictable state of the world in order to imagine a place for oneself within it, as with "Adama the cat" in prison. Time has to be arranged in line with the path to be followed. One must be at peace with one's origins

* "*Mashallah!*" often translated as "God has willed it," is regularly used by young people to rave about a job well done, or a happy event.

to eliminate the feelings of betrayal, self-denial, and subjection that accompany a universal constraint: the need to integrate a sense of what one is becoming with where one came from. Such feelings are defused by a seesaw-like mechanism that punctuates a person's trajectory through society via acts of rupture (being able to present oneself differently on different social stages) and acts of recognition (having points of connection between different spheres that seem distant from one another).[8] Achieving this kind of comfort provides coherence and consideration. It also makes it possible to let go of oneself and have the kind of confidence in the future that invisibly advances the making of a political subject.

And yet the right to such comfort has been severely undermined. First there's the disappearance of grand mobilizing narratives, which for a long time established a framework within which day-to-day experiences could be mobilized – what some call the "end of history" or the "postmodern condition."[9] Then, there are the harmful effects of the rise in inequality, the disruption of the welfare state, and the urban segregation that continually pushes a segment of young people further from the mainstream. On the margins of the city, the era has passed when (despite often miserable work) a "unique generation" of the working class still benefited from the legacy of the postwar era, the early effects of cultural democratization, and the political successes of the workers' movement.[10] Within this anxious context, managing popular fears tends to involve a substitute: public displays of law-and-order politics.[11] Finally, as class mixing has become increasingly notional, stigmatization and shame have spread. These move through a number of channels (neighborhood, skin color, social class, religion, place of birth) and are advanced through two main vehicles: "*la banlieue*" and "Islam." Though a high degree of heterogeneity exists among "*banlieue*-dwellers" or "Muslims," the obligation to confront stigma remains a common denominator. Both young university graduates and residents of the second zone; families who leave the *cités* and those condemned to remain there; Muslims who combine piety with allegiance to the Republic and those who see their faith as incompatible with French laws: all share a common ordeal of social defamation, one that's both intimate and political. In this respect, the second zone is a kind a magnifying mirror that reflects the marginalization of a population deemed redundant. It turns people into straw figures – looked at and spoken about. Yet nothing is possible, or thinkable, without a transformation in how one looks at those who are looking at oneself. From this point of view, the case of Amédy Coulibaly – the son of "model" workers and brother of nine sisters who all achieved greater social success than he did – is hardly trivial. His family tragically encapsulates this heterogeneous world where it's possible to quietly escape yet also likely that one will find oneself trapped in a dead-end. Between these two extremes, there is a struggle to gain distance from the experience of "rejection," an experience well illustrated by an episode recalled by Eric de Sardan:

de Sardan: In the courtroom, Amédy wasn't one of those people who come off super well, because he wasn't very well spoken. You have to be comfortable with language. If you already know you're not comfortable, then you quickly get aggressive. Amédy sensed that, so he would do more or less what I told him to do, but he wouldn't say much. That can easily come off as irritation, aggressiveness.

FT: His demeanor was inappropriate?

de Sardan: Someone who isn't used to guys from the *cité* would say he was aggressive, definitely. To someone a bit more familiar, it's not aggression. It's almost like a sort of irritable awkwardness. For example, when I would talk with him, I didn't get that at all.

FT: You saw a gap …

de Sardan [*interrupting*]: What I saw was that the judges rejected him.

FT: You briefed Amédy on how to act in front of the judge?

de Sardan: Yes, but in the moment he would feel like he was facing an enemy. The judge was his enemy. He wasn't a judge, he was an enemy! They all have this profound feeling of injustice. And they're right! They're treated with contempt. Last week, for example, there was a hearing with this little guy: 18, clean record, possession of 3 grams of cannabis. He got several months' hard time. Because he was very poorly spoken, he couldn't put two words together. So of course he's aggressive and out of line. He's never going to say the right thing, he's always going to do the thing he shouldn't do. But behind all that, the message is: "The problem isn't the 3 grams, it's you! You're poor, you're uneducated, I hate you!" How many people go to jail for selling hash. It's not like coke, heroin, or pickpocketing. What's hated is the poor person, the guy from the *cité*. Embezzlement causes more social damage! A guy from the *cité* is an outcast, I see it every day. There's a total rejection of that class. And it's not a question of skin color. Take a guy who's black, well dressed, well spoken, educated: he'll go over incredibly well! It's about a way of being, of acting. So they respond right back with their demeanor. Amédy's demeanor said: "I either respect you or you can go fuck yourself." Sometimes when they play that game with me, I immediately set them straight. And they say: "But I didn't insult you!" How do I get you to see that you can be even more obnoxious without insulting me? How can I get you to see that if you don't already see it?

Through eyes sharpened by encounters with otherness (he is from a bourgeois background and discovered "a whole universe," in his words, when he became a criminal attorney), de Sardan sees the power of what Pierre Bourdieu called "authorized imaginaries" – that is, shared understandings which, because they are held in common, produce effects on bodies and minds, which gradually conform to those understandings, even though they seek to oppose them.[12] The historian Gérard Noiriel, in trying to grasp the story of Rafael – better known as Chocolat, the famous clown of colonial Belle Époque France – described the same phenomenon:

> The story of Chocolat interested me above all because it has a universal dimension: in an extreme way, it raises the problem of recognition, which affects everyone. To be recognized as a human being, this nameless man had to struggle all his life to make a name for himself. But he did too much. He was stiff, his body was ramrod straight. He knew perfectly well that Parisians who saw a black man wearing tails did not take him seriously and found him ridiculous. He knew his name did not work in his favor. So his body went into resistance and spoke for him. But going too far in the opposite direction like that was unnatural, as if he was always being forced to play a character.[13]

Indeed, it's through displays of the body, through language and exchanged glances, that the struggle against everyday stigmatization unfolds. Undoing Rafael's over-correction or Amédy's "go fuck yourself" requires a degree of distance from this mystique, and a certain amount of confidence in one's own respectability. These things take considerable time, and often involve putting on muscle, the chief outward sign of self-confidence. But when media curiosity is focused more on the spectacle of rupture and the exoticism of the bodies that populate the second zone, these resilient pathways remain invisible. Those who patiently cross the winding path to inner peace disappear from the social radar. And yet, as Howard Becker notes, the reverse would be the more relevant question: why is it that those strongly disposed to remain deviant, and labeled as such, don't advance to the point of action more often, only rarely cutting themselves off from the world?[14]

Safeguards

First, there are the material safeguards. Though far from forming an integrated system, they still have an effect. While the welfare state has undoubtedly retreated as the carceral state has advanced, seeds that are sown do ultimately sprout.[15] Without frequent library visits or his past as an educator, Hassan would not have the spiritual life today that he has. Without the internship that connected his business school with his current company, Radouane would never have been able to afford his training, the cost of which exceeded his father's monthly pay. Without a free and high-quality hospital system, Tarik simply wouldn't be alive. And without the decisive presence of two street educators, his training as a youth coordinator, and his employment with the local government, who can say whether Adama would have been tempted to slide down the slope taken by his best friend Amédy? Not Adama, in any case. And what of subsidized housing or public schools? The wages earned by these boys' parents, however low, were at least steady enough to spare them from becoming victims of the slumlords who thrive off the distress of illegally employed families. The proceeds of the underground economy make an obvious contribution as well. *Le business* is morally censured, but the money it generates keeps the neighborhood afloat. Despite the lopsided distribution of the profits, it helps mitigate the surrounding poverty. Without *le business*, Tarik never would have had a decent wheelchair or a handicapped driver's license. Adama never would have become a homeowner. Marley never would have been able to buy a Mercedes. When they've managed to save, boys with little education, who face discrimination on the labor market, have found exiting crime via self-employment to be a relatively safe path.

And then there are the spiritual safeguards. These create conditions for dialogue with "others," replacing awkward physical demeanors or authorized imaginaries. Learning to face up to difference involves changes and experiences which, little by little, make it possible to connect to oneself and to others. Inside the second zone, bridges to the outside world shrink to vanishing point. Personal connections embodying benevolent forms of otherness – whether social, generational, or cultural – are often nonexistent. School and the streets come to seem like places where educators are no longer guides and emulating peers is the only option. How, then, is one to shift to a new position? Within this void, religion responds to the unarticulated demand for decentering and transcendence. The perpetuation of the act of officialization, critical re-intellectualization, the re-aestheticization of the world, the completion of truth, and the marks of salvation reinforce the sense of a path coming into view. Islam offers a certain sense of history, of collectivity, of heritage, beauty, emotion, the just, the true, the ideal, and loss. It strengthens nascent convictions, forces humility. It expands what Goffman called the "territories of the self,"[16] satisfying desires for intelligence and a broadened world. The parallel with what is, theoretically, the mission of the republican school system is striking. Hassan's time in school was filled with disappointment, but when a conversation turned to the meaning of his faith, happy experiences from school – about which he had thus far been silent – suddenly came back to him. How not to realize that, too often, school remains a thwarted path to an ardent need for spirituality?

> In school, there were a few models.... There was Madame Duffetel, a handicapped teacher with a degenerative illness and the highest math degrees. She came in a wheelchair and no one wanted anything to do with her classes, even when in good health! It was horrible for her to lead a class. That courage impressed me. Everyone adored her. There was Monsieur Taneur, a graduate of the École Polytechnique. He was hated because he drank. But the guy wanted to bring out the best from you. He yelled all day, but the class was magnificent, masterful. There was a real notion of excellence, you know? These were people who liked to outdo themselves. They made you understand that if you wanted to be on their level, you'd have to get up very early! But they were exceptions. Because at an age when you're trying to find yourself, you need things that are fixed, solid. I would ask myself a lot of existential questions. Why are we here? Why is there injustice? And when your teachers are contemptuous, it's like you're facing a swamp.

Religion isn't the only vehicle for establishing "things that are fixed," things acquired by "get[ting] up very early." Involvement in sports, neighborhood groups, or local politics plays a fully comparable role. But today, religion is one of the most widespread channels.

Intimate refuge

There is a more powerful connection, however: the domestic sphere of the couple, and the refuge that the nuclear family represents.[17] Surrounding these is something often given a generic name – love; but that term is less than fully satisfying, either because it idealizes the couple or because it obscures what is actually emancipatory about it. Luc Boltanski shows the word conceals three different ways of relating to the other. "*Eros*" concerns individual desire: the other becomes a possession and a vector for transcendence. With "*phila*," interactions are experienced in the mode of reciprocity, the same logic of gift/counter-gift followed in the circulation of Korans, for example. Finally, "*agape*" corresponds to an attachment that doesn't call for reciprocity:

> The gift of agape has nothing to do with counter-gifts. For a person in a state of *agape*, what is received cannot be related to what he or she has given at an earlier moment. [...] In short, agape does not come equipped with temporal space for calculation, and this is why it is often said to be without limits. This inaptitude for calculation, which, combined with a weak ability to look ahead, inhibits the expectation of any return, also suppresses debt. Persons in the state of agape neither hold onto things nor expect things.[18]

With *agape*, conflicts of loyalty and recognition of debts become irrelevant. The enigma of the gift remains complete. The relationship to religion unquestionably approaches *agape* as the obsession with the *hassanate* fades.

Thus, it is not by chance that Islam tends to become the cement that binds the closest couples: amid romance and piety, there is often an encounter between intimacy, altruism, and transcendence that the sacred text both sets to music and puts into words. Recentering on Islam and the couple makes it possible to continue inhabiting a private morality in harmony with the norms and recognition of debts instilled "by the neighborhood," and religion imbues those norms with the colors of authenticity. For the boys, this recentering brings the comfort of a shared life of solidarity, however mythified. It celebrates loyalty to loved ones and former crewmates, but without the obligation to continue "getting dirty hands." It thus makes it possible to maintain one's allegiance to the neighborhood while turning one's back on *le business*, and, in some cases, on the laws of the "outside" world, which continue to be viewed through the prism of persecution. With or without Islam, refuge is, in any case, what couplehood can offer, becoming a space of assurance, embedded in a meaningful path in which children become the receptacle of hopes.[19] Adama describes this as follows:

> What I love is taking care of them in the mornings, bathing them, dressing them, putting them in the car, taking them to school. For now, I arrange things around them. They can do anything, because they're all about discovery. They don't know, they're learning – what's good, what's not good. I let them do stuff, I try to parent more in a way that captivates them, it's better than getting angry.... Sometimes I get upset with them but it lasts 25 seconds. I'm their father! I'm their mentor! I'm the one who's going to explain things! I'm the one who's going to show them what's right, along with my wife!

From holdup man to mentor; from "little cat" to "shower of what's right": socialization and time have done their work. Our encounter – the ex-holdup man and the former teacher; the educator and the sociologist – probably arose from a coincidence of timing, between Adama's self-fashioning in the world and my desire to understand. For others, Islam nestles at the heart of an existential fear, to the point of leaving no room for anything else, of replacing – as with Adama's friend Amédy – the imaginary of peace with that of war. With something like a final fantasy: "I fight therefore I am."

Kif-kif

What we now call "radicalization" involves the encounter between people's understanding of their trajectory – the circular dead-end – and their entry into Islam, marked by a fascination with the about-turn and the spectacle of rupture. When the past seems too "dirty" and the only imaginable future is a repetition of the present but worse, the present becomes intolerable. Critical re-intellectualization, a re-aestheticization of the world, and the fulfillment of truth seem like promises too beautiful to put at risk from the kinds of changes that come with time. The "radicalized" person refuses to anchor Islam in his own past. He tries to stay within the effervescence of conversion, avoiding the sociological ordeal of reconversion.

Effervescence

The issue is one of reconciling two opposing representations of the world – the fantasy of continuity (I am defending the Muslim community to which I have always belonged) and the fantasy of rupture (I am no longer what I used to be and will become the best – in opposition to my past and to the unbelievers) within a floating political imaginary. These two poles fuel the constant suspicion which, with *takfir*,* singles out "fake Muslims" and combines condemnation with demonstrations of purity. The contradiction is resolved by the manly figure of the religious fighter, the ultimate incarnation of the comfort of de-intellectualization: living to make war and making war to live,

* *Takfir* refers to the practice of excommunication, where those who refuse to believe, renounce their faith, or espouse a faith deemed illegitimate are punished and demeaned by "*takfiris*" – a term now used generically to refer to anyone who advocates an exclusionary religion of combat.

in the fullest realization of the class free-for-all. Now one fights for what one believes in: the completed truth of Allah. The soldier fights, alone, for those close to him and for "himself."

I have tried to show, using ethnography, how these mechanisms are deployed and sustained by our collective history. Clinical psychiatry, for its part, observes the structures of personality that attend them: a hunger for the ideal, narcissistic seduction, identitarian justice, purification, repentance, omnipotence, regeneration, the erasure of the border between life and death. In confusing speeches, sermons, performances, practices, and societal problems, however, we tend to flatten out these processes. From Salafism to jihadism, it's all *kif-kif*:* rigoristic lifestyles, performative practices, verbal support for acts of terrorism, departures for Syria, attacks on national soil.

The notion of a "radicalization of Islam" illustrates this tendency to theorize Islam out of context. Let's return to the first principle of scholarship: making clear how and from where one is speaking. The "radicalization of Islam" describes the ideological hardening of a corpus of global texts. It is the result of painstaking and necessary textual work. That work is done in an office, with an Internet connection and an Arabic dictionary. Gilles Kepel points to a historic break in the year 2005. As YouTube was coming into existence, the Syrian Abu Musab al-Suri published his "*Call for Worldwide Islamic Resistance*" (a text of some 1,600 pages, available in English, but with only two excerpts translated into French) calling for a new decentralized terrorism. Its connection with the *banlieue*, however, hinges on an analogy: the "2005 riots" are described as a Muslim revolt,[20] triggered by rumors of a teargas grenade launched into the Clichy-sous-Bois mosque. While the rumors were no doubt adding oil to the fire, the conflagration started – first and foremost – with the deaths of Zyed Benna and Bouna Traoré. No one who witnessed those repeated confrontations between young people and police could help but observe the jumble of hatred, death, and law enforcement that structures political socialization within the second zone, where the sense of collective existence is truly experienced through combat. References to Islam are rare but revealing – for example, the acronym BAK (Brigade anti-*kafir*†), a play on BAC (Brigade anti-criminalité, i.e. riot police). These religious invocations must be understood for

* A French word imported from Arabic, meaning "same-same," or, roughly, "six of one and half a dozen of the other."

† A *kafir* is an unbeliever or heathen singled out by a *takfiri*.

what they are: a scream. During the confrontations with police that followed demonstrations against the sexual assault on Théo and the death of Adama Traoré in 2017, for example, fewer than 30 boys, among the hundreds of young people who took part in the confrontation, started shouting "*Allah Akbar!*" in Bobigny, amid volleys of makeshift projectiles. To take these performances and the spectacle of rupture as a pure expression of people's thinking or practices amounts to a kind of contempt for primary sources.

Amid this confusion, a text becomes a pretext, an anonymous video becomes a presence on the ground, an unguarded comment becomes an interview. Radical-jihadist Muslims now seem to exist only in press clippings. This is the death of the very concept of scholarship. Every outrageous performance is adduced as evidence for one side or the other. The concrete conditions leading to violent action become a subsidiary issue. Aggressively incanting "*Allah Akbar!*," going to Syria, mounting an attack in France: are these really the same thing? Since the attacks of November 13, 2015, that has been the prevailing view. And that is precisely what their perpetrators want. Two Belgian-Moroccans (Chakib Akrouh, 25; Abdelhamid Abaaoud, 28) and a Frenchman (Brahim Abdelslam, 31) who had come back from Syria and were originally from the Molenbeek-Saint Jean district of Brussels, who were responsible for the killings on the streets of Paris. A Frenchman (Bilal Hadfi, 20), an Iraqi (Ammar Ramadan Mansour Mohamad al Sabaawi, 25), and one person who was not officially identified but had come back from Syria, who were responsible for the attack on the Stade de France. Three Frenchmen back from Syria and Iraq (Foued Mohamed-Aggad, 23, originally from Wissembourg; Ismaël Omar Mostefaï, 29, and a resident of Chartres; Samy Amimour, 29, and from Drancy), who were responsible for the Bataclan massacre. Must we take their narcissistic ravings as gospel? Having lost a friend at the Bataclan that night, I say it in all modesty: this is an error of analysis that heedlessly validates the quotation attributed to Ayman al-Zawahiri,[21] one of Al Qaeda's main leaders, who claimed responsibility for the *Charlie Hebdo* attack: "Media jihad is half the struggle."

Differences

While emphasizing the need to situate the spectacle of rupture in its temporal context, I also believe a distinction must be made between two more radical commitments: that of the "homegrown terrorists" and that of the candidates for departure for Syria or Iraq.

Before going any further, some details about my sources concerning these departures. Although our six characters were questioned about them, the following observations are based mainly on other encounters, about which I chose to keep silent in this book. Crisscrossing the field in an attempt to understand, I came into contact with people close to families affected by this phenomenon. They can be identified. They have daily discussions with friends, neighbors, colleagues, educators, elected officials, and local activists, who are still taken aback. Some of their children died in Syria. Others came back and are in some cases free. Some were imprisoned before they could take action. Here we should take stock of the courage involved in reporting one's own child for his or her own protection. Some families "cover" for their children through the use of ambiguous language, and in one specific case, a disturbing expression of pride.

My sources are drawn from this constellation, the result of little moments of conviviality, direct testimony, and secondhand accounts. I have chosen not to divulge them, out of respect for the individuals I met and in order to be able to continue this work. Who today can claim to have exhausted this issue? I'm aware of the trust this requires from the reader; I simply hope not to disappoint. A number of studies embody my argument better than I could: the work of David Thomson,[22] who traced the trajectories of about 40 young people and their families before, during, and after their departures; the initial travel journals of Montasser Alde'Emeh,[23] who recounted the improvised arrangements for his own departure to Syria; or the ethnographic inquiry by Romain Huët.[24] Other studies are also in progress. They tend to corroborate what I have seen and heard at the neighborhood level. Let us be clear right off the bat: the major difference between departures for Syria or Iraq and attacks in France is the magnitude of the phenomenon. There are more departures, and they're more of a mix, both socially and in gender terms. There are also boys like Radouane who declare themselves open to going to Syria but are repulsed by the idea of committing an attack in France. Being a candidate for departure is a less limited phenomenon than attacks on native soil; treating them as if they were alike is a simplification.

Desires for Syria: going off to war, over there

To ask what this desire for Syria means is to ask about the power of attraction of a particular act – going off to war, over there – and about the driving force behind an aspiration: to flee and repudiate one's country in order to live somewhere else, even if it means losing one's life.

Runaways with a plan

For those seeking exile, departure to a war zone brings relief and liberation more than fear. Rather than a plan, it's more an intention to leave without any return envisioned. In this respect, it looks quite a lot like "running away from home." As Ian Hacking has shown, the emergence of that phenomenon – in France, in the late nineteenth century – represented a new synthesis between happy escape and dangerous secession.[25] On the "virtue" side, running away takes on aspects of romantic tourism and the joys of discovery. On the "vice" side, it has much in common with vagabondage, which frightens polite society. Running away allows one to escape the straitjackets of social conformism by undertaking a rash but limited action, a seductive prospect for a broad spectrum within society.[26]

We find this marriage of "vice" and "virtue" in those who leave for Syria. Between the excitement of initiates and the explanations of experts, the act of leaving involves actions that don't require any particular dispositions aside from strong desire and a little ingenuity. A valid passport and some savings – from the sale of personal items or a credit card – have long been sufficient to make the jump. After a few hours of flying and layovers on the way to Turkey, another world becomes, if not yet possible, at least accessible. The act of arranging the trip easily makes up for the lack of specific plans: getting past the authorities, planning one's itinerary, imagining a new task-profession for oneself (the soldiers of the "Caliphate" are rewarded with war booty), facing an unknown that one hopes will prove familiar. Many accounts resemble tourist guidebooks for specific communities with their own specific needs: the "French brothers" or "European sisters." Jihadists are frequently grouped by nationality or mother tongue. On the ground, casual discussions between battles help French arrivals get up to speed and make connections. Militarily, this seems to represent both an asset (communication is simpler) and a problem (delayed acquisition of Arabic, cultural misunderstandings). The picture this gives is not un-reminiscent of Radouane's experience in Mecca.

At the same time, it's running away *with* a plan: a desire for a radical break, an awareness of danger, an urge to fight, to help establish a more just society. When the trip begins, many kinds of excitements combine: the adventure of tourism, utopian politics, emancipation from family, and the call of the battlefield. Hayat,

Amédy's wife, spoke fervently about this when she arrived in Syria after her husband had taken her to Madrid, a few days before the Hyper Cacher killings. She had taken a plane to Turkey with the help of a dozen or so people making the same trip. In a telephone conversation intercepted by French intelligence, she offered her first impressions of the journey:

> Oh, the people I'm with.... They're treasures! I don't know how to explain it to you.... You really get the sense here that people aren't humiliated. Muslims here aren't humiliated. They live with their honor. They live with our religion. ... There's war, I won't deny it. ... No, where I am ... no, there's no war.... Where I am, it's secure.... Actually, the landscape is a bit like Algeria. There are no shopping centers or any of that.... The houses here are nothing like the houses in the *bled.** ... The houses are really, really big here.... They're a lot more advanced here than in the *bled*. For example, there's Internet at home! There's a telephone! There's water every day![27]

Hayat's exhilaration evokes a new-found feeling of hospitality and recognition. For the children of immigrants, one shouldn't forget the physical pleasure of discovering new smells, colors, an evocative heat and light, without the discomfort of quasi-affiliation with the country of their parents. Hayat didn't go to Syria the same way she would go to Algeria – on vacation or out of family obligation. She was joining a cause, in a place that was something like a "super-*bled*," but without the accusatory glances of the *blédards*.† In short, she seems to feel "a lot more advanced." In the initial months after arrival, displays of rebirth proliferated on social media, at a time when those who went to Syria were still online. Such displays project the desire for Syria with tangible flesh, exemplary embodiment. And Hayat's travel to Syria, where she seemed to drop off the radar after a few months, was used to spur on the commitment of others. One can imagine that, for a time, she must have enjoyed her status as an international female martyr. Daesh didn't fail to capitalize on it, via an interview she gave to *Dar Al-Islam*, its official online French-language publication. Throughout her comments, the same obstacles that hamper reconversion and encourage departures for Syria could be seen: the prevalence of the comfort of de-intellectualization over critical re-intellectualization. ("Of course, we do need science in general but,

* The family village in Algeria.
† Inhabitants of the *bled*, or family village.

praise be to God, Allah generally made the Koran and the Sunnah clear and easy to understand."[28])

Together: the spectacle of morality and its stronghold

One of the strengths of jihadism is that it is a "star machine," in David Thomson's phrase, with untouchable icons (Bin Laden, the "old-timer"), generational heroes (Anwar Al-Awlaki, the son of Yemeni diplomats who lived in the lap of luxury in the United States), controversial figures (Omar Omsen, a native of Nice), and "guy next door" celebrities. These different status grades combine to form a field of passions that sets agendas and defines practices for a whole audience. In the imaginary of rebellion, the contrast between the star's power of visibility and the media coverage of the faceless jihadi rioter is striking.[29]

Islamist propaganda notwithstanding, jihadists aren't pure martyrs. The glorification of their deaths in battle has more to do with the current zeitgeist than with the Prophet. Zygmunt Bauman notes that conceptions of injustice have evolved through a succession of four figures: the martyr, the hero, the victim, and the celebrity. Although the martyr acts out of loyalty to the group, he undertakes a solitary sacrifice. He seeks moral redemption: it is a selfish act. Heroes, by contrast, are servants of a higher cause. The hero is prepared to die usefully: it is an altruistic act on behalf of a community. The victim, in turn, finds suffering intolerable: he seeks compensation by singling out a guilty party. The celebrity, finally, cultivates notoriety because that is what is valued; the particular nature of his actions doesn't really matter. Celebrities are competitive without being in competition. The glory of one doesn't negate that of others. According to Bauman, "liquid modernity" scrambles these traditional distinctions, so that "the most despairing and desperate among the besieged [...] are execrably distorted mutants [of these categories]."[30] The jihadist fighter seems to fit this description: a combination of the selfish pursuit of salvation, altruistic sacrifice, restitution for collective suffering, and a desire for fame.

This "mutant" combination serves as a reminder that departures for Syria cannot be reduced to a mere generational attraction to nihilistic glorification of death. Though death in battle is an integral part of the path taken by those who go, it nevertheless remains a means, not an end in itself. Promises of rewards in the afterlife – sometimes quite materialistic, such as the "72 virgins" in paradise for boys – demonstrate this to the point of absurdity. The attitude toward death is part of the vehemence of the stated beliefs, the terminal point of the perpetuation of the act of officialization. This is how we should understand the popularity of the comment attributed to Bin Laden: "We love death as you love life." This motif is not a defense of death for its own sake. Rather, what it says is that no fears or limits will hold back the drive toward the realization of a collective project (the "Caliphate"), however vague that project may be. "Being modern" can be understood as sharing monotheistic beliefs (colonialism, anarchism, fascism, communism, liberalism, nationalism, Islamism, etc.) by solidifying ever-larger imaginary communities.[31] But when repeated experiences of injustice and the emptiness of politics discredit the vertical relationships that are supposed to give form to such beliefs, a breach is opened, into which armed jihad worms its way. As Scott Atran has shown, terrorists are above all moralists: "Global political cultures arise horizontally among peers with different histories [...]. The attraction [of jihad], to youth especially, lies in its promise of moral simplicity and of a harmonious and egalitarian community whose extent is limitless, and in its call to passion and action on humanity's behalf."[32] Going to Syria exalts a physical opportunity, a geopolitical option, and a chosen form of sociability. It represents a projection into the future, combining rebellion against absurdity, an attempt to escape forward, and a desire to be led. As Montasser Alde'Emeh notes: "Before I went to Syria, I had formed a picture of these fighters. [...] I thought that they went in order to fight. That is not the case. They leave above all to build a new life. They have emigrated."[33] Rarely unhinged or incoherent, what terrorists seek is a solution to the human equation of cooperation and trust. Radouane passionately expressed this view, six months before his departure for the *hajj*. As we hadn't seen each other in a few months, we were looking back on previous episodes. That's when he confided to me that he'd secretly thought about "leaving."

> It was a feeling of rebellion and injustice, you know? I was furious. It got worse with what France is doing in the Middle East. It's enraging! I'm not ungrateful: I was educated well thanks to my parents, I went off to school, I learned a lot of things, I have a good job – thank God. I'm not complaining. But what the government is doing outside this country is frankly disgusting and there's nothing you can do about it, you're powerless! Nowadays, if you open your mouth you go to prison. Frankly, it's sad: they say "freedom of speech" but when you're Muslim, you shut up. You look at what happens in France, in Belgium, it's tragic for the families. But look at what's going on on the other side! Open your eyes! The government we have now is a zero. I'm not for the

> Republic. Their government is rotten. Hollande is a clown. His prime minister is a buffoon. They're crap. They just piss off the whole planet.

At the heart of this desire to leave is a certain disgust for political hypocrisy. It speaks in the name of a fundamental value within Western societies, one which jihadists are often said to spurn: freedom. Radouane had no trouble brandishing the slogan of the French Republic – liberty, equality, fraternity – to justify his leaving. According to Pierre-Jean Luizard, the Syrian conflict offers nothing less than the promise of a conjunction between "a universality transcending all narrow particularisms" and "being rooted in the construction of a concrete 'utopia' on the ground."[34] And as Scott Atran notes, there is always something pornographic about an imaginary affiliation: it rests on a manipulation of passionate inclinations capable of generating a spectacle ("Open your eyes!"). This is where the spectacle of rupture becomes addictive, to the point of believing that simply coming to religion is enough to change everything from top to bottom. In departures for Syria, something resembling a fantasy – enjoying the immediate benefits of conversion without enduring the inevitable costs of reconversion – finds a seductive possibility of fulfillment.

"Raindrops" in the dead of night

The "recruiters" who try to foment departures thrive off this hope for a magical exit from the impasse. The tokens of "street cred" are well known: older boys, belonging to the second zone, equipped with minimal theological baggage, dressed in traditional garb. There aren't many of them. Indeed, an outside observer would have trouble encountering any in a *cité*. Generally reviled by parents and educators, they merely "stop by." Their technique is well practiced: strike up a one-on-one conversation during evening or Friday prayers (the most important of the week); such moments of solitude are propitious for introspection. In the dead of night, crewmembers can be bored and a bit lonely, caught up in identical contradictions. For the most vulnerable, it's always the same process: seeking protection from crewmates and from themselves by frequenting the mosque; returning home to their parents with a soothed conscience; then scorning them, turning the stigma around on them – all at a moment when critical re-intellectualization feels both welcome (rekindling the taste for learning) and troublesome (the difficulty of learning). They stop hanging around with crewmates, instead accompanying the "recruiters," who go back-and-forth between playing the materialist card (paying for their McDonald's) and playing the card of altruistic dispossession (giving food to the homeless). One evening, Tarik recounted his first tragicomic encounter with a "recruiter," which took place well before the Syrian conflict began.

Tarik: I was dealing, I felt good, I had my drink, I needed another bottle.

FT: Whiskey?

Tarik: No, vodka, always! I avoid the mosque when I'm like that. You've gotta respect the house of God. So I come across this guy.

FT: You'd seen him before?

Tarik: Yeah. He knew what I did, but we'd never talked. He said, it's Friday prayers. I said I wasn't praying because I'd been drinking. He starts giving me all this stuff that was true: like, it isn't good not to pray, thinking about God will force you to stop dealing. It was a warning. It started off gentle. He was reeling me in [*laughs*]. He was keeping me from going to buy my bottle. I let him delay my getting wasted awhile, it would give him more *hassanate*. At least we'd see each other again in heaven! Then he tells me: "You're handicapped.... Life goes by fast. Seventy years in a life, for God that's nothing, it's seven minutes." It's true – space-time is different down here than it is up there! Einstein already proved it. Then he starts going off, like: "Your life is shit, a martyrdom action would be wonderful for you."

FT: He said it like that?

Tarik: Yes, like that! And I agreed with him. For example, if France was attacked by the Chinese tomorrow, it's my country, so okay, I'll defend it. If Algeria got attacked, fine. That way I'd be dying as a martyr. But he started reaching far off, with Palestine. I told him bad things are happening everywhere, we've been sending them money for 30 years and there's still no liberation! They're even buying rockets from the Israelis, it's bad! [*laughs*]. And then he tells me "I'm basically offering you a place in heaven, right away. I can contact some people if you're ready, they'll bring you the materials and you blow yourself up. Either in Palestine or here. Because right now, you're going to end up in hell, people know what you're doing, you're a soldier of the devil ..." They were already working out how to hit France, you* see! So I come back with: "No problem.

* Of all the boys in this book, Tarik is the only one who addresses me as *vous* (and calls me "*Monsieur*") – an almost anachronistic vestige of our teacher–student relationship, which I interpret less as a mark of distance than an expression of a kind of "respect," combined with a celebration of the "good old days" that brought us together.

I'll do it. You come with me, I need someone to push me, with the wheelchair. You're going to have to carry me on your back, to help me climb the stairs." He said: "No, we need people to recruit, you'd blow me up, you'd kill me!" So here you have this real asshole who takes money to recruit people to end their lives. He was recruited in prison, he's a big talker, he didn't come out of nowhere. But I knew he didn't have the balls to do something like that. Not the balls ... the stupidity, yes!

In his eight years of dealing, Tarik had two encounters of this kind. The sources of his skepticism can be read between the lines of his account: theological knowledge; an ability to debate; his nationalism; personal experience of war, for which he harbors no fascination. Religious knowledge, critical speaking skills, and attachment to the nation were obvious obstacles. Leaving with a one-way ticket also means having to abandon one's family, something Radouane was not resigned to doing. And, as shown by the trap Tarik laid for his savior, fear of death was probably the primary obstacle. To march toward death with the intention of dealing it out to others requires particular dispositions. "Balls" or "stupidity," as Tarik says. This marks a major difference between attacks on national soil and departures for Syria. Of those who go, almost none is *already* a fighter. They fantasize about battle but seem more like slackers. And sustained encounters with the sordid reality of war then generate a new phenomenon: returns home, the fruit of disappointment. A battle-hardened fighter must be able to handle incoming fire, he must already have seen death close up – if not already dealt it out. The "Caliphate" boasts of its "lions" but mainly gets, to quote Adama, "cats."

Marley also offered a description of this scattered menagerie of "*terros*"* when I saw him recently in the prison visitors' room. I hadn't seen him since his fifth incarceration a few months earlier, in June 2017. His shoulders and "pecs" had grown, and he was still praying. He told me he was "holding up under the shock." Manda was getting clean clothes and a few extras sent to him. As for the person for whom he'd acted as a middleman, he'd "understood" he had to pay what was owed, sending Marley several hundred euros each month.

Marley: The *terros* here go down like raindrops! It's a tiny little scene, just like *le business*. They keep to themselves, in little crews. At the beginning, my whole life got taken over by this one so-called "*terro*,"

* A common abbreviation for "terrorist."

who wanted to do an attack but he didn't do anything. The guy was in the cell below me. He kept yelling "Allah whatever" to his buddy above him, for hours! Fucking attack on my eardrums, it drove me crazy. I caught up with him later. I couldn't take it anymore with his goddam screaming! Those guys haven't done anything, they haven't seen life, they've never gone on vacation, they've never worked. There's this little idiot who wanted to go: he got five years and you can tell he's devastated, poor guy. He's still here but he's not holding up. Being surrounded by nutcases isn't helping! In 10 years, things are gonna blow, that's for sure. When you're working, you don't notice this mass of sadsacks, 'cause they're all scattered, but here there's a mass of them. I'm telling you, it's Guantánamo! When they talk to each other, they find out that one of them knows somebody who knows so-and-so, but they didn't realize it before they got to prison! And then there's the ones who come back, a lot of them are determined. Those guys have nothing to lose. Nobody wants to be with them. They're silent. They've seen things that the clowns from the hood haven't. In here, they're not tempted: they don't see girls, they're not drinking alcohol, there's no sinful stuff, so they're all snug in their beliefs ...

FT: What about you, why won't you get hooked in?

Marley: They're idiots. I like life too much, even if it's shit. But really it's for my mother. If she dies, I'm sure I could do some crazy shit. What I know is that I'm just so tempted to get back into *le business*: there's a guy in my old cell who's in contact with a cartel in Africa, which means we can bring in whatever we want. When I changed buildings, I met another guy who has an in with a customs agent. So I've got two pieces of the puzzle, I just need to get back into the scene. There are guys who'll offer you 800,000-euro scores. That makes you think.... If the piece of shit who put me in jail pays me 50,000 euros when I get out, I'll go off to the country and live my life. If not, I don't know what I'll do to him, but he'll disappear from the face of the earth: I've got too much hate, I think about it every day. That's all I care about.

FT: You still think it's the neighborhood that made you like this?

Marley: It's worse than that. The neighborhood screwed me.

The second zone is a confluence. The "*terro*" crews ape those of *le business*: exclusivity, mutual acquaintance, clandestinity, determination, plans. Prison seems to activate what was already there in embryo ("they didn't realize it before they got to prison"; "there's a mass"; "they're all snug in their beliefs"). While different loyalties seem to separate the "*terros*" from the "bangers" (the buddy of "Allah whatever" versus Monique, who, incidentally, doesn't visit Marley, on his orders), they aren't the only obstacle between Marley and the "nutcases." He remains too attached to material life (the desire for money, plans with Manda, his girlfriend, *le business*, etc.) to be captured by the power of the Muslim floating political imaginary. His sociological reflexivity also seems to protect him, despite his greater pessimism ("The neighborhood screwed me"). For example, it allows him to distinguish between the candidates for departure, whom he identifies by their inexperience ("they haven't seen life, they've never gone on vacation"), and those who've fought for real. The former he sees as more ridiculous than dangerous. While he doesn't hesitate to confront the self-proclaimed "*terro*," to pay him back for "attack[ing his] eardrums," he avoids the ones who are "determined." Still, time in prison risks doing its work, he says ("[it] isn't helping"; "In 10 years, things are gonna blow").

It's this particular test of time that changes the returned, who come back with the imprint of prolonged combat experience. Their new aspirations remain jumbled and they're not all equally engaged by the authorities. The returnees are no longer the people they were when they left.[35] By the time they got to the Bataclan, Foued Mohamed-Aggad, Ismaël Omar Mostefaï, and Samy Amimour were no longer merely idealistic moralists, "cats" seeking to become "lions" or "clowns from the hood." They had survived more than two years in Syria. These were soldiers. They had learned how to plan, to execute, to go all the way. Such dispositions weren't foreign to Amédy. While few "lions" leave for Syria, Bülent, the friend of Amédy and Adama, was an exception. An established crew leader and tower of muscles, he is said to have arranged his flight toward death in advance, entrusting his savings and equipment to a neighborhood friend who would later rejoin him in Syria. He is also said to have discussed his desires with Amédy. Is there something like a "network," then? Why did Bülent leave while Amédy stayed? And what does it mean to be *at war, over here*?

"I am Amédy": at war, over here

Whatever might be said in jihadist encomiums to the grand battle, carrying out an attack in France is an act that differs significantly from leaving for Syria. So far, it has been carried out by a small number of individuals, all with identical profiles: boys from the *cité* with immigrant backgrounds, in their twenties and thirties, trapped in the second zone.[36] That includes Amédy, the first person to have claimed an attack in France in the name of Daesh. The media afterlife of a "martyr" reduces all complexity to some single theme that supposedly sums up the "why" of the crime ("Lion of the Caliphate," "anti-Semite," "enemy of the Republic," "bad Muslim," "mentally unbalanced," "un-socialized youth"). No subjectivity, or sensibility, or history. It's as if the terrorist were animated by external forces – whether demonic or sociopsychological – with no effort made to ask how these actually exerted their effects on him. This crude sociologism fails to make use of the whole toolkit of social science, which has shown that radical commitment stands at a point of confluence between a political option, a social context, *and* the "biographical availability"[37] produced by an individual's trajectory. Seen this way, Amédy's resources, dispositions, hopes, and feelings matter. I have contemplated, like a historian, the reconstruction of his "hypothetical emotions."[38] My argument is a suggestion. Though built from suspicions and hypotheses, it has to stay in contact with reality. It tries to retrace what might have happened instead of imagining or reasoning by analogy. It involves bracketing the horror of the hostage-taking and the murderer's posthumous celebrity to unearth "what that other person regarded as fulfillment, or felt as the emptiness of his or her life [...] the primordial wishes he or she long[ed] to fulfill [...] [which are] not embedded in advance of all experience."[39] My intent is not to detail the structure of his personality. Moreover, we have only one expert evaluation, carried out as part of court proceedings when Amédy was 20 years old. It pointed to a "poor capacity for introspection," a "highly deficient moral sense," "immature and sociopathic characteristics," and a "quest for omnipotence," while not concluding there was any serious pathology.[40] My suggestion aims, rather, to show how certain ways of acting, thinking, and feeling gradually established themselves, until they were able to seize on psychological rifts that resulted from an individual history. It makes more sense to speak of a pathway to terror than of some chimerical "root of terror."[41]

A local boy

Amédy was far from antisocial, though he was hardly an extrovert. He was a taciturn person who didn't flamboyantly take up space to assert his existence. This was probably because, as Tarik put it, people "knew what he did." For former occasional crewmates of his, Amédy evokes a manly triptych: professional respect, camaraderie "like crazy," a chain of loyalty. Someone who presumably never "snitched," and on whom one could count. With these boys, he was voluble and teasing. There is also a smaller group of rivals who had to settle "blood debts" with him. They, by contrast, revile the "bastard." There are fewer of them, or at least it wasn't as easy for me to find them, since their voices were less audible. They are muzzled by ongoing business dealings; and spitting on the dead would mean besmirching the neighborhood. For, in the eyes of the great majority of residents, the familiar memory of the "*bonjour/salam*" Amédy remains – pleasant, helpful, rooted in the town. Amédy was not one of those who acted as the morality police, monitoring women walking in the streets. The only sign of his coming to Islam in that respect was, around the age of 25, when he stopped greeting women with handshakes. "That stuff comes and goes and people don't give a shit," according to a female former classmate. Amédy's relationship with a local woman in her fifties, a sort of "neighborhood mom," nicely sums up his two-sided role in the *cité*: a combination of disrespect for collective rules (as when she would chase him out of basement squats at night with a broom) and unconditional solidarity (as when he would carry her groceries to her landing in the late afternoon, in a building where the elevator was always broken). One afternoon, at his workplace, I met Mickey, a boy of Amédy's generation, not involved in *le business*. A convert to Islam for the last 15 years, he makes clear – with an emotion difficult to share with anyone from outside the neighborhood, given how complicit it could sound – how much Amédy remains a local boy, despite everything:

> Amédy was my neighbor. I don't support what he did, as a Muslim, and especially as a human being. So we were really stung. When I heard his name, I didn't want to believe it! I thought: he couldn't be ours! When I saw his picture, I got shivers up to here, you know? When I saw him in the Hyper Cacher, I knew I'd never see him again, that he would come out feet first. There's a story that still sticks with me. When I was younger, I had a wedding to go to one day. Car trouble. I run into Amédy, and right away he tells me: "Here, take my car, go on!" He really was a guy who'd help you out. I didn't see him every day, but we would exercise together, at the gym. When he was young I saw the good side of him, you could say. Exercise, positive stuff. And then, as you know, he spent time in prison. We'd close our eyes to that, since if you stop talking to people who get up to no good, you won't be talking to one out of every three people! And then there was the turn he took, which floored us all. I think about his parents, all his sisters. It sucks.

If Amédy was so well known in the neighborhood, it was probably because he was suffering inside from a lack of social recognition.

He had no "oven,"* and thus no territory. His exploits as a holdup man were mainly the object of rumors. They earned the respect of a small group of boys without offering any public visibility. The surest route to recognition remained money, which always seemed to be his main impetus, as described by Youssef, a boy three years older than Amédy, employed by the local government:

> People couldn't believe he would get into something like that, 'cause there's no money in it! Or at least, not as far as we know. And even if there is, he would die for that? It's bizarre, 'cause he was really someone who thought about money 24 hours a day. That was his motivation. He wasn't doing holdups because he liked it, it was 'cause there was money to be made in it.

In fact, he never completely cut himself off from connections that might bring him a more legitimate form of recognition. While his past at school was fairly turbulent, there were fond memories of him in the youth centers and sports clubs he'd passed through. On the day of the hostage-taking, more than one youth coordinator in Grigny was in tears. He remained close to neighborhood institutions, where he would interact with the local residents who kept the wheels of organized community life turning. Five days before committing the attacks, he asked to see Foued, the social worker who had helped Adama in prison. He stopped by his office twice while Foued was out. They would never see each other again. To Foued, these two missed connections ring out as a call for help that he might have intercepted. Perhaps they were merely a farewell. Amédy's attitude toward the media is equally revealing. Boys involved in crime generally flee from the media. Amédy, in contrast, seemed to seek out a kind of spotlight or exposure. The film he made in prison in 2007 resulted in an interview with *Le Monde* in 2008 and a pixellated appearance on one of the biggest national television stations in 2009; the same year, as we have seen, he gave an interview to the *Parisien* in a white T-shirt when he met Nicolas Sarkozy at the Élysée, and was one of the young people whom the local government tended to put forward; five years earlier, he gave a lengthy interview, under a pseudonym and with his back turned, to another major national daily; he also appeared in the local press and a number of documentaries filmed in Grigny. Following the example of another killer who targeted Jews and the police, Mohamed Merah, he filmed his hostage-taking with

* See note on p. 75.

a GoPro camera.* In these interventions, he was as much seeking to put himself in the spotlight as to be a spokesman for the injustices affecting young people in his social situation. In the eyes of the biggest *bracos*, his scores were also about the limelight – crimes meant to "cause a stir," as one of his lawyers put it. It's as if he were trying to be noticed too much.

Amédy took reckless risks, for which he paid dearly.† From age 17 to his death at almost 33, he spent practically as much time in prison as outside it. When he belatedly started visiting local mosques, his increased religiosity didn't necessarily earn him any greater consideration. Among the "Malians," prayer is a social matter, re-creating the old country. Caste society reappears on the ground. Boys from the most influential families are seated in front. Amédy sat far behind the families of nobles, hunters, or wise men. This lack of recognition signaled a thwarted bond which, in a sense, can be seen in his final fall. When Bülent left for Syria, he was physically turning his back on France. In contrast, Amédy chose to die *here*, under the gunfire of the national police.

His sense that he didn't really count was certainly kept alive by his visceral hatred of the police and guilt regarding Ali's death. His escape forward into a life of crime dated back to a death that pitted the silence of the police against his own silence: with the institution protecting the killer, the criminal protecting those who fled. He kept quiet, took the hit, and left Ali's family in a desperate quest for the truth, which he accompanied with his mute presence. Even today, the boys who were involved in that affair are unable to put it into words: there is something too obscene in the obvious connection between Ali's death and Amédy's. They did seek revenge, in nights of persistent rioting, in the mid-2000s in particular, when Amédy was part of a small group of boys who shot at the police – with an intent to kill. That aim was fulfilled on January 8, 2015, in Montrouge. Amédy

* On March 11, 2012, Mohamed Merah, 23, killed a soldier, Imad Ibn-Ziaten, 31, in Toulouse. On March 15, he killed two more soldiers, Mohamed Farah Chamse-Dine, 23, and Abel Chennouf, 25, in Montauban. On March 19, he murdered a teacher, Jonathan Sandler, 31, his two children, Arié, 5, and Gabriel, 3, and a school child, Myrian Monsonego, 7, in front of Toulouse's Ozar Hatorah school. Mohamed Merah was both a denizen of the second zone and one of the departed, alternating between prisons days and overseas travel (Turkey, Syria, Egypt, Pakistan, Afghanistan).

† Judging from the video of the hostage-taking, it had much in common with the hits Amédy was accustomed to carrying out, both in terms of his sang-froid when talking to the victims, and a fatal lack of preparation (inability to load images from his camera onto his computer, forgetting to hang up the telephone receiver, ignoring the emergency exit, several weapons that jammed, etc.).

murdered Clarissa Jean-Philippe, 26, with several bullets in the back, near a Jewish school. In that attack, coordinated with the Kouachi brothers, the officer, born in Martinique, was allegedly a premeditated target: "I take the police, they take *Charlie*," he announced in the posthumous video claiming responsibility.* Foued is certain: the turn Amédy took came with Ali's death, without anyone realizing it. After all, he was a boy of few words. And what way was there to cope collectively with the death of a 19-year-old caused by a police officer's bullet?

> As soon as he went to prison, he was living in guilt. He was full of questions and no one was coming to see him. He wasn't able to talk about his friend's death with anyone! Can you imagine? His mate dies next to him, in a situation. He comes out alive. The police kind of created a situation that made Amédy feel responsible for his friend's death. How could he live with that? His only mission was to take vengeance on the police. In religion, he found a reason to live. I mean, no, it was an existential reason. A political reason.

Politics took the form of resentment: persecution. Islam became the floating political imaginary that could give substance to the "we," and a meaning to both death and guilt. In the second zone, for many boys, episodes of premature mourning are experienced far from any adults – alone and in silence. This metaphysical searching found an echo in Amédy's relationship with Djamel Beghal, as in this wiretapped conversation from 2010, shortly before the former's arrest for complicity in a terrorist act: "You know, they say when you die, you shouldn't leave any debts. Are there any circumstances when you can leave with debts?"[42] This "existential" and "political" shield wasn't a sudden bolt from the blue. Beghal merely put things into words. By age 22, Islam had already provided Amédy with a coherent framework, uniting the need for recognition, a righting of injustice, a sense of belonging to a group of hardy soldiers, and the promise of a life regulated like "a watch."

* It is likely that Amédy's initial target in Montrouge was a Jewish school, an action that would have been identical to that of Mohamed Merah. Clarissa Jean-Philippe, her colleague, and two local government workers accompanying them, whom he encountered near the school, may have been second-choice targets. It is quite possible that, under these circumstances, his hatred for the police helped push him to go through with the action. The video claiming responsibility was likely filmed between the Montrouge murder and the hostage-taking at the Hyper Cacher. Thus, his declared intention to "take the police" may have been a way of presenting this murder as a deliberate choice in order to hide his initial "failure."

> Prison doesn't treat inmates equally. I don't see why a child rapist should be treated better, given more support, listened to more than another inmate But that's what actually happens. They put more pressure on people who are in prison for their religious beliefs. It all comes from TV and all that stuff. People who don't know, they watch the TV, they get an image, they're afraid. In prison, TV is the outside. Once you've got TV, you're outside. If you don't want to lose your mind, you have to organize your time, your little life. Once you've got everything down, you're a machine, a watch.[43]

Amédy's feeling of injustice is absolute: "Muslims" are treated worse than "child rapists" (the "dirtiest" category of prisoners, often segregated to ensure their protection) – and, most importantly, "listened to more." Incarceration becomes a punishment for his "beliefs," run by an "outside" world whose ignorance ("TV" makes people "afraid") forces him to remain centered on himself ("a machine").

As he made this journey, Amédy found he had resources and dispositions that were equal to his fantasies. In the 15 years he'd spent slogging through the second zone, he had become a fighter and cultivated the required ethic and dispositions to last in this game. The latter is akin to the credo recalled by a former SS member, "We do not believe at all, in anything, except in action itself. Action for the sake of action. Nothing, only the ability to act."[44] These capacities for action – the art of secrecy, adaptation, a subordination of means to ends, tenacity, methodical rigor, risk-taking, a taste for panache, an ability to negotiate, sang-froid – only needed to be reoriented.

Radicalized continuities

From his point of view, the terrorist act that transformed "Amédy Coulibaly" into "Abou Bassir Abdallah al Ifriq" was a reversal. From a sociological point of view, it was more like a radical continuity. Amédy neither changed nor moved backward. Nor was he returning to any roots, in a community that doesn't exist. He extended and perfected the characteristics of the social being he had become. It was a theatrical dramatization of rupture, but the grotesqueness of the video claiming responsibility for the attack reveals the fragility of this performance. The effectiveness of the appeal to violent jihad resides in this mug's game: playacting renewal to avoid enduring the costs of change. Amédy became a "martyr" by capitalizing on his past and his baggage. Any deviation from established habits posed a risk. To obtain telephones, cars, the motorbike, weapons, and the necessary funds, he activated networks he could trust: the Belgian black market for the guns, and his local crew for various logistics. Despite conspiracy theories pointing to a convergence between some nebulous extremist international (one of the individuals suspected of militarizing the Slovak weapons that Amédy used was a former bodyguard for the National Front) and an Islamist network in the *banlieue*, the reality appears more prosaic. There was no grand plan, merely *le business* as usual. Of the six Grigny boys who helped out with the logistics, none had been in the loop about what Amédy was planning. They were merely doing him favors, of the sort inherent in the moral economy of debts and loyalties that connected them. You give and receive without asking questions because a betrayed secret is lethal to any operation. Those are the rules of the game: don't ask why you're giving, and don't forget what you owe. These rules are obviously subject to interpretation. In the weeks preceding the Hyper Cacher attack, Amédy forcefully intensified his demands. He left one young person for dead in the nearby woods, gave another a dressing-down when the latter, who still owed Amédy for a lost *go-fast* cargo,* wanted to back out ... He was trying to get his investment back in a hurry, and he'd concealed his agenda so well that this insistence mystified one of his close crewmates.

This ability to keep a secret deep inside – to "floor everybody," in Mickey's phrase – was key. The difficulty of doing it can doom the most determined attack plans. For it means the euphoric fighter must stifle the exhilaration of the performance, even though mass killing, in the age of ubiquitous video, is as much a spectacle designed to be shared online as an individual act.[45] This is also part of the appeal of leaving for Syria: the act of leaving itself constitutes a mute spectacle of the unveiling of one's convictions, in what is ultimately a quite Westernized aestheticization and dramatization of politics. This dilemma of officialization was what, on April 19, 2017, gave away an attack plan organized by Mahiedine Merabet (29 years old, with 12 convictions over nine years for ordinary crimes) and Clément Baur (23, one recent conviction alongside Merabet) targeting the first round of the presidential election. Evidently, it was simply too tempting to send a video claiming responsibility for the attack to a police officer they thought was a Daesh member – with a newspaper showing François Fillon, the candidate most reviled for his hypocrisy, photos of Syrian children hung up on the wall, and a pithy phrase:

* A *go-fast* involves using a vehicle to transport drugs. The most common technique is to organize a small convoy on the highway (with a "pilot," a "transporter," and, in some cases, a "follower") prepared to initiate a getaway in the event of being chased by police.

"*loi du talion* [an eye for an eye]," as well as a letter to the Roubaix police station signed by Mahiedine Merabet ("I'm giving you my ID card and my [bank] card since, because of you, I no longer need it. I'll give myself up soon, we'll talk about it [...] I have nothing to say to you, I live on love and cold water,* I meditate, leave me alone, bye").

The ordeal of secrecy is a task in its own right: *taqiya*, or the art of dissimulation. I have no way of knowing when Amédy made a firm decision to carry out an attack. He met Chérif Kouachi and Djamel Beghal in 2005. He left prison in 2009 and was arrested in May 2010 for the attempted escape of Smaïn Aït Ali Belkacem. At a minimum, it is reasonable to suppose that, from 2009, his mind was made up. This was at a time when he was working at Coca-Cola, meeting Nicolas Sarkozy, traveling in Greece or Malaysia, all while training in the Cantal countryside. When he went back to prison in 2010, those who interacted with him didn't see anything coming. The prison administration described a model prisoner; Amédy's lawyer, summoned to reason with him during the hostage-taking, was thunderstruck ("It's horrible to know that, inside, this man I had known was threatening innocent people. It was psychologically impossible for me to connect it to the person I had known, at different points in his life. It's still totally incomprehensible to me"[46]); with a catch in his throat, one of Amédy's very last cellmates recalls a "generous guy, *solidaire*, swear to God," as well as their long PlayStation sessions in the cell. However, a smaller number evoke an uncompromising and proselytizing figure, who had periodic discussions with a small group of coreligionists accustomed to meeting in the few spaces they could share – for example, the laundry room, where they worked to improve their chances of parole and cultivate a shared faith in the certainty of their election, sustaining a feeling of superiority that grew stronger from being shared only with those who were part of it.†

* A French expression indicating a state of exaltation, as when someone falls in love and consequently loses their appetite.

† This ability to change masks with the help of the religious imaginary appears clearly, for example, in the wiretaps of the previously mentioned telephone conversation of May 6, 2010, between Amédy and Djamel Beghal. While he assured the latter that "for me, religion comes first, I don't give a shit about family," in this same period all those close to him, including Hayat, described a person not much concerned with Islam, and who was able to "have a good time."

"Blowups" and "balls": ennobling the second zone

Adopting two different sets of behaviors was nothing new for Amédy. It was probably less a matter of duplicity than of ennobling, by way of *taqiya*, the already familiar dissonance of the second zone. It sanctified the guilty routine of cutting himself off from others: the number of "willful and knowing" accomplices narrowed to a handful of elect comrades and – for the first and last time – money went from being an end to a means. Dealing with a crew of "unknowing" accomplices wasn't hard. As a person close to him confided to me, "Amédy had become a real manager, he could be both gentle and brutal to make the crew work and get what everyone was supposed to produce." "Those who knew," in contrast, were partners. United by similar experiences, they had chosen and recognized one another in a common "cause."[47] This time, rather than a network or a crew, they formed what Georg Simmel called a *secret society*. It was held together by "their energetic consciousness of their life. This life substitutes for the organically more instinctive forces an incessantly regulating will; for growth from within, constructive purposefulness," so that "the separation has the force of an expression of value. There is separation from others because there is unwillingness to give oneself a character common with that of others, because there is desire to signalize one's own superiority as compared with these others."[48]

The aim of my inquiry is not to discover who actually belonged to this secret society – the police investigation will determine that – but rather to approach it by degrees. It seems to have been made up of a handful of Grigny boys who knew each other through local connections in *le business*, along with a group of boys from Seine-Saint-Denis who might conceivably have been in prior contact concerning business dealings. Within the second zone, entries and exits from prison and the logic of business expansion drive interconnections between *banlieues*. This final secret society was, quite certainly, an outgrowth of that. The handful of accomplices who supported the operation remotely, notably by editing the video, claimed affiliation with Daesh. But reading the few text-message conversations that have appeared in the press leaves little room for doubt: the syntax, vocabulary, instructions, and suggestions are the same as those that call the shots in the second zone. In Grigny, Amédy had been at the center of a bitter rivalry between two crews, which quite likely resulted in deadly acts of score-settling. Some managed to escape before things got out of hand. Others reportedly left France and continued handling drug shipments from overseas. And then there were those, like Amédy or Bülent, for whom getting out was apparently not an option.

Bülent is said to have left France in a state of profound emotional distress (his wife had left him, he found it impossible to "wash away" his sins through prayer). He went off to die in a grand battle that he could only envision in Syria. According to a returnee who spent time with him, this signaled a point of difference with Amédy, in terms of their personal analyses of the nobility of combat and the meaning of "innocence." But all three saw the second zone as a dead-end path. The secret society took on the air of a final aristocratic coterie. Its members were the only ones who knew what those around them didn't, what they would learn of only by the force of events. They may not have become the best in this world, but in death they would become the best accomplices. When boys like Bülent and Amédy were determined to go through with something, they were probably unstoppable. Not so much because they'd been transformed into fanatical ideologues, but because they had no fear of death. When radically committed, they knew how to act like automatons. Such a disposition could only be the fruit of long experience. That point was stressed by Moussa, a boy who retired from *le business* several years earlier, as he tried to explain to me "his" Amédy, whom he had seen two weeks before the attacks:

> Amédy was a cool guy. A good guy, as we say. I imagine he had moments of weakness, like most people who get hooked in. So obviously everyone thinks, that could have been one of us! And it's easier with guys who have his profile. Because he's a neighborhood guy, with his record and all that. Somebody, quote-unquote, "with balls." Somebody who just goes at it, who has no fear. He's had some real blowups. 'Cause the two-bit pseudo-jihadists, they don't have that temperament. Everybody hates them because they defile us. They defile our parents' religion. They break our balls all day, playing the bad guys, looking at you coldly, being the anti-Jew beardos. But those people will never go through with it. Amédy, he never talked like that. The guy was calm. He blew a fuse on the inside, he got caught up in it all. And he did what he had to do. Without breaking anybody's balls, except in his last video. But other than that, he didn't play the angry pseudo-Salafist in the streets, yelling kill the Jews and all that shit....

Between disbelief and masculine fatalism ("that could have been one of us"), there is a world of difference between the theater of words ("They break our balls") and war-like action ("Somebody [...] with balls"). In the second zone, silence is bad news ("The guy was calm"). In "Abou Bassir Abdallah al Ifriq"'s final GoPro recording, the long, slow work of a floating political imaginary came to fruition. It had transformed a feeling of persecution into a cause ("You kill women and children everywhere! You think that's how things are?"), convictions into enemy camps ("You're Jews? Well, then, you know why I'm here! *Allah Akbar!*"), combat into justice ("Have I killed any women? So far I haven't killed any women! So far, I'm not like you"*). It clarified and simplified the political terms of the class free-for-all, until it reached its nauseous conclusion.

On January 9, 2015, at the Hyper Cacher in the Porte de Vincennes, four men of the Jewish faith paid the price for this silence: Yohan Cohen, 20; Yoav Hattab, 21; Philippe Braham, 45; François-Michel Saada, 64.

* At that moment, Amédy was evidently unable able to think of his earlier victim, the police officer Clarissa Jean-Philippe, as a woman, illustrating the typical pattern of mental compartmentalization between vulnerable humans ("children," "woman") and persecutors ("Jews," "you," "the police," etc.).

EPILOGUE

> Yet do not let us speculate too much. Let us say that social anthropology, sociology, history – all teach us to perceive how human thought "moves on" (Meyerson). Slowly does it succeed in expressing itself, through time, through societies, their contacts and metamorphoses, along pathways that seem most perilous. Let us labour to demonstrate how we must become aware of ourselves, in order to perfect our thought and to express it better.
>
> Marcel Mauss, "A category of the human mind: the notion of person; the notion of self"

The recurrence of Islamist attacks raises the question of responsibility. I have tried here to address that question using the modest, but conscientious, means of scholarship and social science. When faced with a field of ruins, what else is there to do but struggle to understand? Protect ourselves, to be sure, in an emergency. But from whom and from what?

Today, two images of the threat predominate: the "globalized Islamist network" and the "lone wolf." I find both misleading. On the one hand, the notion of a globalized network haphazardly connecting homegrown terrorists, fundamentalists in Africa, the Middle East, or the Gulf states fuels conspiracy theories positing a secret, intricate system of terrorist financing and a politically united Islamist ideology. That there may be convergences among these viewpoints or interests, no one can doubt. That there may be financial flows among these actors is, barring evidence to the contrary, possible. For my part, however, I have found no trace of it. The notion of an "Islamist network" implies that the threat comes primarily from the outside: "close the borders" and "revoke their citizenship," runs the populist refrain. The reality is that amassing the logistical, material, financial, and human resources needed to carry out an attack in Europe requires no outside help. Confined within the second zone, being caught up in the circular dead-end and having a little "dirty" money suffice. As for the "recruiters," they don't entice with largesse: a bit of newfound attention over a shared kebab is enough to open many ears. It's true that the socialization of the departed in Syrian and Iraqi war zones, and the war booty they've amassed, make them potential threats of a different order. This marks a shift from the days when the intelligence services still thought the handful of departed were headed for certain death. At the time, such departures seemed more like a solution than a problem for France. Perhaps we need to think harder. Why do these departures happen? Why such a desire to fight? The vague image of the "lone wolf," for its part, is simplistic.[1] Whether running away or dying solo, the jihadist is never alone. His body and soul are attached to some context. A better understanding of the social creation of terror is thus a matter of collective responsibility.

From this point of view, the call to monitor "Islam" – its "community" and its places of worship – or "foreigners" (read: Muslim foreigners) entering the West is yet another empty slogan. It would also involve a dubious dilution of the intelligence forces and would be the best way, through crude stereotyping, to reinforce Islam as a floating political imaginary. The immediate danger remains concentrated in the second zone. Despite its constant growth, it contains a narrow population, now being reinforced by some of the departed. In many ways, the government already identifies it, monitors it, sends it through the prison system. It's fashionable to denounce the shortcomings of the intelligence agencies by pointing to the fact that each new terrorist was "well known" to the authorities and consistently "slipped through the net." One week before the January attacks, for example, Amédy and Hayat were stopped by police for an identity check, and the standard procedures relating to his monitoring were followed. Conversely, one might well be amazed they had such precise knowledge: given the extensive information on them in the government's archives, a single day of journalistic investigation would have been enough to reconstruct the trajectories of these new "martyrs."*

* The case of the perpetrator of the Nice massacre, which killed 84 on the Promenade des Anglais on July 14, 2017, seems to diverge somewhat from this pattern, since Mohamed Lahouaiej Bouhlel was relatively less rooted in crime – though he had been known to police since 2010 (and convicted) for threats, violence, and property damage. The fact that he was carrying fake weapons suggests a degree of distance from the world of *le business*. However, the same radical continuity is found between the way the horror was carried out and his previous work skills (he was a truck driver), and, in his engagement

And little is said of the many attacks foiled by the intelligence services, bodies which are more effective and well informed than is commonly reported. It's instructive to compare such attacks with suicide missions in war zones: almost nothing is known about those responsible for the latter. Despite their formidable numbers, they die, under the gaze of the Western powers, without much of an afterthought. While some French people today have declared war against their country, "civil war" remains a chimera. That formula – "at war" – is an abuse of language, a form of avoidance, a mere confession of weakness.

France instead has an internal problem to confront. The long history of the public housing tower blocks, combined with the Syrian hub, the uncertainties of post-Fordism, economic inequality, and the attraction to Islam as a floating political imaginary, has made the second zone explosive. Even as the 2017 presidential campaign ended under a cloud of threat – with a foiled attack in Marseille and the murder of a police officer on the Champs Élysées – France's prisons were shut down by strikes of overwhelmed prison guards, to general indifference.* Often residents of the *banlieues*, always poorly paid, they don't see how they can do their jobs anymore amid constant over-incarceration. At Villepinte, Amédy's final prison stay, the prisoner count exceeded 200 percent of capacity. When endless round-trips to and from prison, the constant presence of a police force on edge, and social disrepute blur the distinction between confinement and freedom, the second zone becomes a time bomb. What do police actions and criminal punishments signify in such conditions, if not perpetual condemnation – a social death penalty? Focused on a segment of the population whose members have no trouble recognizing one another – French by birth, immigrant by descent, and Muslim by belief – such punishments can take on the feeling of organized persecution. When combined with the absence of any higher ideal,

with religion, we find the same fascination with the spectacle of rupture, according to those who knew him. Since then, use of automobiles as battering rams has proliferated. In societies where the automobile is at the heart of daily life and the social imagination, it has clearly become an easily accessible make-shift weapon for anyone lacking the necessary contacts and dispositions to obtain weapons directly.

* On April 18, 2017, a few days before the first round of the election, Mahiedine Merabet and Clément Baur (29 and 33; they met in prison in 2015) were arrested in Marseille while preparing to commit an attack, likely the day of a Marine Le Pen campaign event. Two days later, a police officer, Xavier Jugelé (33), was killed in the name of Daesh on the Champs Élysées by Karim Cheurfi (39), who had been convicted and imprisoned several times – including for having fired on a police officer while in detention at age 23. The following week, protesting their working conditions, several hundred prison guards had blocked access to the jails at Fleury-Mérogis and Villepinte – the two prisons where Amédy had stayed.

they produce "biographical availabilities," fuel imaginaries, and foster a concomitant affinity for combat. This is brought about by *our* Western societies. Should we be shocked that eventually, for a few individuals, they lead to a desire to deal out death in spectacular fashion? Should we be shocked that they mold the necessary resources and dispositions? When action replaces introspection as a way of adjusting to violence (both perpetrated and endured); when a fascination with the about-face, the passion of conversion, and the promise of transcendence all seem likely to ennoble skills and knowledge acquired in the underground, the threat is clear. Such implosions don't happen right away, they take time; meanwhile, the seething rage is palpable. Certain journeys must not begin too soon: a nine-year-old can become a "lookout" for 20 euros a day.

In the end, there has to be a "cause." Islam, however radical, draws the political potency of its imaginary from the circumstances at hand. Though armed jihad is now exploding in France or Syria, this is an "ecological niche" that will be duly replaced in the course of history.[2] As Scott Atran notes, it conceals something more universal: "There is urgency, excitement, ecstasy, and altruistic exaltation in war, a mystic feeling of solidarity with something greater than oneself: a tribe, a nation, a movement, Humanity."[3] And the forms this "something" takes are determined by a known criterion: doing things as a group, in the name of a brotherhood beyond price.[4] This anthropological glue underscores how difficult it is for capitalist reasoning to produce transcendent meanings and solidarities for all. It also suggests that schools will never be able to do everything for us; we already probably ask too much of them. It's hardly surprising that in most Middle Eastern countries, the education of homegrown terrorists is above the average, while in France it is below. These differences testify to the same disappointed expectations toward schooling, in societies where the degree of educational democratization and the scope for economic opportunity – and thus the profile of those rejected – differ.[5] Unless backup is forthcoming, the thirst for emancipation through instruction can be only partially quenched. We can talk all we like about the "problem of the *banlieues*," the "problem of Islam," the "problem of prisons," or the "problem of education," but as long as we mistake these symptoms for causes, our view will remain shortsighted. These are merely the delayed consequences of the contradictions of the economic system. The "global problems" are those of wealth distribution, limitless exploitation, infinite accumulation, the absence of moral meaning and direction for a portion of humanity which, because of its ever more glaring functional uselessness, is shunted aside or punished.

Here, perhaps, is a more pertinent issue than any "culture talk": how long can we continue to push aside a growing number of increasingly combative individuals who have nothing to lose but their lives? How far will the dimensions of the second zone expand?

Here, we have examined its French version. It's worth comparing it to the United States. At a time when Islamophobia has overtaken the US,[6] the Islamist threat remains chiefly tied to American geopolitics. It isn't really a homegrown product.[7] The American second zone simply doesn't need Islam or Syria to resolve its contradictions through bloodshed. The history of racial segregation is not the same as that of colonization. The inner cities are not the same as the *banlieues*. There, homicides, overdoses, suicides, deadly confrontations with police, and mass incarceration have already reached proportions comparable to those of many war zones. There, the state scapegoats the poor, who kill each other to claim their piece of the capitalist pie. That is how the problem of surplus is dealt with.[8] In the US metropolis, combat unfolds through Hollywood imagery, making it almost picaresque. Lacking Islam's floating political imaginary, it's now almost invisible. Lacking any international label, there is little spectacle. Yet in both France and the US, the roots of the second zone lie in the same byproduct of the capitalist economy: the market for drugs and its consequences, for the bodies and minds of the most vulnerable.[9] This "cause" is shockingly absent from debates over the threat to *our* peace – probably because the victims of the collateral damage are separated from those who safely enjoy its benefits by a social border that licenses silence. In a sense, theorizing a radicalization of Islam amounts to an extension of that border, replacing it with catchphrases: the "Islamization of the *banlieue*" and "Muslim anti-Semitism."

The political scientists Diego Gambetta and Steffen Hertog have shown convincingly that Islamic fundamentalism attracts individuals with the same personality traits as those seduced by the ideas of the extreme right. Three traits stand out clearly: a propensity for moral disgust (with an aversion to transgressions against tradition and a desire for social and sexual purity); a need for closure (with an aversion to change and upheaval in the social order); and strong intergroup prejudice (with an aversion to difference). Ideologies are simply the political-psychological reflections of an individual's relationship to the Other, and unless we think it's all genetically determined, a crucial question can be posed: how do we ensure that society avoids making its children, as Theodor Adorno put it, "intolerant of ambiguity"?[10] Questions like these might have emerged as a result of the Islamist attacks that have recently struck Western societies, creating a possibility for open debate – instead of high-handed and imperious assertions. Yet a convergence on moralizing notions about the "Islamization of the *banlieues*" and "Muslim anti-Semitism," some of whose concrete manifestations we have already seen, too often prevents all discussion about what Islamist attacks, the Kouachi brothers, or Amédy Coulibaly represent in poor neighborhoods. A fear of "*yes, but*" has spread – and with good reason. "Intolerance of ambiguity" and a "refusal to think" do indeed exist. They constitute a problem that needs to be precisely specified and discussed. But what can be done when, day in and day out, any opportunity to open a conversation is painted as dangerous? What should be said to those young people who condemn terrorism ("*yes*") even while seeming to excuse it ("*but*" the children in Syria, Palestine, my parents, my religion, the Jews, the rich ...)? Young people who feel "a little bit Amédy" exist. In the language available to them, they are giving expression to social disrepute, symbolic violence, racism, precarious work, a lack of prospects. Should we force them to be silent? We could decide that we don't want to hear them, to replace dialogue with a counter-spectacle. Down with halal! Down with burkinis! Or we could show humility and put into practice that apocryphal quote erroneously attributed to Voltaire: "I do not agree with what you say, but I will defend to the death your right to say it." Far from the media chatter, we might then learn about ourselves, learn from others, who might learn from us as well.

Given the paranoid consequences of parochial insularity, there are two options: a critical, educative approach aiming at a decentering of the self, or a moral condemnation that verges on imprisonment. That means choosing between the slow work of education and the quick action of the spectacle. It raises the question of comfort – a necessity if the educational route is to be taken and not merely gestured at. As Daesh loses ground that it will probably never regain, the cyber-Caliphate, with its forums, its posts, and its aestheticism, will survive it.[11] Likewise, as the National Front approaches the gates of power without (yet) managing to capture it, its voters will continue to place themselves within the party's imaginary as long as what that vote expresses isn't taken into consideration.[12] For it involves just the same "intolerance of ambiguity." Not to choose is to run the risk that the about-turn and the spectacle of rupture will congeal, fulfilling the scenario of the grand battle.

When I asked Marley a stupid question in the visitors' room today ("How are you doing?"), I got a stupid answer back – in the form of a quip ("Could be worse – not a jihadist yet!"). It's as if what connects us makes the expected scenario a little absurd. Recall how he teased Saïfi, as we stood at the edge of the late-night barbecue: "See, it's the neighborhood that made him like that – except with him, he doesn't know!" To understand is already to struggle against resignation. It also means striving to think against fear – fear of our shared history, our collective mistakes, and those of our children, however imperfect they may be. That's part of "the history books."

FT: What stays with you about Amédy?
Adama: His laugh. The image of a big wisecracker.
FT: He was someone who liked to have fun?
Adama: A good wisecracker, yeah. A real man. He had the same flaws as me: blowing things out of proportion over some minor issue that should have taken five minutes to deal with. But he didn't have a lot of flaws. It's not that I'm trying not to stain his memory, Fabien, but nothing is coming to me. He was a good wisecracker. Determined. A good brawler. Someone who liked to play around. A big kid, with the values of a man. Now people are going to be saying stuff about him for years. His name is written in the history books, huh?
FT: I think he wanted to put himself there, no?
Adama: That's right, he's become part of people's history. He's part of people's daily life. Amédy is the story of a quiet guy who came into people's homes.

By breaking his way in.

* * *

One isn't born a warrior, one becomes one. Today, many inhabitants of poor neighborhoods feel, and know, that they've been marginalized. There is no ambiguity in this class free-for-all: all are aware of their subaltern position and the interests that arise from it. One thing is obvious to all: everyone must struggle against adversity to get by. Social disgrace isn't enough to make a "community." But it does generate relationships that, little by little, bring into being a world, a morality, a solidarity. These relationships – in denigrated *cités*, like anywhere else – entail debts and loyalties that must be acknowledged and strengthened, in order for people to make their way. That is how boys become sons, guys, kids, grown-ups, mates, crewmates, spouses, accomplices, old-timers, and one day, probably, fathers. This web has grown increasingly frayed since the economic shift of the 1980s, and the result has been a profound rupture of socialization. Many links to the outside world have been cut, countless internal tutelary connections have been weakened. A fear of betrayal and contempt has set in.

As many institutions faltered, Islam, in a sense, was able to salve some of these wounds. Religion replaced a void, created connections, flexibility, esteem, by celebrating a universal ethic and promising individual salvation. Entering Islam has become an act of officialization, aided by its status as a symbolic alternative with relatively deep roots. It's a route to self-assertion, self-revelation, and tenacity. It is often excessive and vindictive, spurred by the comforting high of an about-turn that says a great deal about the depth of this rupture. With time, religious conversion becomes reconversion. Islam is folded into a now-acceptable past. It forces an acceptance of certain moral failings, and it ennobles daily life. It re-moralizes, re-intellectualizes, re-aestheticizes, re-founds, re-enlarges, in constantly shifting proportions. A meaningful path becomes possible. Yet Islam doesn't necessarily become the measure of all things. It's often eclipsed in the face of far more pressing commitments. In short, it, too, finds its place.

However, controversies over its visibility continue to swell. When requests to build mosques or create Muslim areas in cemeteries are presented as signs of a provocative foreign invasion, it could be objected that wishing to pray and rest in eternity in France are probably the greatest possible marks of integration. The same is true when these "bad seeds" reconvert, an act which, as we have seen, grows out of disillusionment with the meritocratic ideal, a furious desire for intelligence, a quest for truth, and a taste for verbal sparring. Many foreign observers would call such passions typically "French." Disillusionment is always a measure of the promises once believed in – and these, because they are more than simply lies, continue to shine. To observe the periphery of the social world is, ultimately, to see what its center is made of. At the extreme end of any phenomenon stands the radical – that which founds a line of succession and presents a total, almost definitive, picture of the world. The radical does not foretell a rupture. It lays bare the foundations in which continuities and reconversions are rooted. Any situation of domination rests on an ambiguous acceptance of the established order, the tacit creation of a consensus around what is valid and what is not. Such *radicalized loyalties* are a very concrete expression of fidelities to a particular set of individuals who matter, and to what is valid. They're experienced in daily life through gifts and counter-gifts, moral debts, social obligations. Implicitly, they speak to intense feelings of loyalty toward things that elevate loved ones in the neighborhood, but also, more generally, the French nation and the Western economic system. In this respect, they have multiple referents, which intersect and are less in competition with one another than is commonly thought. A commitment to Islam is often a way of injecting a little coherence and nobility into these knots. Commitment to an exclusive and exclusionary Islam is only one possibility among others. First and foremost, it reflects a paucity of things to identify with and believe in. It represents an endpoint – an ultimate loyalty which, like any last stand, is more a caricature than anything else. Capitalism today is the orphan to a counter-narrative. As long as the communist utopia existed, the meaninglessness of materialist accumulation could be armed with a rallying cry. There was, indeed, something larger than profit in the proud struggle against what appeared as a totalitarian threat. Within this void, and in supposedly more connected Western societies, Islam can represent both a cause and a mystery for the nation's "bad seeds." This is the great power of what religion offers: a political imaginary, the enigma of the gift, a celebration of connections, an aestheticism and intellectualization of spirituality, and a newfound morality. But despite the claims of those who seize on it with noisy fanfare, its power of attraction is in no way external to capitalist reason. An imaginary can float, but human behaviors cannot: they remain anchored in the story of each person's sometimes contradictory and turbulent socialization.

On the side of peace, the reconvert fashions his own individuality through an effort of personal bricolage; perpetuating the act of officialization allows him to hang on to his "chosen" values. When tied to the intimacy of a couple, religion helps to cultivate inner reforms that make the world's injustices more acceptable. Religion creates a personal zone of comfort and tenacity. It's not a once-and-for-all revolution, but an individual accommodation with reality. Which isn't nothing.

On the side of war, the jihadist fighter resembles a byproduct of capitalist narcissism. A combination of martyr, hero, victim, and star, he takes competition, predation, a desire for power, and displays of victory, and pushes them to extremes. What shines through is an aestheticization and performatization of politics, in which ideas are replaced by showmanship. But the jihadist fighter, too, dies invoking the superiority of morality over self-interest, in a desperate form of altruistic dispossession. Here is another individual accommodation, by force of arms.

In 1843, Karl Marx wrote that religion was the "opium of the people," because it diverted humankind from what was most important: "The demand to give up illusions about the existing state of affairs is the demand to give up a state of affairs which needs illusions."[13] Today, illusions about the state of the human condition or the direction of history are no longer the problem. Capitalism stands naked. Religion is less an opiate than a pathway. It doesn't conceal. It expresses an unfulfillment, and makes its peace with capitalist reason.[14] Some celebrate this, others lament it. The fact is that, for now, it doesn't have much competition. Not until new and imaginative voices can be made audible and – perhaps – a new political imaginary emerges. One rooted in that rocky soil where human misery thrives.

NOTES

Introduction: The Call of the Ground

1 For an initial study featuring Tarik and Radouane, see Fabien Truong, *Des capuches et des hommes. Trajectoires de "jeunes de banlieue"* (Paris: Buchet-Chastel, 2013). For a second study about the academic trajectories of my former students, see Fabien Truong, *Jeunesses françaises. Bac +5 made in banlieue* (Paris: La Découverte, 2015).
2 Albert Camus, *The Myth of Sisyphus and Other Essays*, trans. Justin O'Brien (New York: Vintage, 1955), pp. 12, 54.
3 Gérôme Truc, *Shell Shocked: The Social Response to Terrorist Attacks*, trans. Andrew Brown (Cambridge: Polity, 2017), p. 225.
4 On the "problem of moral equivalence" posed by the "making of silence" after an attack, see ibid., pp. 108–15. On the "to be or not to be Charlie" debate, see Emmanuel Todd, *Who Is Charlie? Xenophobia and the New Middle Class* (Cambridge: Polity, 2015) and Nonna Mayer and Vincent Tiberj, "Who were the 'Charlie' in the streets? A socio-political approach of the January 11 rallies," *International Review of Social Psychology*, no. 29 (2016), pp. 59–68.
5 See, in order, Michael Rogin, *Les Démons de l'Amérique. Essais d'histoire politique des États-Unis* (Paris: Seuil, 1998); Michael Rogin, *Ronald Reagan, the Movie and Other Episodes in Political Demonology* (Berkeley: University of California Press, 1988); René Girard, *The Scapegoat*, trans. Yvonne Freccero (Baltimore: Johns Hopkins University Press, 1986); Stuart Hall, Brian Roberts, John Clarke, Tony Jefferson, and Chas Critcher, *Policing the Crisis: Mugging, the State, and Law and Order* (London: Macmillan, 1978); Norbert Elias and John L. Scotson, *The Established and the Outsiders: A Sociological Enquiry into Community Problems* (London: Sage Publications, 1994).
6 Mahmood Mamdani, *Good Muslim, Bad Muslim: America, the Cold War, and the Roots of Terror* (New York: Doubleday, 2004).
7 Claude Lévi-Strauss, *Race and History* (Paris: UNESCO, 1952), p. 10.
8 Edward W. Said, *Covering Islam: How the Media and the Experts Determine How We See the Rest of the World* (New York: Vintage, 1997), p. 163.

9 Arun Kundnani, *The Muslims Are Coming! Islamophobia, Extremism, and the Domestic War on Terror* (London: Verso, 2014), p. 58. On the growth of Islamophobia in Europe, see Amnesty International, *Choice and Prejudice: Discrimination Against Muslims in Europe* (2012).

10 See Naji Abu Bakr, *Gestion de la Barbarie. L'Étape par laquelle l'islam devra passer pour restaurer le califat* (Paris: Édition de Paris, 2007 [2004]) and "Qu'Allah maudisse la France," *Dar Al-Islam*, vol. 2 (February 11, 2015).

11 Jean-Paul Sartre, *Anti-Semite and Jew*, trans. George J. Becker (New York: Grove Press, 1960).

12 Moustafa Bayoumi, *How Does It Feel to Be a Problem? Being Young and Arab in America* (London: Penguin, 2009).

13 W.E.B. Du Bois, *The Souls of Black Folk* (New York: Dover Publications, 2016); Moustafa Bayoumi, "Racing religion," *The New Centennial Review*, vol. 6, no. 2 (2006), pp. 267–93.

14 See Alberto Toscano, *Fanaticism: On the Uses of an Idea* (London: Verso, 2010).

15 Peter Neumann, *Perspectives on Radicalisation and Political Violence: Papers from the First International Conference on Radicalisation and Political Violence* (London: International Centre for the Study of Radicalisation and Political Violence, 2008).

16 Annie Collovald and Brigitte Gaïti note that "if radicalization is a process, then we agree to follow it before we can explain it. That means moving from the 'why' to the 'how'" (Annie Collovald and Brigitte Gaïti [eds.], *La Démocratie aux extrêmes. Sur la radicalisation politique* [Paris: La Dispute, 2006]). This "how" has long appeared to be a clear step forward in accounting for individual involvement in violent political action, compared to explanations in terms of ideological manipulation (Mohammed Hafez and Creighton Mullins, "The radicalization puzzle: a theoretical synthesis of empirical approaches to homegrown extremism," *Studies in Conflict & Terrorism*, vol. 38, no. 11 [2015], pp. 958–75). Indeed, it is well established in the social sciences that the resort to terrorism emerges at the intersection of three dimensions: individual motivations and belief system; the nature of strategic decisions within a terrorist movement; and the sociopolitical context (Martha Crenshaw, "The causes of terrorism," *Comparative Politics*, vol. 13, no. 4 [1981], pp. 379–99). But today, the systematic assimilation of this process with Islamist terrorism has changed both the word and the thing, making it into a "buzzword" (Peter Neumann and Scott Kleinmann, "How rigorous is radicalization research?," *Democracy and Security*, vol. 9, no. 4 [2013], pp. 360–82).

17 Guy Debord, *Comments on the Society of the Spectacle*, trans. Malcolm Imrie (New York: Verso, 1998), p. 25.

18 Marc Sageman, *Leaderless Jihad: Terror Networks in the Twenty-First Century* (Philadelphia: University of Pennsylvania Press, 2008) and Marc Sageman, *Misunderstanding Terrorism* (Philadelphia: University of Pennsylvania Press, 2016).

19 Farhad Khosrokhavar, *L'Islam des jeunes* (Paris: Flammarion, 1998).

20 See Mark Sedgwick, "The concept of radicalization as a source of confusion," *Terrorism and Political Violence*, vol. 22, no. 4 (2010), pp. 479–94; David Mandell, "Radicalization: what does it mean?," in Thomas M.

Pick, Anne Speckhard, and Beatrice Jacuch (eds.), *Home-grown terrorism: Understanding and Addressing the Root Causes of Radicalisation among Groups with an Immigrant Heritage in Europe* (Amsterdam: IOS Press, 2009), pp. 101–13; Jørgen Staun, "When, how and why elites frame terrorists: a Wittgensteinian analysis of terror and radicalization," *Critical Studies on Terrorism*, vol. 3, no. 3 (2010), pp. 403–20; Jonathan Githens-Mazer, "The rhetoric and reality: radicalization and political discourse," *International Political Science Review*, vol. 33, no. 5 (2012), pp. 556–67.

21 Fathali M. Moghaddam, "The staircase to terrorism: a psychological exploration," *American Psychologist*, vol. 60, no. 2 (2005), pp. 161–9; and Ragnhild B. Lygre, Jarle Eid, Gerry Larsson, and Magnus Ranstorp, "Terrorism as a process: a critical review of Moghaddam's 'Staircase to terrorism'," *Scandinavian Journal of Psychology*, vol. 52, no. 6 (2011), pp. 609–16.

22 Hall et al., *Policing the Crisis*.

23 Scott Atran, *Statement before the Senate Armed Services Subcommittee on Emerging Threats & Capabilities*, March 10, 2010.

24 Roland Barthes, *Mythologies*, trans. Annette Lavers (New York: Hill & Wang, 2012), p. 255. For an assessment of ten years of "de-radicalization" policies in the United States and the United Kingdom, see "The myth of radicalization," in Kundnani, *The Muslims Are Coming!*, pp. 115–52.

25 My argument is not intended to pit the failings of psychology against the virtues of sociology, but rather to stress the blind spots involved in the underlying psychologization of the radicalization concept when it makes "psychological fragility" into an explanation per se for the attraction to jihadism, without, for example, specifying which psychological traits are actually correlated with which ideological values (see John T. Jost, Jack Glaser, Arie W. Kruglanski, and Frank J. Sulloway, "Political conservatism as motivated social cognition," *Psychological Bulletin*, vol. 129, no. 3 [2003], pp. 339–75). Since September 11, radicalization has lent an ad hoc quasi-psychological substance to a concept deployed in contexts as different as domestic security, social integration, and foreign policy (Sedgwick, "The concept of radicalization as a source of confusion"), conflating prevention, remedial action, and an overall understanding of the terrain on which individual trajectories converge. Psychological or psychoanalytic analysis becomes more relevant when it is applied to a narrowly defined object, such as the *ex-ante* analysis of the psycho-pathological forces that advance propaganda discourses and their interaction with individual fears, desires, or projections (see Fethi Benslama, *Un furieux désir de sacrifice. Le surmusulman* [Paris: Seuil, 2016]), or *ex-post* case studies based on observation of the long-run motivations and themes involved in decisions to take action – a rare situation, since terrorists do not tend to reveal their intentions or survive once an attack has been committed. See Ariel Merari, Ilan Diamant, Arie Bibi, Yoav Broshi, and Giora Zakin, "Personality characteristics of 'self martyrs'/'suicide bombers' and organizers of suicide attacks," *Terrorism and Political Violence*, vol. 22, no. 1 (2009), pp. 87–101.

26 Talal Asad, *The Idea of an Anthropology of Islam* (Occasional Papers Series, Washington, DC: Center for Contemporary Arab Studies, 1986).

27 See Gilles Kepel, *Terror in France: The Rise of Jihad in the West* (Princeton: Princeton University Press, 2017) and Olivier Roy, *Jihad and Death: The*

Global Appeal of Islamic State, trans. Cynthia Schoch (London: C. Hurst & Co, 2017).

28 Figures from the latest TeO study (*Enquêtes Trajectoire et Origine*) published in 2016 and carried out by INSEE (Institut national de la statistique et des études économiques) and INED (Institut national d'études démographiques). Estimates fluctuate between 3 percent and 8 percent of the French population – a range of 2.1 to 5 million individuals – according to the sources. The lower estimates represent individuals claiming Muslim religious belief (TeO), the upper estimates represent individuals of so-called "Muslim culture" (tabulation by the Interior Ministry). For an exploration of the diversity in the daily lives of "ordinary Muslims," see Nilüfer Göle, *The Daily Lives of Muslims: Islam and Public Confrontation in Contemporary Europe* (London: Zed Books, 2017).

29 See Jodie T. Allen, "The French–Muslim connection: is France doing a better job of integration than its critics?" (Pew Research Center, 2006); Ifop, "Analyse: 1989–2009. Enquête sur l'implantation et l'évolution de l'islam en France" (2010) (in which 78 percent of Muslims say they attach "a lot or a fair amount of importance to religion," versus 24 percent of Catholics); Vincent Tiberj and Patrick Simon, "Sécularisation ou regain religieux: la religiosité des immigrés et de leurs descendants," *Document de travail*, no. 196 (2013) (in which religious homophily reaches a score of 68 percent for residents of the "*zones urbaines sensibles*"); Institut Montaigne, "Un islam français est possible" (2016).

30 See Bernard Godard, *La Question musulmane en France. Un état des lieux sans concessions* (Paris: Fayard, 2015); Samir Amghar, *Le Salafisme aujourd'hui* (Paris: Michalon, 2011). Sylvain Brouard and Vincent Tiberj estimate the share of French of Maghrebin, African, and Turkish origin who reject the French identity in favor of a community or religious identity at 5 percent (Sylvain Brouard and Vincent Tiberj, *As French As Everyone Else? A Survey of French Citizens of Maghrebin, African, and Turkish Origin* [Philadelphia: Temple University Press, 2011]). According to the Institut Montaigne, 28 percent of Muslims have "adopted a system of values clearly opposed to the values of the Republic" (Institut Montaigne, "Un islam français est possible," p. 22).

31 Figures from the Interior Ministry and a report from the International Center for the Study of Radicalization and Political Violence, *Foreign Fighter Total in Syria/Iraq Now Exceeds 20,000* (2015).

32 The "psychological fragility" thesis is seldom sustained. See Clark McCauley, "Understanding the 9/11 perpetrators: crazy, lost in hate or martyred?," in Nancy Matuszak (ed.), *History behind the Headlines*, Vol. 5 (New York: Gale, 2002); Edwin Bakker, *Jihadi Terrorists in Europe, Their Characteristics and the Circumstances in which They Joined the Jihad: An Exploratory Study* (The Hague: Clingendael Institute, 2006); Mohammed Hafez, *Suicide Bombers in Iraq: The Strategy and Ideology of Martyrdom* (Washington, DC: United States Institute of Peace, 2007). See also the works by Scott Atran and Marc Sageman cited above.

33 Karl Marx, "On the Jewish question," in Karl Marx and Frederick Engels, *Collected Works*, Vol. 3 (London: Lawrence & Wishart, 1975).

34 Germaine Tillion, *Fragments de vie* (Paris: Points, 2013).

35 This joint study will be presented in a subsequent work.

36 Michael Burawoy, "Revisits: an outline of a theory of reflexive ethnography," *American Sociological Review*, vol. 68, no. 5 (2003), pp. 645–79.
37 Les Back, *The Art of Listening* (Oxford: Berg Publishers, 2007).
38 For a relational approach to the social world, see Pierre Bourdieu, *Practical Reason: On the Theory of Action*, trans. Randall Johnson (Cambridge: Polity Press, 2008).
39 This study looks only at the "bad *guys*." In part this is because since the 2005 riots, they have become "the problem," with the girls thereby remaining "absent." Since the 2015 terrorist attacks, they have continued to be seen as the leading problem, though it is now acknowledged that they can be supported by "submissive girls," a figure that has gradually appeared in public debate since the 2004 headscarf affair (John R. Bowen, *Why the French Don't Like Headscarves: Islam, the State, and Public Space* [Princeton: Princeton University Press, 2008]). The gradual expansion of the terrain of struggle (the urban question was masculine, the religious question will be cultural) and the gendered distribution of the threat associate the clash of civilizations theme with the ordinary patterns of masculine domination which continue to structure Western society. Such a reading minimizes the quite real existence of female violence. It ignores, for example, that in certain contexts (such as Chechnya or the PKK's armed struggle) females make up the majority of terrorists. In the French case, while the "homegrown terrorists" are exclusively young males, those who depart for Syria are, according to estimates, one third female – a significant difference that cannot be ignored (see Carolyn Hoyle, Alexandra Bradford, and Ross Fenett, *Becoming Mulan? Female Western Migrant to ISIS* (London: Institute for Strategic Dialogue, 2015); *European Union Terrorism Situation and Trend* (Report, Europol, July 2016). Finally, the practical logic of ethnographic inquiry induces its own gender biases. I am a man and it is easier for me to achieve a more than nominal degree of proximity with males. Nevertheless, I carried out numerous interviews with women. See for instance, Gerôme Truc and Fabien Truong, "Cinq femmes fortes. Faire face à 'l'insecurité' dans une 'cité de la peur'," *Mouvement*, no. 92 (2017), pp. 94–103.
40 Jean-Claude Passeron, "Biographies, flux, itinéraires, trajectoires," *Revue française de sociologie*, vol. 31, no. 1 (1990), pp. 3–22 (p. 6).
41 Gaston Bachelard, cited in Pierre Bourdieu, Jean-Claude Passeron, and J.-C. Chamboredon, *The Craft of Sociology: Epistemological Preliminaries* (New York: Walter de Gruyter, 1991), p. 11.

Chapter 1 Common Histories

1 Henri Mendras, *La Seconde Révolution française: 1965–1984* (Paris: Gallimard, 1988) and Henri Mendras, *Social Change in the Fifth Republic: Towards a Cultural Anthropology of Modern France*, trans. Alastair Cole (Cambridge: Cambridge University Press, 1991).
2 Abdelmalek Sayad, *L'Immigration ou les paradoxes de l'altérité. La fabrication des identités culturelles* (Paris: Raisons d'Agir, 2014).
3 Olivier Masclet, *La Gauche et les cités. Enquête sur un rendez-vous manqué* (Paris: La Dispute, 2003); Stéphane Beaud and Olivier Masclet, "Des 'marcheurs' de 1983 aux 'émeutiers' de 2005. Deux générations sociales d'enfants d'immigrés," *Annales. Histoire, Sciences Sociales*, vol. 61, no. 4 (2006),

pp. 809–43; Abdellali Hajjat, *La Marche pour l'égalité et contre le racisme* (Paris: Éditions Amsterdam, 2013).

4 On the invisibility of immigration in France, see Gérard Noiriel, *The French Melting Pot: Immigration, Citizenship, and National Identity*, trans. Geoffroy de Laforcade (Minneapolis: University of Minnesota Press, 1996). On the shift from the working class to the working-class condition, see Stéphane Beaud and Michel Pialoux, *Retour sur la condition ouvrière. Enquête aux usines Peugeot de Sochaux-Montbéliard* (Paris: Fayard, 1999).

5 Sylvie Tissot, *L'État et les quartiers. Genèse d'une catégorie de l'action publique* (Paris: Seuil, 2007); Mustafa Dikec, *Badlands of the Republic: Space, Politics and Urban Policy* (Oxford: Wiley-Blackwell, 2011).

6 Loïc Wacquant, *Urban Outcasts: A Comparative Sociology of Advanced Marginality* (Cambridge: Polity, 2010).

7 Alec Hargreaves, *Multi-Ethnic France: Immigration, Politics, Culture and Society* (London: Routledge, 2007); Gérard Noiriel, *À quoi sert "l'identité nationale"* (Marseille: Agone, 2007).

8 Michel Wieviorka (ed.), *La France raciste* (Paris: Seuil, 1992).

9 "L'Événement," TF1, February 19, 1976.

10 Speech in Orléans, June 19, 1991, RPR dinner-debate before 1,300 party militants and sympathizers.

11 See Loïc Wacquant, *Punishing the Poor: The Neoliberal Government of Social Insecurity* (Durham, NC: Duke University Press, 2009); Grégory Salle, *La Part d'ombre de l'État de droit. La question carcérale en France and en République fédérale d'Allemagne depuis 1968* (Paris: Éditions de L'EHESS, 2009); Denis Salas, *La Volonté de punir* (Paris: Fayard/Pluriel, 2010); Didier Fassin, "Prison: l'idéologie de l'enfermement," *Mouvements*, vol. 88, no. 4 (2016), pp. 19–26; Didier Fassin, *Punir. Une passion contemporaine* (Paris: Seuil, 2017).

12 Karim Bellazaar and S. Forbes Dawson, *Reality Taule, au-delà des barreaux* (Grigny: Grignywood/Icetream, 2012).

13 Ivan Boszormenyi-Nagy and Geraldine M. Spark, *Invisible Loyalties* (Hagerstown, MD: Lippincott Williams and Wilkins, 1973). For Boszormenyi-Nagy, feelings of loyalty are experienced on a day-to-day basis through interpersonal, ethical, and existential conflicts.

14 Marcel Mauss, *The Gift: The Form and Reason for Exchange in Archaic Societies*, trans. W.D. Halls (New York: Routledge, 1990), p. 13.

15 Norbert Elias and John L. Scotson, *The Established and the Outsiders: A Sociological Inquiry into Community Problems* (Thousand Oaks, CA: Sage, 1994), p. 7.

16 Pierre Bourdieu writes: "If sociology is difficult and unlikely, that is precisely because people are so caught up in the game that they are not at all disposed to treat it objectively. But treating it objectively is an absolutely extraordinary freedom [...], one can discuss without drama, without naïvety, without interdisciplinary inanities." Pierre Bourdieu, *Sociologie générale*, Vol. 1, *Cours au Collège de France* (Paris: Seuil, 2015), p. 448.

17 See Nikolas Rose, *Governing the Soul: The Shaping of the Private Self* (London: Routledge, 1990), p. 262; Luc Boltanski and Ève Chiapello, *The New Spirit of Capitalism* (London: Verso, 2007); Richard Sennett, *The Corrosion of Character: The Personal Consequences of Work in the New Capitalism* (New York: W.W. Norton, 2015).

18 Karl Marx and Friedrich Engels, *The Communist Manifesto* (London: Penguin, 2015).
19 Richard Hoggart, *The Uses of Literacy* (London: Transaction Publishers, 1957), p. 63.

Chapter 2 On the Margins of the City

1 Paul E. Willis, *Learning to Labor: How Working Class Kids Get Working Class Jobs* (New York: Columbia University Press, 1981), p. 50.
2 As Richard Hoggart pointed out in a different context, "parents were aware of the school but largely ignorant of what today would be called its 'philosophy,' if it had one other than a handful of pragmatic and largely conventional aims and points of view" (Richard Hoggart, *A Local Habitation* [Oxford: Oxford University Press, 1992], p. 142). On the notion of a "badge of dignity," inspired by my own reading of the concept of *badge of ability* (Jonathan Cobb and Richard Sennett, *The Hidden Injuries of Class* [New York: Vintage Books, 1973]), see my book *Jeunesses françaises*.
3 See John Devine, *Maximum Security: The Culture of Violence in Inner-City Schools* (Chicago: University of Chicago Press, 1996); Bowen Paulle, *Toxic Schools: High Poverty Education in New York and Amsterdam* (Chicago: University of Chicago Press, 2013).
4 Willis, *Learning to Labor.*
5 Alexandra Oeser, *Enseigner Hitler. Les adolescents face au passé nazi en Allemagne* (Paris: Maison des Sciences de l'Homme, 2010).
6 Abdelmalek Sayad, *L'École et les enfants de l'immigration. Essais critiques* (Paris: Seuil, 2014), pp. 153–5.
7 Claude Grignon, *L'Ordre des choses. Les fonctions sociales de l'enseignement technique* (Paris: Éditions de Minuit, 1971).
8 Georg Simmel, "The sociology of secrecy and of secret societies," *American Journal of Sociology*, vol. 11, no. 4 (1906), pp. 441–98.
9 Ibid.
10 Max Weber, *The Protestant Ethic and the Spirit of Capitalism*, trans. Talcott Parsons (New York: Routledge, 1992), p. 40.
11 Mary Douglas, *Purity and Danger: An Analysis of Concepts of Pollution and Taboo* (New York: Routledge, 2015).
12 For an anthropology of the carceral world in France, see Didier Fassin, *Prison Worlds: An Ethnography of the Carceral Condition*, trans. Rachel Gomme (Cambridge: Polity, 2016); Farhad Khosrokhavar, *Prisons de France* (Paris: Robert Laffont, 2016).
13 In France, the year 1975, which symbolically signaled the end of the postwar era, marked a rupture. The prison population has grown continually since then. The process accelerated starting in the 2000s. In 1980, there were 36,913 imprisoned individuals; in 2000, there were 51,411, and in 2014 there were 77,883; 85.8 inmates per 100,000 were imprisoned in France in 2000, versus 117.9 per 100,000 in 2014 – of whom 96.5 percent are men (*Séries statistiques des personnes placées sous main de justice, 1980–2014*).
14 Almost one in two prisoners is or was an *ouvrier* (blue-collar worker), and 72 percent of those incarcerated left school at 16 or 17. The risk of incarceration is 3.4 times greater for someone from a family of five children than

for someone with only one brother or sister, and 30 percent of inmates have a father who never spoke French to them during their childhood (Francine Cassan, Laurent Toulemon, and Annie Kensey, "L'histoire familiale des hommes détenus," *Insee Première*, vol. 706 [2000]). In 2014, foreign nationals continued to represent almost 18 percent of incarcerated individuals, while making up only 6.4 percent of the French population (*Huitième Rapport annuel du contrôleur des libertés*). While in 2000 there were 11,971 inmates between the ages of 18 and 25, and 24,277 between 25 and 30, there were, respectively, 18,918 and 36,413 in 2014, an increase of more than 60 percent for both age brackets. In 2000, inmates sentenced to less than one year made up 25.3 percent of the total and those sentenced to between one and three years made up 20.4 percent – versus 36.3 percent and 29.9 percent, respectively, in 2014. Along with this greater number of young people in the prison population and the proliferation of short sentences should be added the explosion in assignments to electronic surveillance, which affected 128 individuals in 2001 versus 23,147 in 2013 (figures from *Séries statistiques des personnes placées sous main de justice, 1980–2014*). The proliferation of short sentences among young people is one of the factors most highly correlated with recidivism, which fluctuates between 35 percent and 61 percent of cases, depending on the study and the methodology.

15 Out of respect for the work of the journalists who gathered this testimony, taken from a series of portraits using pseudonyms, I omit the source here.
16 *Le Parisien*, July 15, 2009.
17 Pierre Bourdieu, "L'illusion biographique," *Actes de la recherche en sciences sociales*, vol. 62, no. 1 (1986), pp. 69–72.
18 Bellazaar and Dawson, *Reality Taule*.
19 Ibid., p. 26.
20 Ibid.
21 Ibid., p. 27.
22 Boris Thiolay, "Coulibaly s'était radicalisé en prison," *L'Express*, January 9, 2015. This view was confirmed by another lawyer who defended him in a different case.
23 However, unlike with the functionary Adolf Eichmann, it is not about serving "the system" or the party hierarchy, but one's personal interest.
24 Bellazaar and Dawson, *Reality Taule*, p. 49.
25 Emeline Cazi, "Amédy Coulibaly 'avait un côté audacieux chien fou,'" *Le Monde*, January 11, 2015.
26 Bellazaar and Dawson, *Reality Taule*, p. 54.
27 Ibid., pp. 90–1.
28 Stephen J. Ducat, *The Wimp Factor: Gender Gaps, Holy Wars* (Boston: Beacon Press, 2005); Frédérique Matonti, *Le Genre présidentiel* (Paris: La Découverte, 2017).
29 Pierre Bourdieu, *Masculine Domination*, trans. Richard Nice (Stanford: Stanford University Press, 2001), pp. 51–2.
30 Philippe Bourgois correctly notes that "although street culture emerges out of a personal search for dignity and a rejection of racism and subjugation, it ultimately becomes an active agent in personal degradation and community ruin" (Philippe I. Bourgois, *In Search of Respect: Selling Crack in El Barrio* [Cambridge: Cambridge University Press, 2010], p. 9).
31 Christopher Lasch analyzed the consequences of this loss of the "spirit of

play" in mass sports: "The emergence of the spectacle as the dominant form of cultural expression [in which] what began as an attempt to invest sport with religious significance, indeed to make it into a surrogate religion in its own right, ends with the demystification of sport, the assimilation of sport to show business" (Christopher Lasch, *The Culture of Narcissism: American Life in an Age of Diminishing Expectations* [New York: W.W. Norton, 1991], p. 124).

32 Samuel Wilson Fussell, *Muscle: Confessions of an Unlikely Bodybuilder* (New York: Open Road Media, 2015).

33 Peter Sloterdijk, *You Must Change Your Life*, trans. Wieland Hoban (Cambridge: Polity, 2013).

34 Lesley A. Hall, *Hidden Anxieties: Male Sexuality, 1900–50* (Cambridge: Polity, 1991); Barry Glassner, "Men and muscles," in Michael S. Kimmel and Michael A. Messner (eds.), *Men's Lives* (New York: Macmillan, 1989).

35 Loïc J. D. Wacquant, "Review article: why men desire muscles," *Body & Society*, vol. 1, no. 1 (1995), p. 164.

36 Hoggart, *The Uses of Literacy*, p. 81.

37 Olivier Schwartz, *Le Monde privé des ouvriers. Hommes et femmes du Nord* (Paris: PUF, 1990), p. 516.

38 On the adoption of one's partner's religion in France, see Loïc Le Pape, "Prendre la religion de l'autre. Lorsque les choix religieux se mêlent aux sentiments amoureux," in Anne-Sophie Lamine, Françoise Lautman, and Séverine Matthieu (eds.), *La Religion de l'Autre. La pluralité religieuse entre concurrence et reconnaissance* (Paris: L'Harmattan, 2008), pp. 57–67.

39 Hayat Boumedienne's statement to police investigators in the inquiry concerning Smaïn Aït Ali Belkacem's escape attempt.

40 Didier Fassin, *Enforcing Order: An Ethnography of Urban Policing*, trans. Rachel Gomme (Cambridge: Polity, 2014). For an explanation of the French police's "doctrinal retrenchment," rejecting the idea of "de-escalation," see Olivier Fillieule and Fabien Jobard, "Un splendide isolement. Les politiques françaises du maintien de l'ordre," *La Vie des idées*, 2016, available online at *www.laviedesidees.fr*.

41 On how the grip of Mafia-type activities on young boys in impoverished neighborhoods can be seen in their attitude toward death, see Roberto Saviano, *Gomorrah: A Personal Journey into the Violent International Empire of Naples' Organized Crime System*, trans. Virginia Jewiss (New York: Farrar, Straus and Giroux, 2007).

42 Göran Therborn, *The Killing Fields of Inequality* (Cambridge: Polity, 2013).

43 Amar Henni, *Grigny la Grande Borne. Des années 1970 aux attentats de January 2015*, doctoral dissertation in anthropology, Université Paris-8, Saint-Denis, 2016.

44 Despite the prevailing notion "that criminal activity (past or present) stands in opposition (for young people in working-class neighborhoods) to the expression of a political or ideological consciousness," a view that is "typical of those rationalizations from above [that amount to an] intellectual set-up job according to which criminals have no political consciousness or disposition for contestation." See Marwan Mohammed, "Les voies de la colère: 'violences urbaines' ou révolte d'ordre 'politique'? L'exemple des Hautes-Noues à Villiers-sur-Marne," *Socio-logos*, no. 2 (2007) (*http://socio-logos.*

revues.org/352). See also Ferdinand Sutterlüty, "The hidden morale of the 2005 French and 2011 English riots," *Thesis Eleven*, vol. 121 (2014), pp. 38–56.

45 On this point, see my conclusions in Fabien Truong, "Total rioting: from metaphysics to politics," *The Sociological Review*, vol. 65, no. 4 (2017), pp. 563–77.

46 Max Weber, *The Sociology of Religion*, trans. Ephraim Fischoff (Boston: Beacon Press, 1993).

Chapter 3 Reconversions

1 Ferdinand Tönnies, *Community and Civil Society*, trans. Jose Harris and Margaret Hollis (Cambridge: Cambridge University Press, 2001), p. 18.

2 See John R. Bowen, *Can Islam be French? Pluralism and Pragmatism in a Secularist State* (Princeton: Princeton University Press, 2009); Solenne Jouanneau, *Les Imams en France. Une autorité religieuse sous contrôle* (Marseille: Agone, 2013); Étienne Pingaud, *L'Implantation de l'islam dans les "quartiers." Contribution à l'analyse du succès d'une offre symbolique*, doctoral dissertation in sociology (EHESS, 2013); Julien Talpin, Julien O'Miel, and Franck Frégosi (eds.), *L'Islam et la Cité. Engagements musulmans dans les quartiers populaires* (Villeneuve-d'Ascq: Presses Universitaires du Septentrion, 2017).

3 David Thomson, *Les Français jihadistes* (Paris: Les Arènes, 2014); David Thomson, *The Returned*, trans. G. Flanders (Cambridge: Polity, 2018).

4 Leïla Babès, *L'Islam positif. La religion des jeunes musulmans de France* (Paris: L'Atelier-Éditions ouvrières, 1997); Jocelyne Cesari, *Musulmans et républicains. Les jeunes, l'islam et la France* (Brussels: Complexe, 1999); Chantal Saint-Blancat, *L'Islam de la diaspora* (Paris: Bayard, 1997); Khosrokhavar, *L'Islam des jeunes*.

5 Sayad, *L'Immigration ou les paradoxes de l'altérité*, pp. 148–9.

6 Danièle Hervieu-Léger, *Catholicisme, la fin d'un monde* (Paris: Bayard, 2003).

7 Olivier Roy, *Globalized Islam: The Search for a New Ummah* (New York: Columbia University Press, 2013), p. 151.

8 Sayad, *L'Immigration ou les paradoxes de l'altérité.*

9 Bourdieu, *Sociologie générale*, Vol. 1.

10 Claude Poliak, *Aux frontières du champ littéraire. Sociologie des écrivains amateurs* (Paris: Economica, 2006).

11 Mauss, *The Gift*, p. 58.

12 As Danièle Hervieu-Léger notes, "The more individuals mix and match the belief system best corresponding to their own needs, the more they aspire to exchange this experience with others who share the same type of spiritual aspirations" (Danièle Hervieu-Léger, *Le Pèlerin et le Converti. La religion en mouvement* [Paris: Flammarion, 1999], pp. 180–1).

13 Maurice Godelier, *The Enigma of the Gift*, trans. Nora Scott (Cambridge: Polity, 1999), p. 201.

14 Ibid., p. 208.

15 Salman Rushdie, *The Satanic Verses* (London: Viking, 1988).

16 Quoted by Les Back in his academic diary: Les Back, *Academic Diary: Or*

Why Higher Education Still Matters (Cambridge, MA: Goldsmiths Press, 2016).
17 Weber, *The Sociology of Religion*, pp. 151–4.
18 Ibid., p. 155.
19 Ibid.
20 The boys' less than total attendance is in line with the national average. According to the latest TeO study (2016), only 20 percent of French Muslims attend a mosque frequently.
21 Florence Weber, *Le Travail à-côté. Une ethnographie des perceptions* (Paris: Éditions de l'EHESS, 2001), p. 197.
22 Paul Ricoeur, *Oneself as Another*, trans. Kathleen Blamey (Chicago: University of Chicago Press, 2008).
23 Weber, *The Sociology of Religion*, p. 192.
24 Ibid., p. 194.
25 Scott Atran, *In Gods We Trust: The Evolutionary Landscape of Religion* (Oxford: Oxford University Press, 2005), p. 227.
26 Ibid., p. 278.
27 Weber, *The Sociology of Religion*, pp. 162, 164–5.
28 Atran, *In Gods We Trust*, p. 120.
29 Benslama, *Un furieux désir de sacrifice*, pp. 9–11.
30 Olivier Roy, *Holy Ignorance: When Religion and Culture Part Ways*, trans. Ros Schwartz (Oxford: Oxford University Press, 2010), p. 117.
31 Olivier Roy, *L'Islam mondialisé* (Paris: Seuil, 2004), p. 102.
32 Romain Badouard, "'Je ne suis pas Charlie.' Pluralité des prises de parole sur le web et les réseaux sociaux," in Pierre Lefébure and Claire Sécail (eds.), *Le Défi Charlie. Les médias à l'épreuve des attentats* (Paris: Lemieux éditeur, 2016).
33 Bourdieu, *Sociologie générale*, Vol. 1, p. 117.
34 Pierre Livet, *Émotions et rationalités morales* (Paris: PUF, 2002), pp. 177–8. That is also what Gérôme Truc observes in the moment of shell-shock after attacks; paradoxically, this moment allows each person to verbalize the meaning they attach to their own existence (Truc, *Shell Shocked*).
35 Michael Walzer, *On Toleration* (New Haven: Yale University Press, 2008).
36 Abram de Swaan, *The Killing Compartments: The Mentality of Mass Murder* (New Haven: Yale University Press, 2015). In other veins, see Jean Hatzfeld, *A Time for Machetes: The Rwandan Genocide – the Killers Speak* (London: Serpent's Tail, 2008); Christopher Browning, *Ordinary Men: Reserve Police Battalion 101 and the Final Solution in Poland* (New York: Harper Perennial, 2017).
37 Through the prism of the "shell-shock" that follows terrorist attacks, Gérôme Truc describes a continuum between "resigned acceptance of difference," "benign indifference to difference," and a maximum degree of openness that leads to "respect" (Truc, *Shell Shocked*, p. 169).
38 Theodor W. Adorno, *The Authoritarian Personality* (New York: W.W. Norton, 1950).
39 This observation implies that "the key point, in this approach, is to recall that once we focus on *trajectories*, no one is working on substantive and stabilized identities: the problem is precisely to have sufficiently flexible tools to mark out the steps in a process which, by definition, cannot be frozen into a definitive description. Religion in modern societies is *in motion*: it is this

motion that we must strive to grasp" (Danièle Hervieu-Léger, *Le Pèlerin et le Converti*, p. 88).

40 Ibid., p. 99.

41 Hyun Mee Kim, "Becoming a city Buddhist among the young generation in Seoul," *International Sociology*, vol. 31, no. 4 (2016), pp. 450–66. See also the concept of "practical Sufism" in Julia Howell, "Indonesian urban's Sufis: challenging stereotypes of Islamic revival," *ISIM Newsletter*, vol. 6 (Leiden, 2000).

42 Loïc Le Pape, "'Tout change, mais rien ne change.' Les conversions religieuses sont-elles des bifurcations?," in Michel Grossetti, Marc Bessin, and Claire Bidart (eds.), *Bifurcations. Les sciences sociales face aux ruptures et à l'événement* (Paris: La Découverte, 2010).

43 Gérôme Truc, Alexandra Bidet, and Louis Quéré, "Ce à quoi nous tenons: Dewey et la formation des valeurs," in John Dewey, *La Formation des valeurs* (Paris: La Découverte, 2011).

44 Patrick Michel, "Introduction. Religion et démocratie: nouvelles situations, nouvelles approaches," in Patrick Michel (ed.), *Religion et démocratie* (Paris: Albin Michel, 2013), p. 2.

Chapter 4 War and Peace

1 Christian Baudelot and Roger Establet, *Avoir 30 ans en 1968 et en 1998* (Paris: Seuil, 2000).

2 The concept of "scarification" is primarily used in quantitative sociological studies to measure the long-term effects of the ruptures and scars that "mark" individual socialization.

3 Donald Winnicott, *Through Paediatrics to Psycho-Analysis* (London: Hogarth Press, 1978).

4 Paul Nizan, *Aden, Arabie*, trans. Joan Pinkham (New York: Columbia University Press, 1987), p. 59.

5 According to Norbert Elias, time is not something that "passes" but rather is the result of a process of representation in which different events are placed in relation to one another. This is linked to a "capacity for synthesis," that is, people's "capacity for having present in their imagination what is not present here and now and being able to connect it with what happens here and now" (Norbert Elias, *Time: An Essay*, trans. Edmund Jephcott [Oxford: Blackwell, 1992], pp. 74–5).

6 See the definition of "square" in Howard S. Becker, *Outsiders: Studies in the Sociology of Deviance* (New York: Free Press, 1997), p. 85.

7 Marie Cartier, Isabelle Coutant, Olivier Masclet, Yasmine Siblot, and Juliette Rogers, *The France of the Little-Middles: A Suburban Housing Development in Greater Paris*, trans. Juliette Rogers (New York: Berghahn, 2016).

8 Truong, *Jeunesses françaises*.

9 Francis Fukuyama, *The End of History and the Last Man* (London: Penguin Books, 2012); Jean-François Lyotard, *The Postmodern Condition: A Report on Knowledge*, trans. Geoff Bennington (Minneapolis: University of Minnesota Press, 2010).

10 Gérard Noiriel, *Workers in French Society in the 19th and 20th Centuries*, trans. Helen McPhail (New York: Berg, 1990).

11 "Fear itself," *The Hedgehog Review*, vol. 5, no. 3 (2003), p. 5.
12 Bourdieu, *Sociologie générale*, Vol. 1, pp. 136–7. Furthermore, this exchange illustrates recent changes in the use of judicial reprimands in relations between young people and judges, cutting against the order of 1945 and the creation of the children's judge. The latter aimed to establish a space for dialogue and concrete appropriation of the law, versus a strictly punitive and procedural approach. For an enlightening analysis of this slide, see Denis Salas, "C'est un adulte qui est le vecteur de la rencontre des jeunes avec la loi," *Diversité*, no. 188 (2017), pp. 11–15.
13 Gérard Noiriel, "Communication aux rendez-vous de l'histoire" (Blois, 2017).
14 Becker, *Outsiders*.
15 Loïc Wacquant, "Crafting the neoliberal state: workfare, prisonfare and social insecurity," *Sociological Forum*, vol. 25 (2010), pp. 197–220.
16 Erving Goffman, *Relations in Public: Microstudies of the Public Order* (New Brunswick, NJ: Transaction Publishers, 2010).
17 Richard Sennett, *Families against the City: Middle-Class Homes of Industrial Chicago, 1872–1890* (Cambridge, MA: Harvard University Press, 1984).
18 Luc Boltanski, *Love and Justice as Competences: Three Essays on the Sociology of Action* (Cambridge: Polity, 2012), pp. 112, 114.
19 As Olivier Schwartz points out, "[I]t must be emphasized that, whatever promise of autonomy it may contain, private life creates no social logic on its own" (Schwartz, *Le Monde privé des ouvriers*, p. 522).
20 Kepel, *Terror in France*.
21 This quote has long been attributed to the Al Qaeda leader. It circulates widely in jihadist circles, though its origin cannot be precisely dated.
22 Thomson, *Les Français jihadistes* and *The Returned*.
23 Montasser Alde'Emeh, *Pourquoi nous sommes tous des djihadistes* (Paris: La Boîte à Pandore, 2015).
24 Romain Huët, "Quand les 'malheureux' deviennent des 'enragés': ethnographie de moudjahidines syriens (2012–2014)," *Cultures & Conflits*, vol. 97 (2015), pp. 31–75.
25 Ian Hacking, *Mad Travelers: Reflections on the Reality of Transient Mental Illnesses* (Cambridge, MA: Harvard University Press, 2006).
26 Ibid.
27 Matthieu Suc, "Hyper Cacher: la veuve d'Amédy Coulibaly confirme dans des écoutes être en Syrie," *Mediapart* (January 10, 2017).
28 "Qu'Allah maudisse la France."
29 John Castles, *Big Stars* (Perth: Network Books, 2007); Nathalie Heinich, *De la visibilité. Excellence et singularité en régime médiatique* (Paris: Gallimard, 2012).
30 Zygmunt Bauman, *Liquid Life* (Cambridge: Polity, 2017), p. 46.
31 John Gray, *Al Qaeda and What It Means to Be Modern* (London: Faber & Faber, 2007).
32 Scott Atran, *Talking to the Enemy: Violent Extremism, Sacred Values, and What It Means to Be Human* (London: Penguin, 2011), p. 42.
33 Alde'Emeh, *Pourquoi nous sommes tous des djihadistes*, p. 224.
34 Pierre-Jean Luizard, *Le Piège Daesh. L'État islamique ou le retour de l'Histoire* (Paris: La Découverte, 2015). For a similar reading of young

Frenchmen's involvement in the Spanish Civil War, see Rémi Skoutelsky, *L'Espoir guidait leurs pas. Les volontaires français dans les Brigades internationales (1936–1939)* (Paris: Grasset, 1998). According to David Mallet, in the 331 conflicts between 1815 and 2005 that he studied, about 20 percent of combatants were foreign (David Mallet, *Foreign Fighters: Transnational Identity in Civil Conflicts* [New York: Oxford University Press, 2013]).

35 Thomson, *The Returned.*

36 As for the few returnees who have finally become homegrown terrorists, one must take into account their effective socialization on the battlefield to understand the gradual acquisition of the warrior's dispositions, qualities, and resources.

37 Doug McAdam, "Recruitment to high risk activism: the case of Freedom Summer," *American Journal of Sociology*, vol. 92, no. 1 (1986), pp. 64–90.

38 Alain Corbin, *The Life of an Unknown: The Rediscovered World of a Clog Maker in Nineteenth-Century France* , trans. Arthur Goldhammer (New York: Columbia University Press, 2001), p. 9.

39 Norbert Elias, *Mozart and Other Essays on Courtly Art*, eds. Eric R. Baker and Stephen Mennell (Dublin: University College of Dublin Press, 2010), pp. 58, 60.

40 Sonya Faure and Patricia Tourancheau, "Amedy Coulibaly, suspect numéro 1 de l'assassinat de Montrouge," *Libération*, January 9, 2015.

41 See Karin Von Hippel, "The roots of terrorism: probing the myths," *The Political Quarterly*, vol. 73 (2002), pp. 25–39; Stephen Vertigans, *Militant Islam: A Sociology of Characteristics, Causes and Consequences* (London: Routledge, 2008); John Horgan, *Walking Away from Terrorism: Accounts of Disengagement from Radical and Extremist Movements* (London: Routledge, 2009). On the perceived differences in "sincerity" between terrorist actions and military actions, see Talal Asad, *On Suicide Bombing* (New York: Columbia University Press, 2007), pp. 26–7.

42 Conversation dated May 6, 2010, recorded by wiretap as part of the investigation into the escape plans of Smaïn Aït Ali Belkacem.

43 Source: the anonymous interview mentioned above and published in a national daily in 2004.

44 Tom Segev, *Soldiers of Evil: Commandants of the Nazi Concentration Camps* (London: Grafton, 1987), pp. 65–6.

45 Jason Burke, *The New Threat from Islamic Militancy* (New York: Vintage, 2016).

46 Isabelle Duriez, "Marie-Alix Canu-Bernard, une pénaliste dans la course au bâtonnat de Paris," *Elle*, June 2015.

47 A cause can be "as limited as the honor of the group, as abstract as social justice, as humane as the future of a people, or as sacred as faith in God." See Diego Gambetta, "Can we make sense of suicide missions?," in Diego Gambetta (ed.), *Making Sense of Suicide Missions* (Oxford: Oxford University Press, 2005), p. 271.

48 Georg Simmel, "The sociology of secrecy and of secret societies," *American Journal of Sociology*, vol. 11, no. 4 (1906), pp. 478, 486.

Epilogue

1 Ramón Spaaij, "The enigma of lone wolf terrorism: an assessment," *Studies in Conflict & Terrorism*, vol. 33, no. 9 (2010), pp. 854–70.
2 Hacking, *Mad Travelers*.
3 Scott Atran, "Why war is never really rational," *Huffington Post*, March 29, 2011.
4 John Macmanus, *Deadly Brotherhood: The American Combat Soldier in World War II* (New York: Presidio Press, 2003); Sageman, *Leaderless Jihad*. On the idea that, on this point, there is no gender difference, see Lindsey A. O'Rourke, "What's special about female suicide terrorism?," *Security Studies*, vol. 18, no. 4 (2009), pp. 681–718.
5 See, for example, Bill Williamson, *Education and Social Change in Egypt and Turkey: A Study in Historical Sociology* (Basingstoke: Palgrave Macmillan, 2013); Diego Gambetta and Steffen Hertog, *Engineers of Jihad: The Curious Connection between Violent Extremism and Education* (Princeton: Princeton University Press, 2016). In examining the overrepresentation of engineers among jihadists in Middle Eastern countries, Gambetta and Hertog show that advances in higher education are accompanied by increased relative frustration; when this frustration encounters specific political, ideological, and personality traits, it can fuel involvement in terrorism.
6 Christopher A. Bail, *Terrified: How Anti-Muslim Fringe Organizations Became Mainstream* (Princeton: Princeton University Press, 2014).
7 Robert Pape, *Dying to Win: The Strategic Logic of Suicide Terrorism* (New York: Random House Inc., 2006).
8 Michelle Alexander, *The New Jim Crow* (New York: The New Press, 2012); Nicolas Duvoux, *Les Oubliés du rêve américain. Philanthropie, État et pauvreté urbaine aux États-Unis* (Paris: PUF, 2015); Matthew Desmond, *Evicted: Poverty and Profit in the American City* (London: Penguin, 2017).
9 Philippe Bourgois and Jeff Schonberg, *Righteous Dopefiend* (Berkeley: University of California Press, 2009); Randol Contreras, *The Stickup Kids: Race, Drugs, Violence, and the American Dream* (Berkeley: University of California Press, 2012); Sudhir Alladi Venkatesh, *Gang Leader for a Day: A Young Sociologist Crosses the Line* (London: Allen Lane, 2008); Alice Goffman, *On the Run: Fugitive Life in an American City* (Chicago: University of Chicago Press, 2014).
10 Adorno, *The Authoritarian Personality*. For an overview of research in political psychology on the connections between "personality" and "ideology," see Alexandra Cichocka and Kristof Dhont, "The personality bases of political ideology and behaviour," in Virgil Zeigler-Hill and Todd K. Shackelford (eds.), *Sage Handbook of Personality and Individual Differences* (London: Sage, 2008). For an assessment of research into "political genes," see Peter K. Hatemi and Rose McDermott, "The genetics of politics: discovery, challenges, and progress," *Trends in Genetics: TIG*, vol. 28, no. 10 (2012), pp. 525–33.
11 Aron Y. Zelin, "The state of global jihad online," 2013, available online at *www.washingtoninstitute.org*.
12 Gérard Mauger and Willy Pelletier (eds.), *Les Classes populaires et le FN. Explications de vote* (Vulaines-sur-Seine: Éditions du Croquant, 2017);

Violaine Girard, *Le Vote FN au village. Trajectoires de ménages populaires du périurbain* (Vulaines-sur-Seine: Éditions du Croquant, 2017).

13 Karl Marx, "A contribution to the critique of Hegel's philosophy or right," in Marx and Engels, *Collected Works*, Vol. 3, pp. 175–6.

14 Overshadowed by "radical Islam," see also "market Islam": Patrick Haenni, *L'Islam de marché* (Paris: Seuil, 2005).

INDEX